International Political Economy Series

General Editor: **Timothy M. Shaw**, Professor of Commonwealth Governance and Development, and Director of the Institute of Commonwealth Studies, School of Advanced Study, University of London.

Titles include:

Hans Abrahamsson
UNDERSTANDING WORLD ORDER AND STRUCTURAL CHANGE
Poverty, Conflict and the Global Arena

Sandra Braman (*editor*)
THE EMERGENT GLOBAL INFORMATION POLICY REGIME

James Busumtwi-Sam and Laurent Dobuzinskis (*editors*)
TURBULENCE AND NEW DIRECTIONS IN GLOBAL POLITICAL ECONOMY

Elizabeth De Boer-Ashworth
THE GLOBAL POLITICAL ECONOMY AND POST-1989 CHANGE
The Place of the Central European Transition

Bill Dunn
GLOBAL RESTRUCTURING AND THE POWER OF LABOUR

Myron J. Frankman
WORLD DEMOCRATIC FEDERALISM
Peace and Justice Indivisible

Helen A. Garten
US FINANCIAL REGULATION AND THE LEVEL PLAYING FIELD

Barry K. Gills (*editor*)
GLOBALIZATION AND THE POLITICS OF RESISTANCE

Richard Grant and John Rennie Short (*editors*)
GLOBALIZATION AND THE MARGINS

Graham Harrison (*editor*)
GLOBAL ENCOUNTERS
International Political Economy, Development and Globalization

Patrick Hayden and Chamsy el-Ojeili (*editors*)
CONFRONTING GLOBALIZATION
Humanity, Justice and the Renewal of Politics

Axel Hülsemeyer (*editor*)
GLOBALIZATION IN THE TWENTY-FIRST CENTURY
Convergence or Divergence?

Helge Hveem and Kristen Nordhaug (*editors*)
PUBLIC POLICY IN THE AGE OF GLOBALIZATION
Responses to Environmental and Economic Crises

Takashi Inoguchi
GLOBAL CHANGE
A Japanese Perspective

Jomo K.S. and Shyamala Nagaraj (*editors*)
GLOBALIZATION VERSUS DEVELOPMENT

Dominic Kelly and Wyn Grant (*editors*)
THE POLITICS OF INTERNATIONAL TRADE IN THE 21st CENTURY
Actors, Issues and Regional Dynamics

Craig N. Murphy (*editor*)
EGALITARIAN POLITICS IN THE AGE OF GLOBALIZATION

John Nauright and Kimberly S. Schimmel (*editors*)
THE POLITICAL ECONOMY OF SPORT

Michael Niemann
A SPATIAL APPROACH TO REGIONALISM IN THE GLOBAL ECONOMY

Morten Ougaard
THE GLOBALIZATION OF POLITICS
Power, Social Forces and Governance

Markus Perkmann and Ngai-Ling Sum (*editors*)
GLOBALIZATION, REGIONALIZATION AND CROSS–BORDER REGIONS

Leonard Seabrooke
US POWER IN INTERNATIONAL FINANCE
The Victory of Dividends

Timothy J. Sinclair and Kenneth P. Thomas (*editors*)
STRUCTURE AND AGENCY IN INTERNATIONAL CAPITAL MOBILITY

Fredrik Söderbaum and Timothy M. Shaw (*editors*)
THEORIES OF NEW REGIONALISM
A Palgrave Reader

Amy Verdun
EUROPEAN RESPONSES TO GLOBALIZATION AND FINANCIAL
MARKET INTEGRATION
Perceptions of Economic and Monetary Union in Britain, France and Germany

International Political Economy Series
Series Standing Order ISBN 0–333–71708–2 hardcover
Series Standing Order ISBN 0–333–71110–6 paperback
(*outside North America only*)

You can receive future titles in this series as they are published by placing a standing order. Please contact your bookseller or, in case of difficulty, write to us at the address below with your name and address, the title of the series and one of the ISBNs quoted above.

Customer Services Department, Macmillan Distribution Ltd, Houndmills, Basingstoke, Hampshire RG21 6XS, England

The Political Economy of Sport

Edited by

John Nauright
Georgia Southern University, USA

and

Kimberly S. Schimmel
Kent State University, USA

First published in 2005 by
PALGRAVE MACMILLAN
Houndmills, Basingstoke, Hampshire RG21 6XS and
175 Fifth Avenue, New York, N.Y. 10010
Companies and representatives throughout the world.

PALGRAVE MACMILLAN is the global academic imprint of the Palgrave
Macmillan division of St. Martin's Press, LLC and of Palgrave Macmillan Ltd.
Macmillan® is a registered trademark in the United States, United Kingdom
and other countries. Palgrave is a registered trademark in the European
Union and other countries.

ISBN-13: 978–0–333–77386–4
ISBN-10: 0–333–77386–1

This book is printed on paper suitable for recycling and made from fully
managed and sustained forest sources.

A catalogue record for this book is available from the British Library.

Library of Congress Cataloging-in-Publication Data
    The political economy of sport / edited by John Nauright and Kimberly
S. Schimmel.
        p. cm.—(International political economy series)
    Includes bibliographical references and index.
        ISBN 0–333–77386–1 (cloth)
        1. Sports—Economic aspects. 2. Sports—Social aspects. I. Nauright,
John, 1962– II. Schimmel, Kimberly S., 1961– III. International political
economy series (Palgrave Macmillan (Firm))
GV716.P65 2005
306.4'83—dc22   2005043775

10 9 8 7 6 5 4 3 2 1
14 13 12 11 10 09 08 07 06 05

Printed and bound in Great Britain by
Antony Rowe Ltd, Chippenham and Eastbourne

Contents

Part III Place Competition: Sport Mega-Events and Urban Development

List of Figures and Tables

Preface and Acknowledgements

We would like to thank the authors for their hard work in producing the chapters and revisions to chapters in a timely fashion. Our editors at Macmillian and now Palgrave Macmillan have been most patient and encouraging as this project has developed. Professor Tim Shaw, the series editor, had the vision several years ago to include a volume on sport in the International Political Economy series. We hope this volume lives up to the traditions of that series and contributes to the growing debate about the political economy of sport.

We would like to thank several people in addition to the contributors who have helped us along the way. John would like to thank John Bale, David Black, Jørn Hansen, Verner Möller, S.W. Pope, Trevor Slack and Patricia Vertinsky. John's colleagues in the Department of Hospitality, Tourism, and Family and Consumer Sciences at Georgia Southern University and his colleagues in the School of Social and Health Sciences and the Division of Sport, Leisure and Tourism at the University of Abertay Dundee have provided much needed encouragement and support during this project. John would also like to thank Dalhousie University in Canada for hospitality during a period of study leave when this project was first conceived and the Universities of Southern Denmark and Copenhagen for supporting him as a Visiting Professor.

Kim is especially grateful to C. Lee Harrington for her tireless encouragement and irrepressible sense of humour. Kim extends a thank you to George H. Sage and Joseph Maguire for their wise counsel and continuing support and to Alan G. Ingham for nurturing her initial interest in political economy. Kim would also like to thank her friends and colleagues in the Department of Sport, Exercise and Health Sciences at the University College Chichester in England for their gracious hospitality during a research leave near the completion of this project and also to acknowledge the resources provided by the School of Exercise, Leisure and Sport at Kent State University throughout the project's duration. We would both like to thank the Australian Research Council for funding of research that led to the production of several contributions to this volume. The external reviewer provided valuable comments that have helped us to strengthen and reshape the book.

Finally we would also like to thank those personally close to us for their love and support. John would especially like to thank his wife Jenni, and daughters Ashley and Lauren, for showing him daily the real meaning of life, and for their love and laughter. He also thanks Lord and Lady Clett for the Grouse, gorse, generosity, and, finally, his parents for their love and patience while he spent many years living far, far away.

Statesboro, Georgia   JOHN NAURIGHT
Kent, Ohio   KIMBERLY S. SCHIMMEL

Notes on the Contributors

Douglas Booth is Professor of Sport and Leisure Studies at the University of Waikato in Hamilton, New Zealand. His primary research interests cover the study of sport as a form of popular culture with a particular emphasis on political relationships and processes. Within this broad framework, specific areas of investigation have included racism in South African sport, the Olympic movement and the beach. He currently serves as an executive member of the Australian Society for Sport History and on the editorial boards of several journals, including *Journal of Sport History*, and *The International Journal of the History of Sport*.

Timothy J.L. Chandler is Professor of Sport Studies in the School of Exercise, Leisure and Sport and Associate Dean for Graduate Studies in the College of Fine & Professional Arts at Kent State University, in Kent, Ohio, USA. He has also taught at Syracuse University and been a visiting lecturer in the School of Physical Education, Sport and Leisure at De Montfort University, Bedford, UK. He is co-editor (with John Nauright) of *Making Men: Rugby and Masculine Identity* and *Making the Rugby World: Race, Gender, Commerce*; and (with Tara Magdalinski) of *With God on Their Side: Sport in the Service of Religion*. He is author of a number of book chapters and articles on sport in the English public schools. His articles have appeared in a range of journals, including *The International Journal of the History of Sport*, the *Canadian Journal of History of Sport*, and *Youth and Society*. He currently serves on the editorial boards of *Sports History Review*, *Football Studies* and *International Sports Studies*.

Mark Falcous is a lecturer in sport and leisure studies in the School of Physical Education at the University of Otago in Dunedin, New Zealand. He received his doctorate from Loughborough University in England. His research has focused on sport, the local–global nexus and identities.

Richard Giulianotti is Senior Lecturer in Sociology at the University of Aberdeen in Scotland. He is the author and editor of numerous books on sport generally and football/soccer more specifically. He is author of *Football: A Sociology of the Global Game*. He is also co-editor (with Gary Armstrong) of the books *Entering the Field: New Perspectives in World Football*, *Football Cultures and Identities*, *Fear and Loathing in World Football* and *Football in Africa*. He has also recently produced *Sport: A*

Critical Sociology, Sport and Modern Social Theorists and *Sport and Human Rights* (with David McArdle).

C. Michael Hall is Professor in the Department of Tourism, University of Otago, Dunedin, New Zealand and an Honorary Professor, Department of Marketing, Stirling University, Scotland. He also holds an associate position in sports management with the University of Alberta, Canada and is the co-editor of *Current Issues in Tourism*. Michael holds wide-ranging interests in tourism, leisure consumption and regional development, with his original interest in sports events generated by the Americas Cup in Fremantle in 1986–7.

John Horne is Senior Lecturer with the Scottish Centre for Physical Education, Sport and Leisure Studies at the University of Edinburgh in Scotland. He has written several articles on sport and leisure in Japanese society as well as *Understanding Sport* (with Alan Tomlinson and Garry Whannel). His most recent major publication is *Football Goes East: Culture and Business of the People's Game in East Asia* (with Wolfram Manzenreiter).

Brett Hutchins teaches sociology and media studies at the University of Tasmania in Australia. He is the author of *Don Bradman: Challenging the Myth* and several journal articles and book chapters that examine the social and cultural dimensions of Australian sport.

Tara Magdalinski is a Senior Lecturer in the Faculty of Arts and Social Sciences at the University of the Sunshine Coast in Australia. She has published several articles and book chapters in the area of sports studies, most recently on the cultural construction of performance enhancement. In addition, she examines the role of 'nature' in the bodies and site of the Sydney 2000 Olympics, the cultural reception of Fastskin and the corporate motives of Olympic education. She co-edited (with Timothy Chandler) *With God on Their Side: Sport in the Service of Religion* and is currently writing a book on performance technologies.

Wolfram Manzenreiter is associated with the Institute of East Asian Studies at the University of Vienna in Austria, where he teaches modern Japanese society. His research interests cover social aspects of Japanese sport, popular culture, technology and labour in a globalizing world. The author of several books and articles on sport and society in Japan, he supports the soccer club SK Rapid Vienna, and he loves long-distance running and snowboarding. His most recent major publication is *Football Goes East: Culture and Business of the People's Game in East Asia* (with John Horne).

John Nauright is Professor of Sport Management and Director of the Graduate Program in Sport Management at Georgia Southern University in Statesboro, Georgia, USA. Prior to Georgia Southern he held several positions internationally, most recently as Professor of Sport and Leisure Studies at the University of Abertay Dundee in Scotland. He has been a visiting professor at the Universities of Copenhagen and Southern Denmark (Odense) in Denmark and Dalhousie University in Canada. For several years he has been the Founding Editor of *Football Studies* and co-editor of *International Sports Studies*. He is author or editor of nine books, including *Sport, Cultures and Identities in South Africa*; *Rugby and the South African Nation* (with David R. Black); *Making Men: Rugby and Masculine Identity* and *Making the Rugby World: Race, Gender, Commerce* (both with Tim Chandler) and *The Essence of Sport* (with Verner Møller). His most recent work has appeared in *Critical Arts, Contours* and *Sport History Review* and his work has appeared in many other journals, including *Sport Marketing Quarterly* and *Policy Options*.

Murray G. Phillips teaches in Sport Studies in the School of Human Movement Studies at The University of Queensland in Brisbane, Australia. His research interests are in the epistemological status of sport history, sport and gender, the football codes, swimming and coaching history. He has published *From Sidelines to Centre Field: A History of Sports Coaching in Australia* and will shortly publish *Sport History into the New Millennium: The Postmodern Challenge*.

Kimberly S. Schimmel is Associate Professor in the Sociology of Sport in the School of Exercise, Leisure and Sport at Kent State University in Kent, Ohio, USA. She is a member of the Extended Board of the International Sociology of Sport Association and currently serves as a book and media reviews editor for the *International Review for the Sociology of Sport*. She has published numerous chapters and articles on topics related to the political economy of sport in urban areas, including professional team sport franchise relocation, production–consumption relations in sport, and regime theory and sport-related urban (re)development.

Bob Stewart is Associate Professor of Sport Management at Victoria University in Melbourne, Australia. He is co-editor (with Rob Hess) of *More than a Game: An Unauthorised History of Australian Rules Football*. A former Australian football player for the Melbourne Demons Football Club, he has written widely over the past 20 years on the history and political economy of Australian football and Australian sport.

Gordon Waitt teaches Geography in the School of Earth and Environmental Sciences at the University of Wollongong, Australia. His research interests include tourism, city cultures, creative industries and cultural policy. He is co-author of *Introducing Human Geography* and is currently co-authoring *Somewhere Over the Rainbow: Understanding Gay Tourism*.

List of Abbreviations

AFL	Australian Football League
ANA	All Nippon Airways
ARL	Australian Rugby League
BBC	British Broadcasting Corporation
FA	Football Association (UK)
FIFA	Fédération Internationale de Football Association
INGO	International Non-Governmental Organization
IOC	International Olympic Committee
ITV	Independent Television (UK)
NBA	National Basketball Association (US)
NFL	National Football League (US)
NRL	National Rugby League (Australia)
OCA	Olympic Coordination Authority (Australia)
RFL	Rugby Football League (UK)
RFU	Rugby Football Union (UK)
SOBL	Sydney Olympic Bid Limited
TNC	trans-national corporation
UEFA	Union of European Football Associations
UK	United Kingdom
USA	United States of America

1
Sport and International Political Economy: An Introduction

Kimberly S. Schimmel

This collection of case studies represents an attempt to capture key aspects of the profound transformations occurring at the beginning of the twenty-first century in sport in advanced capitalist societies. As even a casual observer may recognize, the phenomenon of modern sport bears little resemblance to that of the fairly recent past. At the turn of the twentieth century, sports were occasional and unregulated events played by members of local sport clubs. In the late 1950s and early 1960s, an individual's association with sport might have been limited to participant, spectator or consumer of sport 'news' mainly through radio or newspaper (see Houlihan, 2003). However, as sport became meaningful to more than just the people who played them, the emergence of crowds at local sports club contests provided the opportunity for risk-taking entrepreneurs to turn games into profit-making ventures; for, as William A. Hulbert, one of Major League Baseball's first owners, reasoned, 'Why should we be losing money on games that people love?' (quoted in Peitrusza, 1991: 28). In a relatively short time, traditional community pastimes became today's commercial spectacles. Voluntary participation was replaced by binding contractual arrangements, and small hometown rivalries gave way to regional and international mega-events produced for mass consumption by a global television audience. The extension of capitalism's production–consumption relations into the realm of sport culture is one of the defining features of 'modern' sport (Ingham and Hardy, 1993; Schimmel, 2001). This transformed and transforming environment is the focus of this book.

In line with other volumes in the International Political Economy Series, the contributors of this volume embrace political economy as both focus and mode of analysis. Unlike more traditional texts that might be organized around levels of analysis or major theories that have

1

influenced the evolution of political economy (for example, neoclassical, mercantilist and Marxist), we have not sought to replicate theoretical and analytical categories and boundaries[1] (see also, Busumtwi-Sam and Dobuzinskis, 2003). Instead, the case studies in this volume represent some of the diversity that exists within political–economic perspectives and reflects the broad, emergent trends in sport studies scholarship that defy neat compartmentalization. Although each contributor focuses on some aspect of sport in the international political–economic context, they are eclectic in their use of historical, cultural, economic and socio-logical evidence to support their analyses. The 'political economy' contained in these chapters, then, refers primarily to questions gener-ated from the interactions of economic, political and cultural affairs (see Gilpin, 2001). The political–economic interpretation that emerges identifies powerful economic actors and institutional elites who make decisions and act in ways that advance their own interests, who make a profound impact on the nature and functioning of sport-related indus-tries at the international level and whose actions are experienced at local levels in a variety of ways.

The aim of this volume is to contribute to a greater understanding of sport, in a political–economic context, set against the backdrop of increasing international cultural flows. It is not our goal to arrive at an overarching theoretical synthesis that maps out the precise contours of the current transformation of modern sport; nor is it our aim to grapple explicitly with the continuing debate surrounding the nature of 'the global'.[2] In this respect, following Scholte (2000: xii), this is 'not another book on globalization'.[3] The contributors to this volume view globalization as contested terrain in which economic, technological and cultural features are intertwined (Kellner, 2002). They all recognize, and in some cases provide evidence, that capitalist globalization is often fought against by subcultures of resistance or by activist groups attempting to preserve more traditional or specific forms of culture and society. Thus the case studies contained in this volume do engage the broader debate regarding globalization, and we invite readers to con-sider for themselves the extent to which their own specific viewpoints are supported or not.

The chapters are grouped into three parts, each of which represents a current focus of political economic sport scholarship. Though the parts are grouped thematically for organizational clarity, it is important to rec-ognize that the themes are overlapping and intertwined, as are many of the issues that thread through the chapters in the volume. The chapters offer a remarkably topical discussion of sport while, at the same time, locating sport within certain trends and characteristics of advanced capitalism. Each chapter can stand alone, but, when considered together, they provide evidence of similar forces effecting, and being effected by, the internationalization of sport and sport-related enterprises. A dominant theme that emerges is the accelerated expansion of transnational capitalism and its extension into the sport/cultural realm. Related issues include the expansion of neoliberalist ideology/deregulation, vertical integration of media and sport markets, competition for capital investment at all geographical levels and brand-name marketing of sport and sport-related goods and services. The major actors in these processes are the elites associated with media, transnational corporations (TNCs) and the international non-governmental organizations (INGOs) that control international sport. That TNCs and powerful institutions influence the expansion of transnational capitalism is of no surprise to any reader of political economy, but what these chapters provide is a detailed description of the alliances that form between these actors and the culturally specific manifestation that is sport. In addition the contributors of this volume include perspectives of non-elites: the workers in the sporting goods industry, schoolchildren, grassroots supporters of sport clubs and urban residents.

Transnational alliances: manufacturing, merchandising and brand-name marketing in the sport industry

The first part of the volume concerns the alliances that develop between TNCs and the INGOs that control sport in the global market. These mutually beneficial alliances accelerate the commodification and commercialization of sport and, aided by recent advancements in production and communication technologies, deliver the sport 'product' on ever-increasing scales to international consumers (Hargreaves, 2002; Miller *et al.*, 2001). As Gilpin (2001) points out, in one sense, TNCs are not necessarily new. The Dutch East India Company and the Massachusetts Bay Company are examples of forerunners of today's TNCs such as IBM and Sony. These earlier versions of TNCs were far more powerful than the TNCs we can identify today; they commanded armies and fleets, created self-contained foreign policies and controlled vast expanses of territory. But it is hard to argue that the reach of these earlier TNCs extended as far as their present-day counterparts do, especially when they are allied with sport. Real and Mechikoff (1992) claim that the 'largest number of people ever in human history to engage in one activity at the same time are viewers watching the Olympic Games and the World Cup [of soccer]' (p.324). Toohey and Veal (2000) estimate that a cumulative audience of over 25 billion viewers in over 200 countries watched the television coverage of the 2000 Olympic Games in Sydney. More recently, over 31 billion people cumulatively watched the 2002 FIFA World Cup tournament (Coakley, 2004).

Richard Giulianotti takes up the issue of sport-related transnational enterprises by focusing on the production and brand-name marketing and merchandising of sport itself. Specifically Giulianotti examines the political economy of world soccer and identifies some of the key historical developments within the game's economic structure that have resulted in dramatic changes in the globe's most popular sport. In order to unravel some of the complex threads within world soccer's current political economy that have altered the game since the latter 1990s, his discussion focuses particularly on England, the United Kingdom's largest soccer market. As Guilianotti shows, a key issue there is that media tycoons with soccer interests are able to sit on both sides of the table when television contracts are being negotiated. He highlights the example of the major takeover saga in the UK involving Rupert Murdoch's £623 million bid for the soccer club Manchester United which, in late 1998, following widespread public opposition, was blocked by the Monopolies Commission.

Murdoch's pursuit of the club reflected his marketing philosophy: that televised sport is a 'battering ram' for penetrating and controlling new television markets. This policy has been vigorously pursued in North America, as evidenced by Murdoch's purchase of the major professional sports franchises New York Rangers (ice hockey), New York Knicks (basketball), LA Kings (ice hockey) and the Los Angeles Dodgers (baseball). As Guilianotti points out, the rapacious business practices of Europe's leading soccer clubs have attracted major moralizing criticism and the Fédération Internationale de Football Association (FIFA), which controls world soccer, flirts with a 'legitimation crisis' by its transparent embrace of neoliberalist market practices. Nevertheless these transnational enterprises are able partially to obfuscate their corporate ideology by deploying, through the mass media, significations of soccer clubs' traditionalism and heritage. Again, Manchester United is indicative here. The club is often castigated for readily exploiting the various economies of scale; their European ambitions and peerless finances are deemed to be undermining the domestic game's 'traditions'. However the semiology behind their corporate identity is more multilayered than this suggests. A key strategem in United's marketing, Gulianotti points out, is the commodification of the club's heritage set against the assurance that 'fans do not switch teams'.

Tara Magdalinski, Kimberly S. Schimmel and Timothy J.L. Chandler in Chapter 3 also discuss 'legitimation crisis' and brand-name marketing in their case study of strategies used by the International Olympic Committee (IOC), and its alliance with TNCs, to promote the Olympic Games. These authors suggest that the increasingly overt commercialism of the Games has come at a price: a loss of the 'mystique' of the Olympics, a mystique founded on the general aims outlined in the original Olympic Charter. Magdalinski, Schimmel and Chandler examine an array of Olympic education materials produced by corporations, which are distributed to schools, these authors suggest, as a means of 'selling' the Olympic Games and Olympism to schoolchildren. This chapter focuses on the content, framing and promotion of Olympism and global multinational corporate capitalism as it appears in materials aimed at primary and secondary schoolchildren. In this process, the authors posit that consent for the Olympic movement is manufactured at the same time that corporate brand-name loyalties are inculcated in the young consumers of these 'educational' materials.

Magdalinski, Schimmel and Chandler introduce a number of problematics that surround curricular material that is produced and promoted by the 'partnership' between corporate interests (Olympic sponsors), government agencies (schools), and international non-governmental organizations (the IOC). These include pairing Olympism and nationalism with consumerism in contexts where children are a 'captive audience', mobilizing schoolchildren to assist in the cultural and material sale of the Games, and incorporating schoolteachers to assist in consensus building around the Olympic ideology. The authors suggest that those involved in promoting the Olympic movement have turned increasingly to the 'youth of the world' to reinvigorate the Olympic mystique. The crucial questions addressed by Magdalinski, Schimmel and Chandler are not about how much corporate sponsorship is evident or explicit in these materials, but rather why these partnerships were formed to produce educational materials in the first place, and whose interests they serve. On the one hand, it would seem ironic that, although the IOC prohibits corporate signage in sport stadiums, it apparently has no problems with *delivering* corporate logos to schools. On the other hand, it is also clear that the marketing of Olympism is a successful method of introducing future consumers to corporate identities under the guise of fostering educational opportunities for all and promoting the learning of a socially responsible 'worldview'.

Active moments: capitalist production, cultural change and patterns of resistance

The second part of this volume puts the cultural meanings attached to sport into sharper focus. As was the case in Part I, the transforming impact of capitalist expansion and the extending reach of economic calculus into the realm of sport is the foundation of the chapters that follow. However, in Part II, the authors place more of an emphasis on the disruptions that sometimes occur when groups at more localized levels resist the efforts of sport entrepreneurs to shape sports in ways that serve their own interests. Sport is bound up with a variety of sentiments, place attachments and identities that people find socially meaningful and important. The dislocating effects of the transnational/national restructuring of sport and the marketing and merchandizing of sport cultures are, therefore, seldom seamless or uncontested. Of course, these types of struggle are not limited to the culturally specific form of sport. In recent years, a body of literature has emerged within cultural studies that deals with 'active consumers', which includes sports fans, but that also documents resistance efforts mobilized by fans of television, music and film against the global economic forces in the culture industries (for example, see Marris and Thornham, 1996). These next three chapters of this volume do not engage that broader literature specifically, though each makes a contribution to it. The theme that emerges in this section concerns the 'active constitutive moments' (see Ingham *et al.*, 1987) in the cultural realms of sport that contour capitalist economic forces and relations of production.

Perhaps even more dramatic than the changes occurring in world soccer, previously discussed, are the radical transformations, which began in the 1990s, in the organization of British rugby league. As Mark Falcous shows, the recent developments in rugby league are the result of a complex series of pressures, negotiations and challenges at the local level, intertwined with broader global processes. Various local agents have taken an active role in rugby league's changes, while pressures global in scope, most notably continuing media struggles in Australia, have transformed the sport in Great Britain. Though these changes were sweeping, they, like the actions of TNCs such as Nike, have not been unchallenged. Falcous uses the examples of reactions to the innovations precipitated by the emergence of a Superleague in rugby league to demonstrate that local people are in a (limited) position to make their own interpretations of global cultural impositions. Despite the efforts of 'global promotional culture', local sport supporters ('fans') attempt to maintain their own meanings, values and interpretations, thus retaining notions of distinctiveness and local identity. For example, Falcous documents fan protests that arose as a result of proposed mergers between rugby league clubs to form Superleague. The subsequent development of the game demonstrates that the application of commercial logic is subject to negotiation with wider cultural forces; this is also illustrated by the failure, in economic terms, of a series of crudely implemented commercial strategies regarding league expansion.

Falcous uses the term 'global relocalization' to describe the process whereby negotiation between recipient cultures and the forces of globalization occurs at the interpretive level. This results in global processes, despite rearticulating indigenous cultural features, being subject to local interpretation. Through these processes, the locality undergoes change in the face of the forces of globalization, but maintains the capacity for distinct local meanings and interpretations. However, even given this important proviso in the appropriation of rugby league by global commercial forces, the shifts in the balance of power in the case of rugby league, Falcous urges, should not be underestimated. While levels of interpretation and resistance are possible, commercial forces are pervasive. Indeed the new patterns of consumption associated with Superleague provide a potent example of a local sporting context profoundly altered by a shifting global sports media economy.

Resistance to changes in sport development forced through by media elites and TNCs is also an issue explored by Murray Phillips, Brett Hutchins and Bob Stewart, who focus on Australia's two most popular football codes: rugby league and Australian football. These authors offer a historically grounded Marxist analysis that outlines the similarities and differences between the political economies of rugby league and Australian football, and they assert the importance of understanding specific social and cultural contexts in the formation of the 'media sport cultural complex' (a phrase borrowed from Rowe, 1999). Both in rugby league and in Australian football, beginning in the 1980s, the media sport cultural complex drove the national expansionist programme that resulted in the rationalization agenda that has characterized the last decade. As the authors show, the important dividing dimension of the rugby league and Australian football political economies has been pay television's utilization of sports programming to drive subscriptions.

A central aim for Phillips, Hutchins and Stewart is to incorporate in their analysis sport fans' resistance to the process of rationalization in rugby league and Australian football. As the previous chapter by Falcous demonstrated in the case of British rugby league, fans' emotional attachments to their favourite clubs have been threatened time and time again by league reorganization and team merger, relocation and termination. Phillips, Hutchins and Stewart show that the resistance of fans to prospective club mergers or relocation in rugby league and Australian football has been largely conservative (rather than transformative). They illustrate this point in their case study of South Sydney supporters, whose protests against the media giant News Limited is offered as an example of the ways in which media and commercial corporations coopt and reintegrate community sentiment.

The chapter by Douglas Booth examines local-level attachments through an analysis of the tensions that exist between surfing culture and the world surfing industries. Central to his analysis is the notion of cultural authenticity and the paradoxes that exist in grassroots-level surfing culture, which both rejects and embraces corporate capitalist relations. As Booth describes, surfing culture is one that celebrates social freedom, escape from drudgery and a harmonious interaction with the natural world, and which simultaneously propagates capitalist accumulation, competition and exploitation in its modes of economic and political organization. For millions of people, surfing defines a way of life and manner of living, which Booth refers to as an 'irreverent culture'. Grassroots surfers have rejected Hollywood's effort to appropriate them and are vitriolic in their opposition to corporate capitalism's thrust to transform 'surfing the art form' into 'surfing the sport'. However Booth's multilayered analysis probes beyond the social and artistic meanings of surfing and examines the material dimensions of surfing, critical to the sport's diffusion, which harbours deep contradictions and uneasy paradoxes in surfing culture.

According to Booth, most surfers are only too well aware of the paradoxes of their sport and they reconcile the contradictions in a variety of ways. But political pressures emanate both from within surfing culture and from the broader 'counterculture' movement that has influenced the development of surfing and its subsequent mode of political organization. Moreover, while some optimistic surfing industry insiders believe that the appeal of surfing to the Generation Y market, with its own sense of adventure and style of irreverence, offers surfing unlimited potential, others are more cautious. As Booth points out, wearing surfing emblems and fashions is not tantamount to understanding the spirit of the surfing culture, or of being able to interpret its nuances, much less living by its tenets. It may be possible that the youth market represents a new vibrancy for surfing culture, but it may also be the case that creative agents within surfing are sowing the seeds of a reversal in the fortunes of the surfing industry.

Place competition: sport mega-events and urban development

Part III explores issues related to locality, community and identity as well; however, in these chapters, the analysis shifts to the political economy of place and issues associated with hosting sport 'mega-events' (Roche, 2000). The broader context of these three chapters is the transformations in capitalism, and simultaneously the transformations that have taken place in cities, in the second half of the twentieth century (see Jewson and MacGregor, 1997). The practices employed by new styles of urban governance, often referred to, following Harvey (1989), as 'urban entrepreneurism', are to be understood as both a consequence and component of new global geographies for modern capitalism. For many 'advanced' capitalist nations, a period of economic restructuring and social adjustment, which began in the 1980s, resulted in a shift away from formerly propulsive mass production industries. This shift, combined with the failure of available ideologies (both welfare statism and neoliberalism) to come up with effective policy solutions, generated a series of crises and conflicts including, among others, rising unemployment, increasing polarization between socially excluded groups and the middle classes, and deleterious environmental conditions (Jewson and MacGregor, 1997). Responding to these crises, 'entrepreneurial city' governance embraced growth policies tied to cultural consumption, thus propelling the commodification and marketing of culture (arts, theatre, fashion, sport and 'heritage') to the forefront of the regeneration industry. Thus symbolic and cultural economies have become increasingly important in representing and marketing cities as sites for consumption and leisure (Hall and

Hubbard, 1998; Jewson and MacGregor, 1997; Judd, 2003; Salmon, 2001; Schimmel, 2002; Zukin, 1995).

In Chapter 7, C. Michael Hall examines these contextual transformations with a focus on Sydney's and Toronto's bids to host the 2000 Summer Olympic Games. Hall's exploration of 'hallmark tourist events' highlights the role that 'image' plays in international, national and regional competition for increasingly mobile capital investment. Sports, tourism and urban development are three areas of urban policy in which image construction has assumed vital importance. All three options include issues of commodification of identity and the development of urban products to be sold in the marketplace. All three policies are also intimately interrelated. Hall examines the nature of these relationships and the implications for urban regeneration in cities pursuing sports mega-events. Hall explains that, while large-scale sports events may be glamorous to urban elites and spectators, their hosting does not come without a price.

The 'revitalization of place' requires more than just the development of product and image. The recreation of a sense of place is a process that involves the formulation of urban design strategies based on conceptual models of the city, which are, in turn, founded on notions of civic life and the idea that urban planning should be debated publicly. Unfortunately tourism and place planning, Hall maintains, is often poorly conceptualized with respect to participatory procedures, while the institutional arrangements for many of the public–private partnerships for urban redevelopment actually exclude community participation in the decision-making process. Policy visions for Olympic cities, whether they are for places, for sport, or for tourism, typically fail to be developed in the light of oppositional or critical viewpoints. Instead 'place visions' tend to be developed through the activities of industry experts and urban elites rather than the broad populace. Perhaps this is the case, says Hall, because the vision of the wider public for a place may not be the same as that of civic boosters (local promoters) who have most to gain from the hosting of hallmark events.

Wolfram Manzenreiter and John Horne analyse in Chapter 8 sport policy and sport infrastructure development in present-day Japan, set within a broader context of Japanese public policy, regional development programmes and private sector initiatives. These authors present a case study of the establishment of the Japanese Professional Football League (soccer) or 'J.League' and the successful Japanese/South Korean bid for and hosting of the 2002 FIFA World Cup finals. According to

Manzenreiter and Horne, gradual industrial decline and steady migration into the overcrowded major Japanese cities during the last two decades led to a rapidly aging population and a diminishing income tax base, resulting in severe threats upon the vitality of regions. Within this scenario, sport and leisure have recently been assigned special importance in an attempt to counterbalance the widening gap between centre and peripheries in Japan. Local planners envisioned two general benefits from the development of sport facilities and the promotion of sport culture. First, they assumed sport would be an economic generator. Citizens in numerous cities and municipalities of various population sizes were enthusiastic about the prospects of economic growth fuelled by investment in new sports facilities and theme parks. Thus local governments forged partnerships with private enterprises and other beneficiaries of regional development to construct new sport facilities in hopes of attracting sport consumers and fuelling local economies. Second, planners felt that a modern and enlarged sports infrastructure would enhance the 'quality of life' for local residents. Local planners reasoned that staging major sport events, or having hometown teams compete in the new professional sport leagues, would increase feelings of regional pride, foster feelings of community and create local identity attachments. These intangible benefits, it was hoped, would help prevent younger populations from migrating out of the region and bridge the social gap between established residents and newcomers.

As Manzenreiter and Horne show, however, while the number of football pitches and high-quality sport franchises has increased dramatically in Japan since 1990, the overall concerns about Japanese economic conditions have not been mitigated. With respect to professional sport, despite J.League conditions governing team location, rather than overall league balance, the most economically prosperous franchises have been located in the large population centres stretching out from Chiba Prefecture in the east, to Hiroshima in the west. Also concerns about the usage of large stadiums built for the World Cup continue to be voiced throughout Japan. While some of these facilities serve as venues for J.League teams, it is feared that seating capacity will rarely be reached for regular league matches, leaving taxpayers to cover the annual maintenance costs of the stadiums. Finally, Manzenreiter and Horne suggest, the overall concern with sport mega-events and professional football threatens to deplete the financial base for community sports and undermine Japan's 'sports for all' ideology.

In the final chapter of this volume, Gordon Waitt also focuses on planning for and hosting of sport mega-events. However he argues that an analysis of the hosting of the Olympic Games should not only include the socioeconomic cost and benefits, but should also extend into issues concerning the environment. This is especially true now that 'environmental sustainability' has become a part of the Olympic ideology. According to the Olympic Charter, increased understandings of cooperation, solidarity, tolerance and environmental sustainability are all claimed to be outcomes of hosting an Olympic Games. Waitt's chapter explores environmental sustainability in the context of Sydney 2000's 'green' Games. The Olympic Charter's apolitical social movement claims are juxtaposed in this chapter by examining the games as 'urban spectacle'.

Designing, marketing and constructing Olympic venues within a globalized economy, says Waitt, calls upon establishing an elite urban development authority informed by entrepreneurial urban planning polices of the New Right, where emphasis is given to image over substance and to budgets items over social welfare. His evaluation of Sydney's 'green' games is firmly situated within both the attributes of the Sydney Olympic site, Homebush, and the site's political economy, explaining conflicting appraisals of the site in terms of different ideologies and power relations between actors, both individual and collective. In doing so Waitt, like Hall and Manzenreiter and Horne in previous chapters, helps challenge the commonly held view that the relationship between sport and the state is neutral. The Olympic Charter suggests that the Olympics is a only a social movement, but, in fact, it is also a commercial sporting spectacle requiring huge financial investments from a variety of sources. Furthermore Waitt questions the assumption that the Olympics Games are an appropriate forum for modelling environmentally sustainable development. In the post-Sydney Games context, Homebush's official image remains 'green', as Waitt clearly documents. However he shows how 'greenwashing' can become embedded in the urban planning process and remain as a legacy for urban developers' marketing schemes, leaving actual environmental hazards uncertain, and resting environmental sustainability on mere assertion.

Conclusion

The chapters in this volume provide a look into the transformed and transforming international political economic context of sport in advanced capitalist societies in the early part of the twenty-first century. Taken together, they reveal some of the modern changes in economic, political and cultural relationships that are both a consequence and a component of international sport. They identify political and economic actors whose decisions contour the ways in which sport is produced and consumed within and across nations. They examine struggles that surround attempts by various elites and organizations to redefine or invent sport-related images in ways that mostly benefit themselves. They show that 'politics matters' (to barrow a phrase from Clarence Stone, 1989) in economic processes and outcomes, and also that sport matters, both to elites who manipulate it and to people for whom it represents a lifestyle, a tradition or an identity. Ultimately, then, this volume aims to provide a realist insight into sport as a non-neutral, significant and meaningful aspect of everyday life in modern capitalist societies.

Notes

1. In his discussion of political economy and sport, Sage (2000) distinguishes between classical political economy, neoclassical economics and radical political economy. For a more general analysis of the 'enduring legacy' of Karl Marx for the sociology of sport, see Beamish (2002).
2. For an overview of the ways in which sport studies scholars have conceptualized and debated sport and global processes, see for example, Bairner (2001), Donnelly (1996), Hargreaves (2002), Maguire (1999, 2000) and Miller *et al.* (2001).
3. Scholte's phrase is quoted by Busumtwi-Sam and Dobuzinskis (2003) in their introduction to *Turbulence and new directions in global political economy*.

References

Bairner, A. (2001), *Sport, nationalism, and globalization: European and American perspectives*, Albany, NY: State University of New York.

Beamish, R. (2002), 'Karl Marx's enduring legacy for the sociology of sport', in J. Maguire and K. Young (eds), *Theory, sport & society*, London: Elsevier Science, pp.25–39.

Busumtwi-Sam, J. and L. Dobuzinskis (eds) (2003), *Turbulence and new directions in global political economy*, London: Palgrave Macmillan.

Coakley, J. (2004), *Sport in society: issues & controversies*, 8th edn, New York: McGraw-Hill.

Donnelly, P. (1996), 'The local and the global: globalization in the sociology of sport', *Journal of Sport and Social Issues*, **20** (3), 239–57.

Gilpin, R. (2001), *Global poltical economy: understanding the international economic order*, Princeton, NJ: Princeton University.

Hall, T. and P. Hubbard (eds) (1998), *The entrepreneurial city: geographies of politics, regime, and representation*, New York: Wiley.

Hargreaves, J. (2002), 'Globalization theory, global sport, and nations and nationalism', in J. Sugden and A. Tomlinson (eds), *Power games: a critical sociology of sport*, London: Routledge, pp.25–43.

Harvey, D. (1989), *The condition of postmodernity: an inquiry into the origins of cultural change*, Oxford: Blackwell.

Houlihan, B. (2003), 'Introduction', in B. Houlihan (ed.), *Sport and society: a student introduction*, London: Sage, pp.1–7.

Ingham, A.G. and S. Hardy (1993), 'Introduction: sport studies through the eyes of Raymond Williams', in A. Ingham and J. Loy (eds), *Sport and social development: traditions, transitions, and transformation*, Champaign, IL: Human Kinetics, pp.1–19.

Ingham, A.G., J. Howell and T. Schilperoort (1987), 'Professional sport and community: a review and exegesis', *Exercise and Sport Science Reviews*, **15**, 427–65.

Jewson, N. and S. MacGregor (eds) (1997), *Transforming cities: contested governance and new spatial divisions*, London: Routledge.

Judd, D. (ed.) (2003), *The infrastructure of play: building the tourist city*, London: M.E. Sharpe.

Kellner, D. (2002), 'Theorizing globalization', *Sociological Theory*, **20** (3), 285–305.

Maguire, J. (1999), *Global sport: identities, societies, civilizations*, Cambridge: Polity.

Maguire, J. (2000), 'Sport and globalization', in J. Coakley and E. Dunning (eds), *Handbook of sport studies*, London: Sage, pp. 356–69.

Marris, P. and S. Thornham (eds) (1996), *Media studies: a reader*, Edinburgh: Edinburgh University.

Miller, T., G. Lawrence, J. McKay and D. Rowe (2001), *Globalization and sport: playing the world*, London: Sage.

Peitrusza, D. (1991), *Major leagues: the formation, sometimes absorption, and mostly inevitable demise of 18 professional baseball associations, 1871 to present*, Jefferson, NJ: McFarland and Co.

Real, M. and R.A. Mechikoff (1992), 'Deep fan: mythic identification, technology, and advertising in spectator sports', *Sociology of Sport Journal*, **9**, 323–9.

Roche, M. (2000), *Mega events and modernity: Olympics and expos in the growth of global culture*, London: Routledge.

Rowe, D. (1999), *Sport, culture and the media*, Buckingham: Open University.

Sage, G. (2000), 'Political economy and sport', in J. Coakley and E. Dunning (eds), *Handbook of sport studies*, London: Sage, pp.260–76.

Salmon, S. (2001), 'Imagineering the inner city: landscapes of pleasure and the commodification of cultural spectacle in the postmodern city', in C.L. Harrington and D.D. Bielby (eds), *Popular culture: production and consumption*, Oxford: Blackwell, pp.106–19.

Schimmel, K. (2001), 'Take me out to the ballgame: the transformation of production–consumption relations in professional team sport', in C.L. Harrington and D.D. Bielby (eds), *Popular culture: production and consumption*, Oxford: Blackwell, pp.36–52.

Schimmel, K. (2002), 'The political economy of place: urban and sport studies perspectives', in J. Maguire and K. Young (eds), *Theory, sport & society*, London: Elsevier Science, pp.335–51.

Scholte, J.A. (2000), *Globalization: a critical introduction*, Basingstoke: Macmillan.

Stone, C. (1989), *Regime politics*, Lawrence, KS: University of Kansas.
Sudgen, J. (2002), 'Network football', in J. Sugden and A. Tomlinson (eds), *Power games: a critical sociology of sport*, London: Routledge, pp. 62–80.
Toohey, K. and A.J. Veal (2000), *The Olympic Games: a social science perspective*, New York: CABI.
Veseth, M. (1998), *Selling globalization: the myth of the global economy*, London: Lynne Rienner.
Zukin, S. (1995), *Loft living: culture and capital in urban change*, Cambridge, MA: Blackwell.

Part I

Transnational Alliances: Manufacturing, Merchandising and Brand-Name Marketing in the Sport Industry

Part I

2
Playing an Aerial Game: The New Political Economy of Soccer

Richard Giulianotti

Association football, otherwise known as soccer, is without question the world's most popular sport. Globally soccer is played and watched by more people than any other game. While the American professional basketball (NBA) and football/gridiron (NFL) leagues struggle to cultivate a massive European following, soccer has been successfully transplanted into the apparently infertile territory of the United States, resulting in 18 million direct participants (Andrews, 1999). Soccer's flagship tournament, the World Cup finals, is fast approaching the Olympic Games as sport's most extravagant mega-event. Soccer constitutes a lingua franca *qua* body culture to peoples otherwise divided by language, religion or custom. Politically the game has been considered to spark wars in Central America and revolutions in Eastern Europe (Kapuscinski, 1992),[1] as well as promote ceasefires and conflict resolutions in Africa (Murray, 1996; Richards, 1997). Yet soccer's global centrality is most commonly measured in financial terms. Some estimates valued annual soccer-related business at over £250 billion in the year 2001.

In this chapter I unravel some of the complex threads within world soccer's political economy. To discuss the major trends, I examine in particular the United Kingdom (UK) club game, which contained ten of the world's top 20 clubs in terms of turnover for the season 2001–2. I also examine some central features of soccer finance in other countries, notably in Latin America and continental Europe.

Sociological discourses on soccer finance

Sociologists have shown a rather cyclical interest in soccer's political economy. Early commentators adopted an orthodox Marxist perspective and thus concentrated upon economic structures. Gerhard Vinnai (1973) explored the rise of an alienating, 'scientific' control over players as rooted in the industrial commodification of soccer. Ian Taylor (1970, 1971) confirmed that English club directors were seeking to wrest soccer from its working-class and community roots. He averred that the 'participatory democracy' within the club was being replaced by a more profitable, bourgeois enterprise. Although ethically positive, this argument rather romanticized UK soccer's social history. Most English clubs have been genuine businesses since the late nineteenth century; since then, few fans have truly believed that club politics were essentially democratic.

The rise of soccer hooliganism by the 1980s switched academic attention towards explaining this 'problem', with some sociologists again emphasizing a materialist analysis. Taylor had initially argued that hooligans were 'resistance fighters' opposed to soccer's commodification. Switching tack, he claimed that hooligans were racist, chauvinistic and deeply xenophobic: direct products of New Right policies and a real problem for working-class communities (Taylor, 1982a, 1982b, 1987, 1989). Meanwhile, the emerging Leicester School of sociologists drew on Norbert Elias to explain hooliganism according to the 'civilizing process' (Dunning *et al.*, 1988). Ultimately, if indirectly, the key to their explanation lay in the alleged socioeconomic status of soccer hooligans. Most fan violence, it was claimed, emanated from lower working-class fans, particularly those from rough housing estates where young males were socialized into aggressive masculine identities. Neither Taylor nor the Leicester researchers put forward persuasive fieldwork with hooligan groups to support their arguments. Later researchers separated analytically the economic and cultural structures within soccer (Armstrong, 1998; Back, Crabbe and Solomos, 1996; Giulianotti, 1999a, 1999b). Hence participation in violent activities is not reducible to pure class dynamics; other factors predominate, notably social identity that is rooted geographically (at local, regional and national levels) and subculturally (youth aesthetics and styles) (Giulianotti, 1999a).

Hooliganism remained a major if more intermittent subject of academic and popular discussion through the late 1990s, though other issues emerged, notably the financial boom within soccer and its sudden fashionable status after the 1990 World Cup finals. Financial growth was based on lucrative television deals, new sponsorship and merchandizing practices, rising income from ticket sales and a greater global circulation of professional players. Rogan Taylor has been the most publicly trenchant critic of soccer's commodification and the 'disgusting', multi-million pound profits reaped by a handful of beneficiaries. For its proponents, soccer's 'commodification' has been presented as the only form of 'modernization' that was possible to 'save' the game. Yet, as Adam Brown (1998) points out, these modernizers construct a highly caricatured, sociopathic picture of the old soccer crowd. Elsewhere I have endeavoured to trace a genealogy of soccer's political economy in the UK with regard to its traditional, modern and post-modern phases (Giulianotti, 1999a). I favour the analyses of more mainstream writers by drawing attention to the new politics of access within soccer *qua* field of popular culture (Conn, 1997; Dempsey and Reilly, 1998; Horton, 1997). The relatively decomposed working class is excluded financially from attending the increasingly expensive live matches, while the communicative codes surrounding soccer have been colonized by a cadre of metropolitan middle-class spectators. Soccer in this sense has been ensnared by neoliberal policies and thinking that otherwise predominate in the West. In the discussion that follows here, I seek to examine some of the key historical and economic changes within the game.

Proto-commodification: merchandising the early 'brand-name'

European soccer finances have developed rapidly in recent years. In the early 1980s, Western clubs still relied heavily on gate-money to survive and compete. Northern European clubs retained an antediluvian corporate structure with ownership and control reposing within one family or small clique of shareholders. The clubs' entry to stock markets – the logical step for expansion – was eschewed for several reasons. First, during the 1980s, several European leagues faced declining crowds and general uncertainty about soccer's financial future. Market capitalization at some clubs (such as Brondby in Denmark) backfired, leaving them near to liquidation. Second, in nations like Germany and Italy, legal regulations prevented capitalization or required the exercise of exceptional austerity prior to going public. Elsewhere soccer accountancy was a relatively murky affair, where 'bungs' (bribes) to managers during transfers or an extra few thousand supporters at matches failed to materialize on tax returns. Capitalization would risk exposing this underworld for an uncertain market return. Third, we must consider the financial and egotistical persona of many top club owners. For some, absolute ownership and control of a major club was a vital conduit towards sustaining a charismatic public identity. For others, the 'family' club reflected the owner's petit-bourgeois business habitus: paternalism, hard work, low employee turnover, limited diversification (Raspaud, 1994). Until the late 1980s, few clubs were controlled by flamboyant entrepreneurs with a penchant for risky financial ventures. Most club owners comprised, instead, a rentier class of local businessmen with an ingrained compulsion to balance the books (Hopcraft, 1988). Fourth, in southern Europe, notably Spain and Portugal, clubs like Barcelona are private member associations, and therefore still 'owned' by *socios* or club members who pay monthly or annual subscriptions.

Nevertheless, by the early 1980s, the leading clubs in northern Europe were beginning to employ brand marketing and merchandising in a more wholehearted fashion to maximize their revenues and keep up with competitors. Trackside advertising was revamped, shirt sponsorship was established, larger deals with shirt manufacturers were signed, corporate hospitality and conference facilities were created, and executive boxes were carved into the main stands. Meanwhile the price of admission to matches multiplied, well beyond inflation levels. Subsequently a smorgasbord of products was manufactured under club names: beer, whisky, tomato ketchup, radios, hi-fis, bedspreads and leisurewear. Banks, credit card companies, building societies and holiday firms have joined with clubs to offer special consumer packages to supporters. In effect, the club name has become a floating signifier that can be appended to any product to facilitate the latter's fetishization among consumers. This post-modern marketing strategy still relies ultimately on two deeply traditionalist principles of soccer culture: that fans identify automatically with their team 'sign' no matter where it sits, thus generating 'inelastic demand' (Conn, 1997: 155), and that fans do not switch teams (hence will not switch brands).

As clubs were switched into brands, market capitalization duly followed, netting astronomical profits for the original shareholders. At Scotland's top two clubs, the Rangers chairman David Murray saw his £6 million investment multiply to £100 million within six years; Celtic's Fergus McCann saw his £13 million investment become £50 million within three years. In England, similar paper profits were reaped by Alan Sugar at Tottenham, David Dein at Arsenal and Sir John Hall at Newcastle. The greatest profits fell to businessmen who had invested in the early 1980s, when soccer was in a parlous financial condition. For example, Doug Ellis at Aston Villa held a post-flotation fortune of over £50 million, based on his stake of £500,000 in 1982 (Sloane, 1997). Clubs in Italy, Spain and Turkey are looking closely at following this model, with Lazio among the earliest and most prominent observers of the capitalization trend. Yet, since the late 1980s, the biggest influence on soccer's political economy has come from television, the medium that makes brand marketing a mass possibility.

Television money and soccer divisions

The relationship between soccer and television has not always been comfortable. During the 1960s and 1970s, UK club officials feared that television directly undermined spectator attendances, the clubs' major source of revenue (Walvin, 1975: 168–71). Live soccer matches were few and far between, hence post-match highlights packages were the order of the day. In the UK, highlights packages were distributed between the public sector BBC and the sole independent station, ITV. The fees were strikingly low: a four-year highlights deal between the BBC and the English Football League was signed for £9.8 million in 1978. Five years later, some live English matches were secured for the very moderate fee of £2.6 million (Szymanski and Smith, 1997).

At the 1985 European Cup final in Belgium, Liverpool fans attacked their Juventus rivals inside the Heysel Stadium. The Italians' attempts to escape led to a wall collapsing and crowd crushing, resulting in 39 deaths. English clubs were immediately banned from international competition, leaving them and the sports broadcasters with a vacuum in prestige fixtures. A subsequent rise of televised league soccer helped to repair that problem, but sowed the seeds of a major political schism between English clubs. The so-called 'Big 5' (Everton, Liverpool, Arsenal, Tottenham and Manchester United) gained markedly from television coverage. Their fixtures were shown far more regularly than those involving other clubs, enabling them to make millions from trackside advertising that was beamed into all UK homes. Aspiring clubs like Chelsea were unable to tap that lucrative, elite income (Fynn and Guest, 1994).

In 1991, English First Division clubs were lured to join an FA-controlled breakaway league. One major attraction had been the FA's offer to divide all television money between the top clubs. Clubs in the lower divisions that had benefited from earlier television deals were excluded from the new agreement. The greatest fillip for the new FA Premier League was the landmark broadcasting deal signed to begin during the inaugural season of 1992–3. The contract guaranteed the Premier League an astronomical £304 million over five years: £191.5 million came from the satellite station BSkyB, who would feature 60 live matches each season on subscription sports channels. The BBC paid £22.5 million for regular match highlights, with £90 million coming from sponsorship and overseas television rights. Significantly, each club was guaranteed an equal share of half of this total; the rest was divided according to final league position and the frequency of television appearances. In November 1995, the FA coffers were further swollen when an ITV–BSkyB partnership paid

£115 million for a four-year FA Cup package. The controlling interest in BSkyB is held by Rupert Murdoch, whose News Corporation company bore the heavy start-up costs for satellite television. By the end of 2003, BSkyB had turned into Sky digital television and possessed around seven million UK subscribers, most of whom bought soccer packages. The global networking of Murdoch's corporation ensures that live European sports fixtures can be watched in all corners. BSkyB has sister companies throughout Europe (notably Sky Italia), in Australia (Foxtel), the United States (Fox) and the Far East (Star TV).

The new relationship between English soccer and satellite television has been replicated overseas. FIFA, soccer's governing body, utilized satellite television income to accelerate its conversion from a sports-oriented association to a transnational corporation. FIFA accrued a relatively modest £84 million for television rights to the 1998 World Cup finals, mainly from terrestrial broadcasting networks such as the EBU (European Broadcasting Union). The 2002 and 2006 tournaments were sold for £1.16 billion to satellite broadcasters through FIFA's marketing arm, which in a reflection of the governing body's murky financial activities subsequently fell into bankruptcy. In Italy, France, Germany and Spain, the top divisions have all come under the aegis of subscription television stations. While these deals mirrored England in apportioning revenues relatively equally, the remaining differences and spin-off marketing benefits have deepened divisions between an elite few in each league and the remaining clubs. Thus Europe's national leagues are faced by a crisis in the 'uncertainty of outcome' as economic power overdetermines soccer success.

The institutional framework of club soccer in Europe and South America has always been bedevilled by this problem. The groundwork for the oldest leagues was established prior to the First World War. In Western Europe, most clubs were established as limited companies, committed to attracting supporters to survive financially and maximize profits. The league competition emerged to satisfy these needs. The most powerful clubs cemented their hegemony by offering high transfer fees and salary contracts to the best players available within the market. Unlike sports leagues in the United States and Australia, soccer leagues do not operate a 'draft' system of player recruitment. Clubs at the foot of the league are not compensated the next season by receiving first option on junior players; they are instead relegated into lower divisions. There is no salary cap to ensure the wealthiest clubs do not outbid their opponents for top players. Nor is match-day income pooled by the league administrators, then distributed between clubs; instead all gate money from league games is retained by the home club, allowing the most popular clubs to enjoy the greatest profits. Inevitably the economies of scale come to prevail, and there is increasingly little 'glory' to be found in the struggle to survive among the lower clubs.

Recent changes within English club soccer's political economy seem likely to exaggerate the inequalities. First, from the late 1990s, as stock markets fell into troughs, the capitalization of clubs became a less secure way of gaining new revenues. Instead attention turned again to investments from extremely rich individuals, most spectacularly at Chelsea in the summer of 2003, with the arrival of Russian oligarch Roman Abramovich, and an immediate player transfer budget of over £100 million. Second, clubs in the Nationwide League (below the Premiership) suffered a massive loss of revenue (around £180 million) when their main broadcasting partner, ITV Digital, went into receivership in April 2002. Although an alternative deal was signed with Sky television, the loss of revenues has further widened the gulf between Premiership clubs and those in the lower leagues. Third, uncertainty surrounding future television deals with Sky has been intensified by the intervention of the European Commission, on the grounds that the current deal with the Premiership amounts to a monopoly. While England's top few clubs can look to the European Champions League tournament for at least around £10 million in annual income, other clubs are dependent on the continuation of high revenues from Sky. When Sky can no longer seriously claim 'exclusive' (that is, monopoly) access to live English football, then the financial lifeline between the broadcaster and many English clubs will be broken. Fourth, attempting to break into the European elite through heavy speculation is extremely risky. Leeds United spent massively in a bid to guarantee a regular place in the Champions League, but failed, and thus at time of writing look certain to enter administration with unserviceable debts of £80 million. Fifth, future technological breakthroughs such as digital television might enable individual clubs to exercise complete control over the broadcasting of their home matches. If this occurs, alongside the rise of pay-per-view, the financial differences between teams like Manchester United and Southampton will be further magnified.

The influence of television finance over soccer's organization and playing inequalities is more explicit in Latin America. Mexican soccer is basically run by television companies that own the best clubs and the national stadium (Magazine, 2001). Brazilian soccer's dependency on television is such that fixture calendars and tournaments are rescheduled at very short notice to suit broadcasting schedules, while Brazil is seen as an ideal laboratory by FIFA for testing innovations (such as the time-out) that suit network controllers. In Argentina, a new, double-league championship system was introduced at television's behest to spread the likelihood of victory among the nation's five great clubs. Football's room for manoeuvre is curtailed by the long agreements that the media giant *T y C* holds with the Argentinian, Uruguayan and Paraguayan federations. Generally South American soccer's political economy represents a study in the capacity of transnational corporations to redefine the institutional administration, and reshape the cultural production, within a central component of the continent's civil societies. In McLuhanian terms, via Castells (1996: 337–42), we find the soccer 'message' being essentially determined by the medium through which it is experienced, the mass media stations themselves.

In Western Europe, the distinction between soccer clubs and media organizations *qua* discrete institutional actors is becoming increasingly blurred. A trend towards vertical integration has seen major media companies buying large or controlling interests in top European clubs. In France, the leading club, Paris Saint-Germain, is owned by Canal Plus; in England, Caspian bought into Leeds United; in Spain, Antenne 3 bought into Real Madrid; in Germany, Bertelsmann have helped to revitalize Hertha Berlin; in the Netherlands, Phillips propelled PSV Eindhoven to the European Cup in the early 1980s; in Turkey, the owner of Star TV was controller of Istanbulspor. The most compelling case for soccer-media ownership comes from Italy, where Silvio Berlusconi's Mediaset SpA empire acquired the ailing giant AC Milan in the early 1980s. Milan soon purchased a huge squad of the world's leading players to become Europe's premier club during the late 1980s and early 1990s. That pre-eminence encouraged Berlusconi to purchase the television rights to the top Italian league (Serie A) for his subscription channels. Later Berlusconi founded a right-wing political party as Italy's Christian Democrats imploded in the midst of corruption scandals and the fall of the Eastern bloc. Significantly, Berlusconi owed election victory in 1993 to his use of soccer metaphors and discourses. Even the party, *Forza Italia!*, was named after a popular soccer slogan (Semino and Masci, 1996).

The vertical integration of media and soccer institutions is reflected in other culture industries, particularly through takeovers and mergers involving film, music and telecommunications companies, all of this enabled by the legal deregulation of media corporate activities. Subsequently the old 'modern' boundaries between institutions that produce and those that mediate cultural practices are becoming increasingly obsolete. A further consequence is that media tycoons are seeking soccer interests to sit on both sides of the table when negotiating broadcasting contracts. A major takeover saga in the UK involved Rupert Murdoch's £623 million bid for Manchester United, which was eventually blocked by the Monopolies Commission in late 1998 following widespread public opposition. Murdoch's interest reflected his marketing philosophy that televised sport is a 'battering ram' for penetrating and controlling new television markets. That policy has been soundly exploited in North America by buying into four major sports franchises: the New York Rangers (ice hockey), New York Knicks (basketball), LA Dodgers (baseball) and the LA Kings (ice hockey). Moreover the soccer club represents more than a mere security option for satellite television. Manchester United's annual budget is nearly twice that of Italy's two biggest sides, Internazionale and Juventus. The Murdoch–Manchester United courtship sparked a frenzy of takeover speculation and share purchasing involving media companies and clubs as rival stations strove to position themselves for future deals. In the longer term, the promise of digital television encourages Europe's top clubs to follow Manchester United's lead by founding their own subscription channels, or establishing marketing deals with those media companies that take smallholdings within the club.

Finally there has long been a content-based connection between football and other forms of cultural entertainment, since players have endorsed many products, but it has only been in the last decade or so that the world's leading superstars have become massive global icons with media-dependent followings that extend well beyond football. David Beckham's transfer from Manchester United to Real Madrid, for example, caught not only the imagination of football audiences, but also, for example, the celebrity-focused attentions of millions of females in China where, less than coincidentally, his new club played some pre-season friendly matches in 2003.

Soccer's global market system

European soccer's boom has direct consequences throughout the world. The major clubs in Latin America are under increasing pressure to match their European counterparts or face the exile of more and more players in richer pastures. Uruguayan league clubs have been beyond that point since the early 1980s. Over 400 Uruguayan players play abroad, in the larger South American leagues or (preferably for them) in Europe – a figure sufficient to fill the squads of the national league's top two divisions. The institutionalization of elite labour migration is pivotal to the underdevelopment of the Uruguayan national side, which struggles even to qualify for the World Cup finals (Giulianotti, 1999c). Argentinian club soccer faces similar problems. Top players now migrate to Europe at younger and younger ages, the transfer of the brilliant minor Cambiasso to Real Madrid being indicative. Meanwhile the cream of the Argentinian game is also willing to 'make do' by playing for moderate European club sides (that pay handsomely) rather than top home sides (Alabarces, 1999). As in Uruguay, the Argentinian clubs confront a 'legitimation crisis' as they struggle to sustain public interest in a weakened league, an inferiority rendered even more transparent by constant television coverage of glamorous European clubs. Meanwhile the economic collapse of Argentina and Uruguay means fans struggle to pay admission fees while clubs cannot pay the interest on their debts and retain revenues to pay players. Certainly there can be no criticism of moves to eliminate corruption at Latin American clubs through the introduction of more professional administration, as witnessed, for example, initially at the bankrupt Racing Club of Buenos Aires. However, strong political and moral criticisms can be advanced towards arguments that Latin American clubs should abandon the *socio* model of organization for a neoliberal model defined by market capitalization.

The changes to soccer's financescape have helped to establish a new market order within the global game, which may be summarized as follows. First, the core soccer powers remain in Europe, primarily with the richest clubs in the 'Big Five' leagues (England, Spain, Italy, Germany and France), who make up most of the 18 clubs that now comprise the 'G14' business group of elite European teams.[2]

Second, an outer core or semi-periphery of clubs exists among the larger clubs in smaller soccer markets (such as Portugal, Holland, Belgium and Scotland). Some have secured or are on the fringes of G14 membership. Collectively these clubs spend heavily in attracting promising overseas stars from across Europe and Latin America, while losing their finest players to the richest clubs in the biggest European leagues. The biggest clubs in Scotland, Portugal, Belgium, Holland and Austria are trapped inside small television markets, cannot match the standard television incomes afforded to clubs in large markets, and so have most to gain comparatively from a radical restructuring of European club soccer. One approach would involve an enlarged European Superleague. Another possibility, mooted at the end of the millennium, would see teams from Scandinavia, the Low Countries and Scotland forming an Atlantic League, to deliver potentially a combined television audience of over 50 million.

Third, at a more peripheral level, we find the strongest and wealthiest clubs in weaker soccer markets, such as the old Eastern bloc (such as Croatia, Russia, Yugoslavia) or Latin America (Brazil, Argentina). The feeder role of these clubs for the G14 sides is much more transparent, while their capital growth is restricted by slow expansion in their nation's service economies.

Finally, we have those societies on the geographic, economic and symbolic periphery of the world soccer system. Most domestic clubs need to function as feeders to stronger soccer markets in order to survive. Africa, Australasia and poorer South American nations such as Paraguay and Uruguay are noteworthy in this regard, although this periphery is itself internally stratified. For example, South African clubs attract the better southern African players, while some Australian clubs purchase players from the Pacific islands.

The structure of this world soccer system is being cemented by strong vertical integration of global clubs, whereby the elite contract with or purchase shares in smaller sides at home or abroad to ensure first options on emerging young talents. For example, Manchester United has entered an agreement with Royal Antwerp to exploit Belgium's more relaxed labour regulations towards non-EC nationals. In theory, emerging non-EC players may be signed or farmed out to Antwerp to learn their trade and quickly acquire an EC work permit. Other partnership deals exist between United and teams in Scotland (Livingston), France (Nantes) and Portugal (Sporting Lisbon).

Disorganized capitalism and the deconstruction of the nation: global club power and cultural mythology

The current transformations and restructuring of soccer's power relations can be explained in terms of the emergence of a 'disorganized' form of capitalism. Disorganized capitalism is a new epoch in which 'culture, consumption, the global, the local, and concern for the environment' predominate (Lash and Urry, 1994: 258). Globalization of economic and cultural practices is particularly influential, as 'the flows of subjects and objects are progressively less synchronized within national boundaries' (ibid.: 10). The old institutions and organizations, that had arisen under 'organized capitalism' to regulate and control economic and cultural practices, embark upon an often terminal decline in the late twentieth century (Lash, 1994: 213–14; Lash and Urry, 1987).

There are signs of this 'disorganizing' process within the political economy of world soccer. Soccer's old organizational pyramid had imagined FIFA at the apex, followed by the continental associations (such as UEFA in Europe), the national associations, the clubs, the players and the fans (literally 'the supporters' at the base) in a neatly administered hierarchy, with their own specific fiefdoms and spheres of varying economic influence. That arrangement is now undermined in a plethora of ways.

First, FIFA, the continental, and the national associations encounter greater clashes of interest, such as the legal and financial control over world soccer's congested fixture calendar. For example, FIFA's 'World Club Championship' opened in 2000 to serious criticism from national and continental associations, because of its extra burden on players and its inopportune relationship to other club and national fixtures.

Second, in true post-modern style, the transnational persona of G14 clubs is undermining the traditionally subservient relationship with national soccer associations, UEFA (European soccer's governing body) and FIFA. A threatened breakaway league of top European clubs was only averted in the summer of 1998 after UEFA acceded to club demands for a revamp of existing European competitions, to create the 'Champions League' that provided for far more lucrative competition involving the richest European clubs. The national soccer associations, UEFA and FIFA, are empowered to head off a breakaway by ejecting any clubs from their competitions and placing worldwide bans on 'rebel' players.[3] Yet major, regular alterations to European competition are certain to be put forward by the G14 with the game's governing authorities under increasing pressure to comply.

A further struggle surrounds the claim that nations make on club players to play in international fixtures. Clubs complain that they pay players' wages but have few rights over controlling the timing and the number of international fixtures involving these employees. If players are injured during internationals, or return exhausted, it is the clubs that pay the financial penalty. Conversely football's governing bodies argue that international fixtures represent football's highest level, are extremely popular with fans and increase these players' prestige and transfer value. Nevertheless, in many nations, there are suspicions that top club managers exert undue influence over the team selection of national coaches. For coaches of small or poor nations, it can be particularly hard to secure the best players who play abroad in rich leagues; these talents can come under severe club pressure to remain at home rather than travel abroad.

Third, top soccer players are the centre of complex power struggles between an array of institutional actors. The European Community's *Bosman*[4] ruling, which had been opposed by the soccer authorities and the clubs, effectively removed the juridicoadministrative barriers on player mobility, allowing top European (and often global) players to move freely between clubs and nations. Player wage inflation is encouraging clubs to oppose FIFA's edict that all players be available for international matches, irrespective of league fixtures. The clubs argue that the national associations must pay players' wages when on international duty, an argument given greater piquancy by FIFA's determination to oversee more and more international competitions.[5] The growing symbolic capital of soccer players, and the expansion of a supportive service sector, ensure that they have far greater personal commitments to major non-soccer transnational corporations, such as Nike, Adidas and BSkyB television. Since Nike's arrival in world soccer in the early 1990s, most merchandise companies have become heavily committed to marketing products through individual players. Conflicts of interest arise when one company hires a player for endorsement purposes, but the player's club or national association endorses a rival product. Symbolically soccer tournaments also become 'matches' between transnational corporations and their affiliated players (Bourdieu, 1999). At the 1998 World Cup, Adidas struggled to project its stars in a positive light: Beckham, Kluivert and Zidane were all sent off in different matches. Ultimately Adidas outperformed Nike: Zidane scored the winning goals in the final, while Nike's flagship player (Ronaldo) and team (Brazil) lost the match amidst intense controversy.

Fourth, as noted, the conversion of soccer's governing cultural institutions into corporate organizations is disturbingly transparent. FIFA flirts with a 'legitimation crisis' as it struggles to square its traditionalist, cultural discourses (universalism, sportsmanship), with its transparently neoliberal market practices (such as selling World Cup television rights to subscription television in Europe). Europe's leading clubs attract political criticism for their rapacious, transnational restructuring. Nevertheless some clubs obfuscate these transnational ambitions by mediating significations of their traditionalism and heritage.

For example, Manchester United has adroitly commodified its club heritage. The successes of the 1950s and 1960s ensured that the club became an international soccer symbol, a key signifier in the universal mediation of the club game. Hence United's belated revival in the late 1980s could be understood as a reclaiming of that majestic heritage. While many clubs have sought to reinvent themselves to generate a new 'corporate' identity, Manchester United has remained symbolically in touch with this past mythology. The club continues to play at Old Trafford, to trade with a 'Red Devils' motif, to employ the legendary Bobby Charlton as a director, to retain the long-term manager, Sir Alex Ferguson, for an exceptional

18 years. The prevailing 'humanity' of the club is signified by a continuing association with the deeply existential. Few 'soccer people' are unmoved by the personal narratives and imagery that surround the 1958 Munich air crash, when United's extraordinarily gifted young team was all but wiped out. Moreover United's soccer side remains a traditional metonym for an attacking, aesthetically exciting playing style that has drawn on the best talents from throughout the UK: Scotland's Dennis Law, England's Charlton and Edwards, Wales's Hughes and Giggs and, most sublimely of all, George Best from Northern Ireland, British soccer's first genuine superstar.

The commodification of this club is neatly encapsulated in a late-1990s club advert. A film mixes images of former players to show them joining forces to score an epic goal. The moving ball unites the various players, and thus the markedly different epochs to which they belong, all in a singular, eternal cause. This mythical construction of 'Manchester United' *qua* traditional institution manages to secrete the club's transnational financial essence. Yet a crucial index of this underlying global appeal is the club's comparative transcendence of 'traditional' regional and national ties. At national level, in England, the club now germinates temporary, neotribal networks of opposition among rival fans who will support most if not all of United's opponents; and also through the fan chants among English fans of 'Stand Up If You Hate Man U' at both club and England matches. Additionally United do not connote the regional or national significations that some of Europe's richest clubs possess: for example, Barcelona with Catalonia, Rangers in Glasgow with Protestant Unionism, Newcastle with the 'Geordie' North-East of England, Bayern Munich with Bavaria. In this way United avoid the wider present-day problem of the post-national milieu: being pulled in opposing directions by strong regional or national identities on one side, and transnational business interests on the other.[6]

The *Bosman* Case and beyond: post-Fordism and player migration

In the deconstruction of soccer's national boundaries, the *Bosman* ruling by the European Courts has revolutionized the international division of elite labour. This process is manifested through the greater mobility of professionals, multiplication of their salaries and the potential collapse of national boundaries between clubs and league systems. *Bosman*'s initial influence was to promote the migration of European players to other European nations. As a result of the *Bosman* ruling, the free market opened up for player transfers within all European Union nations.

Post-*Bosman*, the transfer fees that would have exchanged hands between clubs were largely redirected into player salaries and signing-on fees. In England, wage inflation rose by around 40 per cent in the 1997–8 season. Top players like Ravanelli, Shearer, Bergkamp and Zola were paid £25,000–£50,000 a week; wages for leading players at clubs like Manchester United and Arsenal now exceed £100,000 a week. Meanwhile the remaining income from share issues, television fees and takeover deals has helped to service a spiralling transfer market. The clubs that manage to retain a few, highly coveted players on long-term contracts may demand ever-greater fees for their exceptionally immobile assets.

Most public and academic commentary on *Bosman* has assessed the benefits bestowed on players. Further consideration should be given to *Bosman*'s role in enhancing the clubs' market interests and industrial relations. *Bosman* encourages clubs to adopt a post-Fordist strategy of flexible accumulation in their engagement of human resources. Fewer players will spend more than four or five years at one club, or follow soccer's equivalent of Fordist relations of production in playing under the same manager or within the same team formation throughout their career. Long-term commitments are sought by elite clubs for the most valued players, whose exchange value should ideally appreciate throughout the contract's duration. Shorter player contracts enable club coaches to adapt and change the team personnel and formation, while ensuring that expensive players can be offloaded if the club is relegated. In post-Fordist fashion, there is a pursuit of the 'just in time' team, which gels a diversity of player characteristics, appeals to spectator tastes and contrasts well with competitors who are themselves constantly modifying, dissolving and reinventing their own soccer brands. The dynamic 'free market' has had few obvious benefits for players at the lower ends of the soccer spectrum. Jean-Marc Bosman himself earned little reward from pursuing his dispute. In less developed countries, many player agents adopt overtly predatory strategies towards their human traffic. In Africa, some European agents and club coaches have been described as modern slave-traders owing to their profiteering from the sale of young players (Broere and van der Drift, 1997: 94–7).

Grounds for complaint? The new politics of access in soccer

Throughout the soccer world, neoliberalism has exacerbated social and cultural divisions. This is evident, as we have noted, at the national and international levels among clubs and players, but is also obvious among soccer supporters. Soccer's financial boom has transformed the relations of consumption, particularly between the club and its paying spectators. The 1990 Taylor Report was a major catalyst, decreeing that all major UK stadiums should become all-seated by the summer of 1994. UEFA and FIFA adopted equivalent policies for major international fixtures and tournaments. Subsequently the informal and, at times, unruly public association across the soccer terraces has been replaced by individuated regimes of spectator consumption. Spectators are encouraged to attend with their family to integrate these new soccer consumers. Marketing and public relations at clubs serve to reify this familial, spectating norm. Omnipresent CCTV systems and 'proactive' stewarding make for a pacified spectator experience (Armstrong and Giulianotti, 1998; Giulianotti, 2001). Clubs struggle to reignite 'atmosphere' within the deadened stands. Some, such as Arsenal or Hearts (from Edinburgh), have introduced designated 'singing ends', a sure index of what Marcuse termed the 'repressive desublimation' experienced within capitalist society. Meanwhile the soccer authorities resist the calls of many hard-core fans for the return of some terracing inside grounds.

The international soccer organizations (notably FIFA) take little interest in ensuring that soccer's most dedicated supporters can attend major tournaments. The 1998 World Cup in France witnessed a farcically unjust system of ticket distribution. Major corporate sponsors paid $20 million apiece to secure privileged advertising and seating spaces. The remaining allocation of tickets through national soccer associations, French citizens and licensed operators resulted in a chaotic black market. In one infamous case, hundreds of Japanese fans at Tokyo airport were told there were no tickets for them. Throughout France, the vast majority of visiting fans were forced to purchase tickets through local scalpers (touts) who, on occasion, included the local gendarmerie. To register their collective disgust at the ticketing fiasco, Scottish soccer fans loudly booed the FIFA president, a visibly irritated Joao Havelange, during the tournament's opening ceremony in the Stade de France. The subsequent tournament in Japan/South Korea in 2002 offered little improvement, with further inflated spectator admission prices and a failed computerized system for selling tickets, resulting in many matches kicking off in half-empty stadiums.

Numerous arguments have been advanced regarding how football can begin to reform itself in a more democratic and inclusive manner, from reformulating the game's governing bodies to contributing more financially to the grassroots infrastructure. Here I wish to advocate a more philosophical response with reference to a reconstructed version of critical theory that is rooted in the 'liberal art of separation'. This position favours 'carving up the social world in ways that protect particular spheres of life from outside interference' (Morgan, 1994: 169). Accordingly the commodification of soccer and other areas of cultural life should be prevented from restricting public access to activities and practices that had been relatively open (Walzer, 1983; Walsh, 1998). Strategically, however, that goal can only be a long-term one; the commodification of elite sports, including soccer, is now so advanced that the 'separate and protect' philosophy must proceed incrementally, almost on a match-to-match basis. Lobbying for more just systems of ticket distribution at the World Cup finals, or to protect flagship soccer matches (such as Cup finals or league 'deciders') from transferring to pay-per-view television, are two examples of ways in which the 'separate and protect' principle may be pursued strategically within sports.

Notes

1. See Kapuscinski (1992). The 1989 riots in Bucharest which led to the overthrow of President Ceauşescu were sparked initially by crowd celebrations upon Romania's qualification for the 1990 World Cup finals.
2. The G14 clubs comprise Inter Milan, Juventus, AC Milan (Italy); Barcelona, Real Madrid, Valencia (Spain); Bayern Munich, Bayer Leverkusen, Borussia Dortmund (Germany); Ajax, PSV Eindhoven (Holland); Arsenal, Liverpool, Manchester United (England); Olympique Lyonnais, Olympique Marseille, PSG (France); Porto (Portugal). The Italian and Spanish clubs are the prime movers within this group.
3. This occurred during the early 1950s, when an ill-fated rebel league in Colombia, known as *Di Mayor*, was introduced and attracted many leading internationalists from South America and Europe (see Del Burgo, 1995; Mason, 1994).
4. In December 1995, the European Court ruled in favour of the Belgian player, Jean-Marc Bosman, in his civil case against the Belgian FA. Bosman had argued that any 'out-of-contract' player should be free to join a new club without any transfer fee to his former club. The Court also ruled that restrictions on the number of non-national players within a club team were a restraint of trade and therefore illegal under European labour laws (Greenfield and Osborn, 1998). *Bosman* established a free market in the movement of out-of-contract players.
5. The most recent and ill-starred FIFA tournament is the 'Confederations Cup', which directly interferes with the established soccer calendar. The new FIFA President Sepp Blatter set off further alarm bells among the clubs and soccer writers when he stated that the World Cup should be played every two years rather than the current four. The plan would provide further immense profits for FIFA, but would devalue the World Cup's current value and risk player burnout, given that the tournament is played during the European summer, soccer's 'closed season'.
6. See, for example, Chomsky's (1995: 48–9) identification of this dialectic within European politics.

References

Alabarces, P. (1999), 'Post-modern times: identities and violence in Argentine football', in G. Armstrong and R. Giulianotti (eds), *Football, cultures and identities*, Basingstoke: Macmillan, pp.77–85.

Andrews, D. (1999), 'Contextualising suburban soccer: consumer culture, lifestyle differentiation and suburban America', *Culture, Sport, Society*, 2 (3), 31–53.

Armstrong, G. (1998), *Football hooligans: knowing the score*, Oxford: Berg.

Armstrong, G. and R. Giulianotti (1998), 'From Another Angle: surveillance and football hooligans', in C. Norris, G. Armstrong and J. Moran (eds), *Surveillance, CCTV and Social Control*, Aldershot: Avebury/Gower, pp.191–223.

Back, L., T. Crabbe and J. Solomos (1996), 'Campaign trail', *When Saturday Comes*, December.

Bourdieu, P. (1999), 'The state, economics and sport', *Culture, Sport, Society*, 1 (2), 10–19.

Broere, M. and R. van der Drift (1997), *Football Africa!*, Amsterdam: KIT.

Brown, A. (ed.) (1998), *Fanatics! power, race, nationality and fandom in European football*, London: Routledge.

Castells, M. (1996), *The rise of the network society*, Oxford: Blackwell.

Chomsky, N. (1995), 'The politics of language', in R. Kearney (ed.), *States of mind: dialogues with contemporary thinkers on the European mind*, Manchester: Manchester University Press, pp.31–48.

Conn, D. (1997), *The football business*, Edinburgh: Mainstream.

Del Burgo, M.B. (1995), 'Don't stop the carnival: football in the societies of Latin America', in S. Wagg (ed.), *Giving the game away*, Leicester: Leicester University Press, pp.52–71.

Dempsey, P. and K. Reilly (1998), *Big money, beautiful game: saving soccer from itself*, Edinburgh: Mainstream.

Dunning, E., P. Murphy and J. Williams (1988), *The roots of football hooliganism*, London: Routledge.

Fynn, A. and L. Guest (1994), *Out of time: why football isn't working*, London: Simon & Schuster.

Giulianotti, R. (1999a), *Football: a sociology of the global game*, Cambridge: Polity.

Giulianotti, R. (1999b), 'Hooligans and Carnival fans: Scottish football supporter identities', in G. Armstrong and R. Giulianotti (eds), *Football, cultures and identities*, Basingstoke: Macmillan, pp.29–40.

Giulianotti, R. (1999c), 'Built by the two Valeras: the rise and fall of football culture and national identity in Uruguay', *Culture, Sport, Society*, 2 (3), 134–54.

Giulianotti, R. (2001), 'Conducting play', *Youth and Policy*, 73, 45–65.

Greenfield, S. and G. Osborn (1998), 'From feudal serf to big spender: the influence of legal intervention on the status of English professional footballers', *Culture, Sport, Society*, 1 (1), 1–23.

Hopcraft, A. (1988), *The football man*, London: Simon & Schuster.

Horton, E. (1997), *Moving the goalposts*, Edinburgh: Mainstream.

Kapuscinski, R. (1992), *The soccer war*, New York: Vintage International.

Lash, S. (1994), 'Expert-systems or situated interpretation?', in U. Beck, A. Giddens and S. Lash (eds), *Reflexive modernization*, Cambridge: Polity.

Lash, S. and J. Urry (1987), *The end of organized capitalism*, Cambridge: Polity.

Lash, S. and J. Urry (1994), *Economies of signs and space*, London: Sage.

Magazine, R. (2001), 'The colours make me sick: America FC and political corruption in Mexico', in G. Armstrong and R. Giulianotti (eds), *Fear and loathing in world football*, Oxford: Berg, pp.187–98.

Mason, T. (1994), 'The Bogotà Affair', in J. Bale and J. Maguire (eds), *The global sports arena*, London: Frank Cass, pp.39–48.

Morgan, W.J. (1994), *Leftist theories of sport: a critique and reconstruction*, Urbana: University of Illinois.

Murray, B. (1996), *The world's game: a history of soccer*, Urbana: University of Illinois.

Raspaud, M. (1994), 'From Saint-Etienne to Marseilles: tradition and modernity in French soccer and society', in R. Giulianotti and J. Williams (eds), *Game without frontiers: football, identity and modernity*, Aldershot: Avebury, pp.103–27.

Richards, P. (1997), 'Soccer and Violence in War-Torn Africa: soccer and social rehabilitation in Sierra Leone', in G. Armstrong and R. Giulianotti (eds), *Entering the field: new perspectives on world football*, Oxford: Berg, pp.141–58.

Semino, E. and M. Masci (1996), 'Politics is football: metaphor in the discourse of Silvio Berlusconi in Italy', *Discourse and Society*, 7 (2), 243–69.

Sloane, P.J. (1997), 'The economics of sport: an overview', *Economic Affairs*, 17 (3), 2–6.

Szymanski, S. and R. Smith (1997), 'The English football industry: profit, perform-ance and industrial structure', *International Review of Applied Economics*, 11 (1), 135–53.

Taylor, I. (1970), 'Football mad: a speculative sociology of soccer hooliganism', in E. Dunning (ed.), *The sociology of sport*, London: Frank Cass, pp 346–73.

Taylor, I. (1971), 'Soccer consciousness and soccer hooliganism', in S. Cohen (ed.), *Images of deviance*, Harmondsworth: Penguin, pp.147–66.

Taylor, I. (1982a), 'On the sports-violence question: soccer hooliganism revisited', in J. Hargreaves (ed.), *Sport, culture and ideology*, London: Routledge and Kegan Paul, pp.173–99.

Taylor, I. (1982b), 'Class, violence and sport: the case of soccer hooliganism', in H. Cantelon and R. Gruneau (eds), *Sport, culture and the modern state*, Toronto: Toronto University, pp.35–83.

Taylor, I. (1987), 'Putting the boot into a working class sport: British soccer after Bradford and Brussels', *Sociology of Sport Journal*, 4, 171–91.

Taylor, I. (1989), Hillsborough: 15 April 1989. Some personal contemplations', *New Left Review*, 177, 89–110.

Vinnai, G. (1973), *Football mania*, London: Ocean.

Walsh, A.J. (1998), 'Market pathology and the range of commodity exchange: a preliminary sketch', *Public Affairs Quarterly*, 12 (2), 203–19.

Walvin, J. (1975), *The people's game*, London: Hutchinson.

Walzer, M. (1983), *Spheres of justice*, Oxford: Basil Blackwell.

3
Recapturing Olympic Mystique: The Corporate Invasion of the Classroom

Tara Magdalinski, Kimberly S. Schimmel and
Timothy J.L. Chandler

Since the inception of the modern Olympic Games, there has existed a philosophy of 'Olympism' that purports to promote the ideals and spirit of sport as represented by the Olympic Games. Among the guiding principles that underpinned the original Olympic Charter prepared by founder Baron Pierre de Coubertin were a number of general aims that included developing physical and moral qualities, building a better and more peaceful world and creating friendship and international goodwill through sporting competition (see Binder, 2001). Despite the homage to democracy and inclusion expressed by continuing proponents of the Olympic movement, the ideals promoted within this movement are rooted in Eurocentric, masculinist and elitist ideologies. These sporting ideologies have centred on the doctrine of 'amateurism', an exclusive concept that gradually evolved to mean participation in sporting competition for its own sake, or for success without direct material reward. In the past 30 years the ideologies of Olympism have diverged from this amateurist ethos to incorporate professionalism and form what Peter Donnelly (1996) calls a global sporting monoculture centred on the values of success, capitalism and monetary reward for top-level performances. These ideals, which he labels 'prolympism', are today linked inextricably to a consumer culture that is divisive in terms of both class associations and economic status. In this context, the Sydney 2000 Olympics was representative of the incorporation of sport into multinational advertising and marketing strategies. Such strategies are antithetical to those in sport that promote mass participation, physical education for lifelong health and the ideologies of sport that promote cooperation rather than those that foreground competition and victory. Thus the Olympic movement, centred on the activities of the International Olympic Committee (IOC), National Olympic committees and organizing committees for Olympic Games, is now firmly entrenched in the global capitalist system and its attendant ideologies. In this chapter we argue that the increasingly overt commercialism of the Olympics has come at a price, and that price has been a loss of the mystique of the Olympics – a mystique founded on those general aims that de Coubertin outlined in the original Olympic Charter.

In order to reproduce the global multinational corporatist system, large corporations have made children the target in their use of specific marketing strategies and involvement in educational institutions through sponsorship, curriculum development and provision of free 'educational' materials for schools. Thus, as we highlight below, the primary school education kit for the 2000 Sydney games had as one educational activity the designing of an Australian uniform incorporating the logos of all team sponsors. This chapter examines an array of Olympic education materials, produced by corporations, and which are distributed to schools, we suggest, as a means of 'selling' the Olympic Games and Olympism to schoolchildren. We are interested in the content, framing and promotion of Olympism and global multinational corporate capitalism as it appeared in materials aimed at primary and secondary schoolchildren. In this process, we posit that consent for the Olympic movement is manufactured at the same time that corporate loyalties are inculcated in the consumers of these 'educational' materials.

We introduce a number of problematics that surround curricular material that is produced and promoted by the 'partnership' between corporate interests, government agencies and not-for-profit foundations. These include pairing Olympism and nationalism with consumerism in contexts where children are a 'captive audience'; mobilizing schoolchildren to assist in the cultural and material sale of the Games; and incorporating teachers to assist in consensus building around the Olympic ideology. Others have suggested additional problematics such as the perpetuation/celebration of an agenda that encourages the local populace to share the aspirations of local and global elites; and the fundamental contradiction between internationalist and nationalist discourses (Tomlinson, 1986). Of most interest here, however, is the increasing use of children in the 'marketing' of the Olympics and Olympism. It has been as a result of trying to recast prolympism as idealistic (even naive) Olympism that those involved in promoting the Olympic movement have turned increasingly to the youth of the world to reinvigorate the Olympic mystique.

Exploiting children

Identifying children as a separate consumer demographic remains a post-Second World War phenomenon, though children in North America have been targets of directed marketing campaigns since the early 1900s. A few farsighted advertisers realized that, in addition to marketing to adults directly, children could be enlisted to help business sell products to parents. Beginning as early as the 1920s, American advertising campaigns have focused on children as *influencers* of consumer spending. By the Second World War, however, marketers had broadened their vision regarding the potential of children to stimulate consumer spending, recognising that they possess what Ellen Seiter (1995: 103) has labelled a 'three-in-one' appeal: firstly, children exercise a significant influence over parents in decisions about commodity purchases; secondly, children will eventually spend significant amounts of money themselves; and thirdly, children represent future markets and thus advertising provides opportunities to 'inculcate brand loyalty at an early age'.

Competition in children's goods and services became so intense during the 1980s that marketing campaigns aimed at young people became an almost taken-for-granted aspect of American consumerist culture. During this decade an explosion of media was directed at schoolchildren: child-specific television and radio networks, magazines and newspapers were all introduced or increased. In addition, children-based retail expanded beyond the traditional markets of fast food and toys to include clothing, books and even banking and hospitality. Marketers have recognised the importance of the child consumer and appeal to clients' desire to develop new markets. Thus, not only are children to be viewed as influencers of their parents' purchases, but also they are a target market in their own right, 'consumers in training' (Kincheloe, 1997: 255). In addition, developing 'Kid Konsumer's' 'brand loyalty' has become a coveted corporate prize. As Vance Packard noted:

> It takes time, yes, but if you expect to be in business for any length of time, think of what it can mean to your firm in profits if you can condition a million or ten million children who will grow up into adults trained to buy your products as soldiers are trained to advance when they hear the trigger words 'forward march'. (Cited in Harty, 1979: 11)

Exploitation of children throughout the post-Second World War era has been simplified by the emergence of television. Throughout the 1950s, broadcasters developed children's programming, presenting it as largely 'educational' and free of commercials, in an attempt to entice parents to purchase television sets (Seiter, 1995). Disney became one of the first corporations to directly produce children's television, relying on the production of the *Disneyland* series to raise money for the development of the Disneyland theme park. The series was enormously successful, functioning as an advertisement both for the theme park and for forthcoming Disney films (Bryman, 1995) and revealed to other corporations that children's television could be a lucrative advertising medium. By the 1980s, children's television programming was little more than lengthy advertisements, with cartoons in particular designed simply as advertising vehicles for a range of toys and other consumer items (Seiter, 1995). Despite the success of TV in appealing directly to children, the actual effects of these advertising strategies have been notoriously difficult to assess, and advertisers have sought more certain ways of reaching children. One way has been through school computers.

ScreenAd sells advertising space on screensavers that are directly beamed onto networked computers in educational and other environments. The website for this organization points out to potential clients the benefits of concentrating on children and young adults. Under the fact sheet 'Some interesting facts about our smallest consumers', ScreenAd argues: 'You Grow your Consumers from Childhood ... There are two sources of new business: one involves trying to convince customers to switch to you over your competitors; the other is children. The former strategy often generates only short-term loyalty and presumes consumer disloyalty; the latter builds for the long term and is based on nurturing customer loyalty' (*ScreenAd*, 2001). Appealing to young people is thus regarded as 'a golden opportunity to encourage the bonding that could last a lifetime'.

Increasingly the classroom has become a prized venue for direct marketing as large corporations have moved from merely advertising their products and services to young people to direct involvement in educational programmes and institutions and the production of curriculum resources. Because education is compulsory, schools deliver a 'captive audience' of millions of potential consumers.

School-based advertising

School-based advertising is not a recent phenomenon, but the mechanisms by which corporations have inveigled their way into the classroom are becoming more sophisticated. Throughout most of the twentieth century, schools have been supplied with free pencils and workbooks embossed with business logos, as well as materials for classroom exercises that were often related to specific consumer goods. A 1957 survey of US schools published in *School Executive* found that 97 per cent of teachers surveyed used sponsored materials (Burk, 1957); few of these teachers used any 'ethical standard' in determining whether to use the materials; and none of them received guidance from school administrators (Molnar, 1996: 39). Given that placing advertisements in schools has traditionally been regarded as problematic, businesses have entered into sponsorship arrangements with schools, donating 'educational materials' that generally direct students' attention to products or corporate names. In addition, the business community has distributed videotapes, curricular packages and free sample products to schoolrooms, so that learning often means learning *about* particular products. We suggest that these 'free' commodities and accompanying 'lesson plans' are product advertising packaged as pedagogy.

According to Erika Shaker (1998), the school setting provides an atmosphere conducive to receiving advertising messages. It is 'an environment of trust and familiarity' that can exploit 'future consumers' by 'ensuring that vital messages can be delivered where they may most effectively change behaviour or attitudes' (ibid.: 2). Indeed is there a better place to teach future consumers about products and services than in an environment designed specifically for learning? Advertisers are able to enhance their corporate image by invoking a more altruistic motivation, arguing that they are simply 'giving back to the community', while the school, an 'uncluttered' advertising environment in which a company's message will 'stand out', provides a quasi-endorsement of the products advertised on its grounds (ibid.). School-based advertising comes in several forms; however, for this analysis, it is the development of corporate-friendly curriculum materials that is of most interest. As Shaker points out: 'In-school advertising takes on a very different significance when it is disguised as curriculum. Not only do the corporate products and ads appear to be endorsed by the school environment, but the corporate messages – some more blatantly commercial than others – are actually taught as a classroom lesson' (ibid.: 7).

While there has been public concern about the extent of blatant advertising to children, since the late 1980s commercials have been beamed in live to over 8,000 schools representing around 8.1 million teens across the USA. In 1989, Chris Whittle, a marketing executive, introduced the controversial Channel One television station. Backed by publishing multinationals, Channel One was designed to transmit current events and local news directly to classrooms at no cost to the schools. Revenue for this project was generated from advertisements that, along with the 'educational' content, were also played in the classroom (Cassidy, 2000; Giroux, 1994). Schools were provided with $50,000 of 'free' electronic equipment if they signed a three-year contract guaranteeing that a 12-minute Channel One programme (ten minutes of current events and news with two minutes of commercials) would be shown on at least 90 per cent of the days school was in session, ensuring that at least 85 per cent of the students watched it, and that advertisements were not edited out. In addition, schools had to record their viewing patterns in a log that could be reviewed at any time by Channel One administrators. Advertisers were willing to part with around $200,000 per 30-second spot for, as the Channel One promotion literature suggests, 'We have the UNDIVIDED ATTENTION of millions of teenagers for 12 minutes a day ... And since they're not channel surfing, talking on the phone or getting snacks from the kitchen, they're tuning in to the world and to you' (*Advertising Age*, 1998).

Product awareness is well cultivated amongst school students when the advertising messages are linked to the curriculum and thereby given status and a quasi-endorsement by the school. Most commonly they appear in the form of sponsored programmes that are enormously successful, reaching a target audience of several million children each day. For example, the Pizza Hut BOOK IT!® programme, which rewards children with pizza vouchers upon meeting reading goals, attracts over 20 million schoolchildren in 800,000 classrooms annually in the USA, with millions more participating internationally. The cumulative annual exposure generated by this programme cannot be guaranteed by any amount of mainstream advertising and conveys an extremely high level of product awareness. Fast food and other concerns have also started producing curriculum materials, relying on familiar cartoon figures to teach children primary school subjects. Activities within the McDonald's educational packs distributed to schools in the United Kingdom include visiting a local McDonald's to gather information about the store and then returning as a consumer to buy a meal; drawing plans of the store; making a model of the store using Lego; marking on a map the location of McDonald's stores that the children had visited; inventing words to 'Old McDonald had a store', to the tune of 'Old McDonald had a farm'; and finally, selecting items from a list of McDonald's products to include in a diagram of what the child likes to eat (*McSpotlight website*, 2001a).

Relationships between schools and corporations are further entrenched with some companies insisting on exclusive contractual arrangements while, in one well-documented case, students who choose not to participate in their school's corporate environment face severe consequences.

In March 1998, a student in Georgia was suspended from school for wearing a Pepsi shirt on the school's Coke Day: 'School officials say the shirt was an insult to Coca-Cola executives visiting from Atlanta and ruined a school picture in which students spelled out "Coke" ' (Anon, 1998). Exclusive contracts with corporations such as Coca-Cola are often devised to ensure that the company only need pay out promised monies if schools maintain target sales, thereby providing institutions with financial incentives to promote the corporation's products (Molnar and Morales, 2000).

A brief examination of the various 'educational' programmes developed by multinationals reveals that product awareness is only one of the outcomes of school-based advertising initiatives. Not only do these programmes raise product and brand awareness, the corporate presence in classrooms also cultivates an appreciation of corporate thinking and business practices, designed to introduce children to the principles of the labour market. It is thus of little surprise that many of these programmes are concentrated and flourish in inner-city public schools that are suffering from cuts to public funding (Giroux, 1994). As public money is withheld, and governments insist that schools should focus on providing trained employment for the workforce, introducing children to the world of work becomes an imperative that is well met by the increasing relationships between educational institutions and corporate interests. Once again, McDonald's provides an excellent example of this alliance.

In 1993, McDonald's established the McDonald's Education Service in response to the 'changing nature of education today and the increasing need for schools to prepare young people for the world of work'. Within this programme, 'the McDonald's Education Service aims to offer our restaurants as resources to schools in their communities' (*McSpotlight*, 2001b). McDonald's provides educational kits for under-resourced primary schools, which include activities such as recreating a McDonald's outlet in the school with students role-playing various jobs and re-enacting other parts of the corporate structure, such as Head Office, suppliers and consumers, thus introducing students to the world of non-unionized, minimum wage labour. In addition, McDonald's established a Mini-McDonald's at a school in Detroit, at which children could redeem points earned from taking quizzes and reading. Students could 'apply' at the school's 'employment office' for the right to serve other students (Molnar and Morales, 2000). In Australia, the relationship between McDonald's and education has been further cemented in an arrangement in the state of Victoria, whereby secondary school students can gain course credit towards their school leaving certificate by working at

McDonald's. While McDonald's labour is ostensibly a 'school subject', schools themselves are unable to manage what precisely is being taught through the McDonald's training programmes, as this programme is run and assessed by McDonald's staff, not teachers (Shaker, 1998).

These examples reveal clear evidence of corporate intrusion into schools and the mechanisms by which children develop consumer loyalty and learn industrial discipline. That is, multinational corporations dictate curricula activities in order to instil brand awareness in children and introduce children to the world of corporate consumerism and (non-unionized) labour. Corporate ideologies are presented as learning outcomes while students are variously constructed as evolving consumers, future workers or both. It is upon such a foundation that the corporate ideology of the modern Olympics has been built as the IOC has attempted to develop consumer loyalty to Olympism and to the Olympic Games.

Packaging Olympism/Olympic packaging

While children are exposed to corporate interests in more and more aspects of their lives, including the relative sanctity of the classroom, leisure and sporting activities have traditionally been regarded as areas that have not succumbed to the corporate imperative, associated as they are with healthy lifestyles and character building. Of course, major sporting competitions have become increasingly commercialized over the past 40 years and, as the largest multi-sport international event, the Olympic Games is no exception. Although companies have used the Olympics as an advertising vehicle since 1896, in recent decades the financial impact of sponsors cannot be underestimated. Since the early 1980s, the movement has generated over 15 billion dollars from corporate supporters (*Olympic Marketing Matters*, 1999b: 7).

While professional sporting leagues and international sports events have openly flirted with corporate sponsorship for decades, the Olympic movement has sought to control commercialization on its own terms, deciding only recently to create an elite core of major sponsors in The Olympic Programme (TOP), including Coca-Cola, IBM, Kodak, McDonald's, John Hancock, Panasonic, Sports Illustrated/Time, UPS, Visa and Xerox. TOP has been the IOC's means of promoting exclusivity for the sponsors. These companies provide equipment and funding to the IOC and National Olympic Committees and in exchange receive exclusive access to all Olympic symbols and logos that can be used in their advertising. The Olympics with its attendant 'philosophy' and values is highly regarded by advertisers wishing to associate their product with the 'noble' aims of the Olympic movement. Indeed, the IOC insists that their sponsors actively promote Olympism through their marketing. In other words, money is raised through selling the Olympic ideal, and the games themselves have become part of the global capital market and a product to be sold to the global consumer. Of course, the more these sponsors provide, the greater the return on advertising they will expect. This partnership between sponsor and movement has solidified the rapid process of commodifying the Olympics as a 'product' and has established a clear link between the future success of the Olympic movement and leveraged its ability to attract capital funding from external supporters.

The relationship between the IOC and its sponsors has not always been so well defined. These commercial arrangements developed only after the financial disaster of the Montreal Olympics in 1976 and the corporately profitable 1984 Games that returned little financial gain to the IOC itself. When the games were first hosted in the southern hemisphere, the political credibility of the IOC and the economic viability of the Olympic Games depended upon the city of Melbourne's willingness to support the ideals of Olympism and foot the entire bill. Sponsors only had a limited role in the financing, while local civic boosters, city councillors and business leaders were required to generate the necessary revenue for the event (Davison, 1997). The risks inherent in this sort of partnership model became clear 20 years later, when Montreal suffered economic hardship and massive debt after staging the 1976 Games. The political issues that plagued the Moscow Games in 1980 further exacerbated these economic problems. Together these political and economic problems led to important changes in the way the Olympic Games have been organized and funded since the games returned to Los Angeles in 1984. In brief, for the Los Angeles Games, a more hierarchical partnership model replaced the original dyadic organizational structure involving a partnership between the IOC and local government agencies in the host city. This change signified a transformation of the Olympics into an increasingly market-oriented project where 'a more fully developed expression of the incorporation of sporting practice into the ever-expanding marketplace of international capitalism' is now manifested (Gruneau and Cantelon, 1988: 347). The IOC proclaimed the Los Angeles Olympics a success, for their relatively uneventful nature in political terms (compared with Moscow and the crises in Munich and Montreal) and an enormous success in economic terms, making a substantial profit for the first time. Nevertheless, for many, the Los Angeles Games came 'to symbolize new heights in the corruption of sport

[and] … any remaining vestiges of Olympic ideals seemed to vanish as a result of these "Corporate Games" ' (ibid.: 346).

Though successful in economic terms, the triumph of entrepreneurial capitalism and (American) consumer culture embodied in the Olympics since 1984 has had an undermining effect: the IOC's new partnership model demystified the relationship between global corporate capital and the games as a commodified product. It is unlikely, however, that any loss of 'Olympic mystique' (Nixon, 1988) went unnoticed by the IOC. The overt commercialism of the Olympics has come at a price: it has threatened a legitimation crisis for the Olympic movement and its buttressing Olympic ideals. The problem then, for Olympic officials, is not so much how to *maximize profit* but rather how to *recapture mystique*. If the games are to be 'successful' into the twenty-first century, they will have both to attract more global consumers and (re)create the notion that the Olympics are more than just another global (sport) commodity. We suggest that one of the strategies currently employed by the IOC and its corporate partners is to mobilize schoolchildren to assist in the cultural and material sale of the games, thereby attempting to parallel the purity and innocence of the Olympic movement with purity and innocence of youth. Through the use of 'Olympic Education Kits', Olympism is recast as idealism and the Olympics (as commodity) are marketed to future consumers. It is to the context of schools that we now turn.

Recapturing mystique: the Olympic education strategy

Since the 1980s, the Olympic movement has increasingly coopted children into the business of attracting and selling the games. Competitions are organized, encouraging young people to represent artistically the themes of Olympism, with winning entries appearing on Olympic merchandise and in the corporate advertising of sponsors. At the same time, schools are encouraged to enter their students in a range of 'educational' programmes designed to teach their charges the 'real' meaning of the Olympics. The Sydney 2000 bid became something of a model of how to incorporate children into the marketing of potential host cities, while the construction of elaborate 'educational programmes' has taught future hosts how to generate the widest possible market for their advertisers. In 1992, IOC members received petitions from 160,000 schoolchildren in Australia asking that Sydney be chosen as the site of the 2000 Olympic Games. As a show of 'grassroots community support' 120 schools were paired with individual IOC members who were then personally lobbied. Whenever IOC members visited Sydney, they were taken to 'their' school and presented with scrapbooks prepared by the students and that contained messages of support (Booth and Tatz, 1994). During the final bid presentation, a schoolgirl was used as a 'secret weapon', and has been credited with securing the games for Sydney after she addressed the IOC directly on behalf of the 'children of Australia'. Most significant, however, was the corporate intrusion into the classroom under the guise of 'educating' children about the Olympic movement.

The IOC has long regarded education as crucial to its promotional activities. Olympic founder Pierre de Coubertin believed that a remedy to the social ills in the France of the late nineteenth century could be found in educational reform and his dedication to sport as a means for change underpinned his philosophy of Olympism. The IOC has revived Coubertin's firm belief in the primacy of culture and education in the IOC's Commission for Culture and Olympic Education, which has amongst its tasks the dissemination of Olympism. Most recently the responsibility for communicating this philosophy has been handed to local organizing committees which, in conjunction with TOP and local partners, have produced educational programmes designed to promote interest in the Olympic movement amongst schoolchildren. While these groups argue the educational merits of such products, the school-based curriculum guides are little more than corporate advertising vehicles. The project of raising Olympic awareness thus equates with generating brand recognition amongst young Olympic consumers. Given that the Olympic Education Kits are literally framed by corporate logos, and recommended activities include identifying brand names, it is clear that the objectives of such kits have less to do with education and more to do with developing a consumer basis and raising the profile of corporations.

By far the most comprehensive involvement of children in preparations for Olympic Games are through 'education' kits, produced by Education Departments in conjunction with corporate sponsors and distributed free of charge to schools. After Sydney was chosen as host for the games, a complete 'Olympic Schools Strategy' was released to the public. Through this programme, every schoolchild was provided with access to corporatized Olympic 'educational' materials produced by sponsors directly, as well as regular newspapers and competitions. Part of this 'strategy' included an Olympic Education Resource Kit, which provided extensive and detailed instructions (primary grades to high school and inclusive of all subjects) for bringing Olympism and the Olympic Games into every classroom. Developed by the New South Wales Department of Education, endorsed by the Australian and International Olympic

Committees and sponsored by Coca-Cola and IBM, the kit was issued to every school in Australia.

The primary purpose of such educational programmes is to promote the 'real' ideals of Olympism, and thereby restore the tarnished 'mystique' of the Olympic movement. Promoting a philosophy rather than a product has proved to be a successful marketing technique for the IOC. Through its campaigns, such as 'Celebrate Humanity', and its attempts to secure a Nobel Peace Prize, the Olympic movement is not just selling corporate identity, but it is also commodifying social conscience. Indeed the IOC presents the movement as 'not about selling [commodities] but social responsibility, and it is [an organization] that represents less a product than a lifestyle and a worldview' (Giroux, 1994: 9). While he was referring specifically to clothing manufacturer Benetton, Henry Giroux's comments have currency in the analysis of the Olympics. When companies promote their products through campaigns that rely on identifying social causes, their advertising strategy makes the actual purchase and consumption of products a direct expression of social responsibility. Consumers can feel confident about their commodity choices; the corporation tells them so. Since the 1970s, when public confidence in large companies was declining, corporate leaders have tried to counter their public image as 'greedy' and 'uninterested in the public good' (Steinberg and Kincheloe, 1997: 13). As a result, corporations have spent phenomenal amounts of money on public relations advertising devised to 'promote corporate images and ideological dispositions' (ibid.). Olympic sponsors recognized the appeal of Olympism and worked successfully to link their products and brands with this ethos. The IOC benefits as consumers develop brand loyalty *to* the games, while its TOP partners rely on consumers developing brand loyalty *via* the games.

Such activity is not limited to TOP partners. To this end, Westpac, an Australian financial institution, implemented the Westpac Olympic Youth Program, which was part of the overall Sydney 2000 National Olympic Education Program, of which Westpac was the Presenting Partner. This programme highlights well the processes of reaching children through in-school advertising, while promulgating a 'corporate responsibility' to the nation's youth. According to Westpac's website, the programme was designed to 'leave a legacy for future generations ... by helping them learn about Olympic ideals' (*Westpac Olympic Youth Program*, 2000). Westpac claims that, through its school strategy, it was able to reach 3.1 million schoolchildren and help them 'experience' the Olympic Ideals which it identifies as 'Goal Setting, Teamwork, Fair Play, Friendship, Challenge, Performance and Achievement – values that will help them achieve later in life' (ibid.). Aspects of this advertising strategy included the provision of *O-News* newspaper to every schoolchild in Australia, the creation of *aspire*, a schools resource kit, and 'Kids' internet pages on the Sydney 2000 website. Each of these was branded with Westpac, IBM and *Sydney Morning Herald* logos, and *O-News* featured full-page and half-page advertisements for, among others, Westpac and IBM.

O-News was distributed ostensibly to every schoolchild in Australia several times a year and introduced children to prominent Australian athletes, Olympic mascots and a range of 'human interest' stories. Out of a total of 15 pages (excluding the cover), *O-News* included three full page advertisements as well as two half-page ads featuring popular Olympic athletes as well as competitions and press-clipping services. Within this text, the line between advertising and content was effectively blurred with the 'newsy' athlete profiles replicated in full-page advertisements in both content and style. On page five of the March 2000 issue of *O-News*, Westpac presented a 'special feature', designed to take 'a closer look at Olympic ideals'. In this issue students were encouraged to 'learn about the ideals of Focus and Experience with help from Matthew Dunn and Susie O'Neill'. The banner headline introducing the profile on Dunn stated 'Matthew Dunn: focus takes you further', while a quotation, in large print, apparently taken from the swimmer, concluded the profile: 'Concentrate your energies in one direction and the path to your goals become clear.' Five pages later in the newspaper, the first full-page advertisement for Westpac appears. Featuring a large photograph of Dunn, the banner quotes the swimmer: 'Shut out distractions. Just focus on success and go for it.' Westpac's own slogan, located at the foot of the page, repeats the sentiments from Dunn's profile: 'Decide what's most important to you, then put all your energy into achieving it.' Similarly the O'Neill profile headlines: 'Susie O'Neill: better for the experience' and she is quoted as saying: 'Every experience, good or bad, makes you stronger and smarter for next time.' On the final page of the newspaper, a full-page advertisement for Westpac features a large photograph of O'Neill, with the banner quotation: 'Every experience, good or bad, brings you closer to success.' Again the athlete's 'quotations' are replicated in Westpac's slogan at the end of the page: 'Make the most of *every* experience, they all make you stronger and smarter for next time.' The photographs used in both the profiles and the advertisements were taken from the same photo shoot, making the athletes more readily identifiable, and the line between Olympic athlete and corporate spokesperson less clear.

In *O-News*, the philosophies of the Olympic movement and corporate sponsor are conflated. Whereas newspapers traditionally distinguish between advertising and news content, in *O-News*, the news and advertising are interchangeable: the news *is* the advertising and vice versa. The articles mirror the spirit of the Olympic movement that in turn is reflected in the corporate philosophy of the sponsor. Thus articles refer to the advertisements that refer to the movement in a never-ending cycle. These links are perpetuated in every aspect of Olympic Education materials. The introduction to the Sydney 2000 Olympic Education Kit, written by Australian Olympic Committee President John Coates, suggested that the aim of the resource material was to 'assist young Australians to understand the values and spirit of the Olympic movement and the Olympic Games'. Yet, despite the rhetoric, we suggest that activities in the kit were designed to foster consent about the structure and function of the Olympic movement as well as to raise awareness of the corporations that sponsor the event.

Many of the activities and all of the resources that comprise these resource packages either were heavily branded or attempted to direct children to view advertising materials as part of the classroom activity. For example, the 1998 Nagano Winter Olympics Education Kit distributed to Australian schools insisted that students view an accompanying video, which contained a series of short features on different aspects of the Olympics; each segment of the video was separated from the next with a collage of sponsors' logos. In addition, many of the activities required that students view the local television coverage of the Olympics, visit official Olympic internet sites, and collect clippings from newspapers, in order to analyse their content. These activities necessarily and deliberately exposed children to the advertising by Olympic sponsors in these different media and some activities went so far as to ask children to identify corporate sponsors. The primary school education kit, designed for the Sydney 2000 Games, included activities such as designing an Australian uniform incorporating *all* the sponsors of the team, and collecting pictures of athletes in order to identify brand names and distinguishing between corporate sponsorship and sporting logos. Leading questions for discussion were listed, indicating that 'Students [should] discuss how commercialism has positively influenced the Games.'

As part of its discussion of Olympic Marketing, the Teacher's Notes refer to the history of Coca-Cola's relationship with the Olympic movement. This is of little surprise, given that Coca-Cola was a co-producer of the package. Not only did Australian Olympic Committee President John Coates thank Coca-Cola in the introduction, but also the company was afforded a page to communicate its own aims for the education kit, revealing its own 'rich history ... as a member of the Olympic family'.

The company's message is clear: we've been supporters all along and our level of commitment to the games has increased over time. Again, the aims of the corporation and of the Olympic movement are conflated, blurring the distinction between advertising and education.

Future trends

For our purposes here, the crucial questions have not been about *how much* corporate sponsorship is evident or explicit in these materials; but rather *why* these partnerships were formed to produce educational materials in the first place, and whose interests they serve. On the one hand it would seem ironic that, although the IOC prohibits corporate signage in sport stadiums, they apparently have no problems with *delivering* corporate logos to schools. In the case of the Sydney Olympics this was done under the guise of providing 'all school children with the opportunity to be involved with the year 2000 Olympic Games through ongoing educational programs and special strategies which further the Olympic ideals while developing a range of understanding, skills and effective learning' (Sydney Organising Committee for the Olympic Games, 2000). On the other hand, it is also clear that the marketing of Olympism is a successful method of introducing future consumers to corporate identities under the guise of fostering educational opportunities for all and promoting the learning of a socially responsible 'worldview'.

Finally, we question the notion that educating children about Olympism through a curriculum sponsored by the IOC is necessarily an appropriate endeavour for schools to undertake. Does this constitute a breach of trust between schools and parents about the nature and purposes of educational materials? With other corporate-sponsored educational materials in the USA, learning about a product is often synonymous with being socialized to consume it. Developing brand loyalty to a particular product is a coveted prize for US marketers. What makes the Olympic product so different? Perhaps the Olympics *are* more capable of naturalizing, even mystifying, capitalist relations than are other forms of collective consumption. Australian schools have had a somewhat limited corporatized history by comparison with their American cousins. What the Sydney case provides is evidence of the potential for increasing corporate involvement in schools and even the globalization of (in)corporated curricula. So, even if Australian schools had traditionally served as safe havens from the bombardment of corporate advertising, the Sydney Olympics went a long way towards changing this. The cover page of the Sydney's Olympic Education Kit states:

> Coca-Cola in Australia is pleased to be associated with the Olympic Education Kit. ... The Future of the Olympic Movement lies in the youth of today and with this in mind, the kit has been developed by the Australian Olympic Committee in conjunction with educational authorities to provide a valuable teaching resource.

The act of enlisting school children has the potential to dramatize and (re)create the Olympic mystique, thereby strengthening the IOC's attempts to package the Olympic Games as *the* global celebration of the human spirit (Binder, 2001). Through these programmes, however, the IOC's grasp has been extended to include the world's youth as consumers of present and future games and their 'official' products. Such an analysis puts a different complexion on the IOC president's exhortations at the close of every Olympiad to 'call upon the youth of the world to assemble four years from now'. Might this now be read as an attempt to perpetuate prolympism, socialize young global consumers and ensure the 'success' of future Olympic Games, as much as remystifying the event for future generations?

References

Advertising Age (1998), Channel One advertisement, 11 May.

Anon. (1998), 'Pepsi shirt on Coke Day means suspension', *Cincinnati Enquirer*, 26 March, p.A2.

Binder, D. (2001), ' "Olympism" revisited as context for global education: implications for physical education', *Quest*, 53(1), 14–34.

Booth, D. and C. Tatz (1994), 'Swimming with the big boys? The politics of Sydney's 2000 Olympic bid', *Sporting Traditions*, 11(1), 3–23.

Bryman, A. (1995), *Disney and his worlds*, London: Routledge.

Burk, D. (1957), 'Free teaching materials – assets or liabilities?', *School Executive*, 76 (12), 55–7.

Cassidy, M. (2000), 'Commercial media and corporate presence in the K-12 classroom', in R. Andersen and L. Strate (eds), *Critical studies in media commercialism*, New York: Oxford University Press, pp.264–75.

Davison, G. (1997), 'Welcoming the world: the 1956 Melbourne Olympic Games and the re-presentation of Melbourne', *Australian Historical Studies*, 28(109), 64–76.

Donnelly, P. (1996), 'Prolympism: sport monoculture as crisis and opportunity', *Quest*, 48(1), 25–42.

Giroux, H. (1994), *Disturbing pleasures: learning popular culture*, New York: Routledge.

Gruneau, R. and H. Cantelon (1988), 'Capitalism, commercialism and the Olympics', in J. Seagrave and D. Chu (eds), *The Olympic games in transition*, Champaign: Human Kinetics, pp.245–64.

Harty, S. (1979), *Hucksters in the classroom: a review of industry propaganda in schools*, Washington, DC: Center for Study of Responsive Law.

Kincheloe Joe, L. (1997), 'McDonald's, power, and children: Ronald McDonald (aka Ray Kroc) does it all for you', in Shirley R. Steinberg and Joe L. Kincheloe (eds), *Kinderculture: The Corporate Construction of Childhood*, Boulder, CO: Westview, pp.249–66.

McSpotlight (2001a), 'Extracts from the activity school pack', retrieved 13 March 2001 from the World Wide Web: http://www.mcspotlight.org/company/publications/ schools_pack.html.

McSpotlight (2001b), 'Growing up together', retrieved 13 March 2001 from the World Wide Web: http://www.mcspotlight.org/company/publications/ schools_review.html.

Molnar, A. (1996), *Giving kids the business: the commercialization of America's schools*, Boulder, CO: Westview.

Molnar, A. and Jennifer, M. (2000), Commercialism@Schools.com. The Third Annual Report on Trends in Schoolhouse Commercialism, Center for the Analysis of Commercialism in Education. Retrieved 5 March 2001 from the World Wide Web: http://uwm.edu/Dept/CACE/documents/cace-00-02.htm

Nixon, H. (1988), 'The background, nature, and implications of the organization of the "capitalist Olympics"', in J. Seagrave and D. Chu (eds), *The Olympic Games in transition*, Champaign: Human Kinetics, pp.237–51.

'Olympic Education Kit', retrieved 17 November 1997 from the World Wide Web: http://www.australian.olympic.org.au/educate/.

Olympic Marketing Matters (1999), 'The finances of the IOC: where the money goes', *The Olympic Marketing Newsletter*, **15** (June), p.7.

ScreenAd (2001), 'Some interesting facts about our smallest consumers', retrieved 13 March 2001 from the World Wide Web: http://www.screenad.com/pages/kids.

Seiter, E. (1995), *Sold separately: parents and children in consumer culture*, New Brunswick, NJ: Rutgers University.

Shaker, E. (1998), *Corporate content: inside and outside the classroom*, Education Limited. CCPA Education Project, **1**(2), pp.1–35.

Steinberg, Shirley, R. and Kincheloe Joe, L. (1997), 'Introduction: no more secrets – kinderculture, information saturation, and the postmodem childhood,' in Shirley R. Steinberg and Kincheloe Joe, L. (eds), *The Corporate Construction of Childhood*, Boulder, CO: Westview, pp.249–66.

Sydney Organizing Committee for the Olympic Games (2000), retrieved from the World Wide Web 10 August 2000: http://www.sydney.olympic.org.au.

Tomlinson, A. (1986), 'Going global: the FIFA story', in A. Tomlinson and G. Whannel (eds), *Off the ball: The 1986 World Cup*, London: Pluto.

Westpac Olympic Youth Program (2000), retrieved 14 September 2000 from the World Wide Web: http://www.westpac.com.au.

Part II

Active Moments: Capitalist Production, Cultural Change and Patterns of Resistance

4
Global Struggles, Local Impacts: Rugby League, Rupert Murdoch's 'Global Vision' and Cultural Identities

Mark Falcous

The profound local impacts of the reconfiguration of the global media sports economy were demonstrated by tumultuous changes within British rugby league during the 1990s. Entwined with wider configurations of the media industries, the attempted global takeover of the sport by Rupert Murdoch in 1995 culminated in the emergence of a 'European Superleague' competition. While signalling a departure from the historic playing structure of the game, the implications extended beyond simple shifts toward media and corporate alignment as central to the structure, ethos and formats. Significantly the transition exerted pressures on the historically rooted cultural attachments of the game.

In this chapter I extend earlier work (Falcous, 1998) that discussed the interplay between the incorporation of rugby league within more instrumentally rational approaches to capital accumulation and the cultural ties of the game. I revisit these issues in the context of subsequent developments. Notably I seek to address the interdependence of economic processes and the social contexts that have historically informed the extent of commercialization in sport. Such discussions are grounded in Ingham *et al.*'s (1987) observations that the pressures exerted by logics of capital accumulation can never fully determine social, political and cultural relationships. While, in part, determined by economic forces, these relations they note, do have their own 'active constitutive moments' (p.427). This chapter explores the interplay of economic processes and those 'active constitutive moments' in informing the character, structures and cultural resonance of British rugby league.

The case study also provides scope to explore questions regarding the nature of the 'global age' (Albrow, 1996). The consequences of global interconnectedness have been one of the most debated topics of modern society, as Giulianotti outlined for soccer in Chapter 2. Notably the interplay of global processes and local conjunctural dynamics (the local–global nexus) has been seen as pivotal in informing the current social condition. In this regard, sport is a frequently potent and highly visible feature of localism. As Featherstone (1991: 49) notes, 'the common sedimented experiences and cultural forms which are associated with a place are crucial to a local culture'. The rituals, histories and symbols of sport that inherently link people to places are potent examples of those 'cultural forms' that inform senses of locality. Hence there is a need to ground local–global interdependence empirically through sport as a social field. Approaching such issues, I am attuned to the tendency, noted by Robertson (1995), to falsely conceive of processes, global in scope, as necessarily global *versus* local.[1] Such polarization falsely conceives of 'local' and 'global' in homogenous and oppositional terms.

The commodification of British rugby league provides a fruitful case study to explore these conceptual issues thanks to the fractious interplay between the trenchant cultural attachments surrounding the game and the pervasive impact of the emergent global sports media economy.

Global processes and the changing cultural landscape of sport

Recent shifts in locales beyond North America characterized by an accelerated phase of corporate–media–sport alignment have resulted in sport being linked with more instrumentally rational approaches to capital accumulation. In Britain, for example, the commercial character of sports underwent unprecedented acceleration during the 1990s. The consequence was the reformulation of the structures, ethos and governance of commercial sport. These shifts were associated with reconfiguring power relations, the commercial realignment of playing structures, media dependence, corporate alignment, shifting ownership and control, revamped administrative structures, and revolutionized spectator provisions and event presentation. The historical legacies of paternalistic amateurism, limited entrepreneurial investment, which had previously constrained commercial activity, and decrepit infrastructure were rapidly surpassed. Such transformations exerted pressures on the historically grounded cultural attachments surrounding British sport.

These shifts can be situated within, and are symptomatic of, wider processes of heightened global interdependence. Central to this are developments in the economics, technology and regulation of media delivery

(Morley and Robins, 1995; Herman and McChesney, 1997). Specifically, media conglomerations offering economies of scale have emerged against a backdrop of neoliberal 'deregulation'[2] of national markets and the marketization of public service media outlets. Accordingly strategies of global expansion emerged to characterize media groups' operations. Sport rapidly emerged as a core feature of media distributors' strategies of market penetration (Herman and McChesney, 1997; Alger, 1998; McAllister, 2000; Miller *et al.*, 2001). Subsequently the global mediation of sport has been characterized by new services, including dedicated generic sports channels; new delivery systems, for instance satellite and cable distribution networks; and new forms of payment, such as pay-per-view and subscription networks and events. As a result, national media markets have been transformed as existing structures and institutions underwent transformation or accommodation within the transnational features of the 'new media order' (Morley and Robins, 1995: 12).

The consequences of these processes for sports, as Boyle and Haynes (2000) note, were global in scope. For example, McKay and Miller (1991) and Phillips, Hutchins and Stewart in the present volume report a series of similar, and virtually simultaneous, shifts in Australia. This change, McKay and Miller document, included a realignment of sport with the interests of corporate investment and the managerial tenets of advertising, marketing and public relations. Similarly, Andrews *et al.* (1996) document the reconfiguration of New Zealand sport characterized by media–sports synergies and corporate promotion. As in Britain, these cases represent shifts toward a more rationally instrumental approach to capital accumulation.

Such shifts, Whitson (1998: 59) suggests, characterize the incorporation of sport into a 'global promotional culture' characterized by the push toward 'new revenue streams'. These include, first, the sale of ancillary goods beyond the 'core' sports product of games and events, such as merchandising; second, the marketing of 'stars' that becomes central to the visibility and 'brand imaging' of events and competitions. Pivotal to the promotion of these marketable 'personas' is the media exposure through which they attain their status as popular cultural icons. A third element concerns the 'vertical integration' of the communication and 'infotainment' industries, which has opened up new possibilities for revenue generation surrounding sport. Notably the growth of subscription television technology has heightened the market value of sports events so that cross-ownership of competitions, teams and leagues can afford significant competitive advantages. Such sport–media cross-ownership affords further opportunities for promotional synergies. The emergence of these characteristics, Whitson (1998) suggests, represents a new stage in the commodification of sport, such that it may be gradually detached from meanings based on place attachments and loyalties. In the place of, and supplemental to, geographical loyalties come the discourses of personal and consumer choice.

The commercial transformation of British sport

As noted, global transformations in commercial sport were entwined with wider processes implicated in restructuring national media industries. Accordingly a central dimension of the move toward a more instrumentally rational approach to accumulation in Britain was a TV market 'transformed more in the early part of the decade, than any other period in its history' (*European TV Sports Databook*, 1995: 135). Specifically the 1990 Broadcasting Act was the catalyst for much of the upheaval and heralded major implications for sports coverage. In the terrestrial private sector changes were manifest in Independent Television (ITV) revisions to allow mergers to form conglomerates able to compete globally. The restructuring of Channel 4 and the tendering of the licence for a new terrestrial broadcaster, Channel 5, further increased competition. Within public sector broadcasting, government capping of the licence fee forced the British Broadcasting Corporation (BBC) to engage more efficient working practices to compete globally (*European TV Sports Databook*, 1995). Finally satellite and cable subscription-based television, in particular the Rupert Murdoch-controlled BSkyB network, emerged to compete fiercely for programme rights. The result was a more competitive domestic marketplace for sports broadcast rights.

The securing of major 'marquee' sports events was a key strategy of satellite distributors seeking to break into the British market, most notably BSkyB. The relatively low cost of broadcasting sport in comparison to alternative programming, and its wide popular appeal, made it ideal for new satellite channels. The prominent role of sport in their strategies led to a BSkyB-dominated 'stampede' to secure live and exclusive rights to major sporting events during the mid-1990s (Boyle and Haynes, 2000; Whannel, 2000). The aggressive strategies adopted by BSkyB effectively dissolved the long-standing ITV–BBC 'duopoly' on British sporting events. BSkyB secured the bulk of the lucrative broadcast rights, with the exception of 'listed' sporting events, such as the FA Cup Final, to ensure terrestrial access to viewers.

Conjunctural issues were also significant in reshaping the commercial footing of sport. For example, the consequences of the Taylor Report following the 1989 Hillsborough disaster, in which 96 football supporters died, focused attention on the infrastructure of grounds and facilities and, ultimately, the relationship of clubs with supporters (see Conn, 1997). These events, shifting ideologies and subsequent legislation affected numerous sports, which underwent rapid and marked changes. Additionally the operations of Murdoch's executives, entrepreneurial and corporate investment in sport, and increased corporate sponsorship and advertising combined to underpin the shift toward an accelerated commercial ethos.

English association football was central to the accelerated commercialization of British sport. Entwined with BSkyB and corporate investment, as Giulianotti outlines in Chapter 2 of this volume, the game underwent a substantive transformation during the 1990s (see also King, 1997, 1998; Conn, 1997; Hamil *et al.*, 1999), subsequently cementing its domination of the British commercial sporting landscape. This heightened commercial footing was underpinned by extensive media exposure, aggressive and wide-scale merchandising operations, and mutually reinforcing corporate alliances. Alongside football, virtually every major sport in the United Kingdom became aligned with BSkyB. Notably test match cricket, including prestige England versus Australia Ashes test matches, a series of key boxing promotion, the British ice-hockey 'superleague', British basketball, rugby league and rugby union (notably England internationals) were incorporated within the 'satellite revolution'. Such realignment of the sport–media relationship was accompanied by shifts toward marketing concerns, diversified accumulation through the sale and promotion of ancillary branded products and expansion to global markets.

These transformations affected significantly the consumption of, access to and cultural attachments surrounding sport. The result was friction at numerous points. The scope for tensions was nowhere more apparent than in the case of rugby league, which provides a potent example of a local sporting context profoundly altered by the shifting global sports media economy. The nature of the transformation in the case of British rugby league resulted from the game becoming a tool in a wider media struggle between Kerry Packer and Rupert Murdoch for dominance in the lucrative Australian Pay TV market (see Falcous, 1998; Rowe, 1997; Rowe and McKay, 1999; Phillips and Hutchins, 1998, 2003). The role of the game within a struggle between media leviathans and the strong cultural attachments to locality surrounding the game rendered the shifts particularly rapid.

Commercialism and community in British rugby league

The strength of the cultural ties inherent to British rugby league stems from the origins of the game which resulted from the secession of northern clubs from the southern based Rugby Football Union (RFU) in 1895 (see Collins, 1998a; Delaney, 1993). Subsequently two rugby 'codes', union and league, emerged, operating under separate governing bodies. Ostensibly centring on the issue of amateurism and professionalism, the divide also symbolized wider cultural and geographical divides. Rugby league's heartland was largely confined to the industrial towns of Yorkshire, Cumberland and parts of Lancashire in the north of England. The legacy of the late-Victorian genesis of the game was far-reaching in cementing the cultural ties of the game throughout the twentieth century (Gate, 1986). As Collins (1998a) outlines, rugby league became rooted uniquely within a particularly trenchant, regionally based, working class, white, masculine culture. The cultural significance of the game and strength of allegiances was heightened in that the game suffered from RFU discrimination against any player who had played rugby league (see Hinchliffe, 2000), and thus was forged upon a sense of cultural marginality.[3]

Attachments to the game were embodied in fierce and parochial team loyalties that surrounded live spectating rituals (Spraklen, 2001; Collins, 1998b). The strength of such loyalties, Collins (1998b: 236) explains, 'were combined with a sense of injustice and righteousness to produce a potency of sporting ideology equal to that fuelled by national or racial pride'. While the genesis of the game was underpinned by patrons who spied commercial opportunity in the deeply entrenched nature of the game within communities, commercial activity was constrained. Clubs were historically run on a break-even basis under the patronage of local business elites investing for civic prestige, rather than for direct profit. Semi-professional players were largely drawn from within the locality they represented, thus providing a clear link between team and community. Additionally, by means of a centrally collected gate levy, money was diverted from the elite clubs to the lower playing strata, thus sustaining smaller communities' ties with the game. Hence commercialization was tempered by deep-rooted social contexts that limited the scale of activities. The collision of these cultural attachments with the wider processes noted above revolutionized the game. The tension between traditional supporters, wider social contexts and commercial processes continue to shape the sport's development, cultural attachments and meanings.

Packer versus Murdoch: media struggles and British rugby league

The tumultuous transformation of British rugby league resulted from the struggle to secure dominance of the pay-per-view television market in Australia between media moguls Rupert Murdoch and Kerry Packer in 1995. The two became embroiled in a struggle to broadcast rugby league in Australia as part of their competition for pay television subscribers. Subsequently Murdoch's News Ltd (the Australian branch of News Corporation) approached the Australian Rugby League (ARL) with proposals to establish an elite ten-team competition that would provide the TV product it needed. This plan was rebuffed by the ARL. Consequently News Ltd decided to build its own 'rebel' league competition to show on pay TV, and began secretly to recruit elite players, a task made easier by the fact that a salary cap had previously depressed earnings (see Coleman, 1996, ch. 5). As the plans surfaced, a player bidding battle resulted between Murdoch and Packer, the former signing players to set up his 'Superleague' to ensure the TV product his News Ltd-Foxtel network needed. Packer on the other hand backed the traditional body (the ARL) to secure his existing pay TV interests.

In an attempt to win this struggle, Murdoch's parent organization, News Corporation, turned its attention to Britain. In April of 1995, an £89 million five-year deal was agreed with the British governing body, the Rugby Football League (RFL) to establish a shrunken elite competition of 14 teams to be known as the 'European Superleague'. Since the deal was designed to isolate the ARL and Packer, it specified that Great Britain could play only Superleague opposition at international level. The hastily established plan included proposals to merge several teams based on geographical proximity, and incorporated only those with the best 'markets'. It also included a switch from the traditional winter playing season to a summer one (thus breaking the tradition of 100 years). The reason for this change was to air rugby league matches in the summer when soccer competitions were not running and to run a common season with the Australian competition. In the interests of 'market expansion', the plan included a London team and two new French 'franchises', providing the tenuous basis of the 'European' title of the competition.

This new competition was shown in Britain on BSkyB. The remaining excluded English clubs were to play in a feeder division. Within this new structure, the climax was to be a global tournament between the top European and Australian sides. Such matches were a possibility with the alignment of playing seasons. The Murdoch organization additionally signed en-bloc the elite competitions in France, New Zealand, Papua New Guinea and Fiji. In this manner News Corporation hoped to ensure credibility for its fledgling Australian Superleague, by adding an international dimension, thus winning the struggle for a pay TV product in Australia.

Dovetailing with Rupert Murdoch's extensive media empire, the establishment of the Superleague organization on a global basis (following protracted legal wrangling in Australia) was underpinned by the opportunities to gain access to new markets. The Superleague heralded major changes within the British game which, as noted above, had traditionally existed on a semi-professional basis, with minimal commercial activity. As Murdoch himself noted, however, the intention was to 'make Rugby league look like you've never seen it before' (quoted in Hadfield, 1995a: 22). The pre-eminence of commercial concerns in this transformation was reinforced by a comment of John Ribot, chief executive of the Australian Super League. He reasoned, 'Do you know what's going to be great about Super League? We're going to take the product to the world. So when Manfred in Germany is watching Canberra versus London on pay-TV, he'll be able to pick up his phone and order Ricky Stuart's number seven jumper there and then' (cited in *Open Rugby Magazine*, January 1996: 34).

Identifiable in Ribot's rhetoric of the 'global vision' (a phrase oft repeated by Murdoch executives) was the worldwide scope of marketing opportunities and the centrality of Pay TV to the generation of alternative revenue streams such as merchandising in new global markets. Tellingly this 'vision' conforms precisely to the features of the global promotional culture noted above: the sale of ancillary products (jumpers), promotion of 'stars' (Ricky Stuart) and the centrality of media–sport integration (Pay TV). The plans for the game in Britain were, however, beset with problems. What made sense in marketing terms was replete with difficulties at the local level as the historical legacy of attachments to the game were intense and conflicted with the market logics propounded by the likes of Ribot in a variety of ways.

Local resistance to the Superleague

While reaction among followers of the game, in some quarters, was divided, supporters of British clubs that would lose their identity to the proposed mergers were outraged. At the first games following the announcement of the Superleague proposals, there were impassioned fan protests against the plans. Keighley, a club that by right had won promotion to the elite division, but was to be excluded from the Superleague, announced plans to claim damages in the High Court. Keighley fans meanwhile marched on RFL headquarters at Chapletown Road, Leeds to protest. The Professional Players Association also voiced reservations about the loss of jobs that would inevitably result from team mergers. A Labour-backed petition called for government action on the Superleague proposals. Additionally Members of Parliament investigated legal challenges to the plans, including a possible reference to the Monopolies and Mergers Commission, and called for the National Heritage Select Committee to investigate the Superleague plans (Hinchliffe, 2000).

The passions aroused were best illustrated in West Yorkshire, where a book opposing the Superleague merger plans, entitled *Merging on the Ridiculous*, was written and published within one week of the announcement, largely in response to the proposed merging of historic Yorkshire rivals Featherstone Rovers, Castleford and Wakefield Trinity into a new single club to be named Calder. At a match between the first two of these clubs, supporters of both teams occupied the playing field at half-time in protest against the merger plan. This act received substantial coverage and Channel 4 aired a documentary on the merger issue. The huge amount of media attention that the proposed Superleague attracted meant that this resistance received maximum exposure, and resulted in a great deal of unwanted negative publicity for News Corporation. Underlying much of the protests were fears of television executives controlling the game in future at the expense of those perceived as the historical 'owners' of the game – the fans.

Subsequently, less than one month after the original plans were announced, the structure of the Superleague was reassessed. While Murdoch retained broadcast rights, the game was reorganized into a three-tier competition including an elite Superleague and two feeder leagues. Under the revised plan, no clubs were merged and none was lost. Local resistance had seemingly fought off the market-driven globalizing tendencies of a media magnate. The game in Britain received a vast amount of money to retain a similar playing structure to that which predated Superleague, yet subsequent developments heightened fears of control of the sport by a media organization and demonstrated the transformative role of the media–sport axis on the cultural attachments surrounding the game. As Giulianotti argues above, resistant strategies on the part of fans can achieve some successes, though they do so in limited ways. Rugby league has been no different to soccer or Australian football in this respect, as media conglomerates and markets clash with local fans and tradition.

The commodification of rugby league

The issue that had raised the most consternation among English rugby league fans was the proposed mergers between clubs, which marked a direct threat to the parochial attachments of fans and spectators for whom clubs played an important role in cultural identity. These concerns were in contrast to News Corporation's wish to complement and strengthen their Australian interests, with the corollary of an attractive television product with appeal beyond the traditional rugby league strongholds in northern England. They also ran counter to several influential administrators of elite clubs who aligned themselves with shifts toward a commercially lucrative and expanded game. Although team mergers were successfully averted, and subsequently 'shelved', the shifts toward a more market-oriented structure were undiminished.

For example, within the revised Superleague, only one team from the proposed merger areas was admitted. Teams whose playing record had previously seen them in the top flight, but did not represent attractive markets, were relegated to the lower 'feeder' divisions from which promotion was no longer guaranteed. The goals of News Corporation, with the support of new investors in elite clubs, to consolidate spectator and television markets were therefore still achieved. Clubs faced the dilemma of losing their identity, in several cases forged through 100 years, or alternatively forgoing the right to compete at the elite level of the Superleague. Although mergers were avoided, this came at the cost of *changing* identity. Those teams and fans excluded, while maintaining their identities, had been condemned to a lower playing level. Additionally the greater revenue subsequently channelled to the clubs in the revised Superleague meant that the excluded clubs would find it harder to compete with these clubs in playing terms; therefore the pressure to attract greater revenue by merging and combining markets remained. This pressure was reinforced by the RFL mechanism of 'fast-tracking' that allowed teams to be artificially promoted to the Superleague if they fulfilled certain, largely market-based, criteria. Thus clubs were presented with the incentive to sever local cultural attachments in favour of the financial inducements of the new competition.

Following acceptance of the revised Superleague plan, several developments heightened fears of the influence of the media interests within the game. For example, rule changes were implemented prior to the start of the opening of the first summer season, arousing fears for the autonomy of the game. What was particularly significant about these changes was that they were introduced to align Murdoch's global interests, thus strengthening his position in the struggle for Australian market domination. This was the result of the Australian branch of the Superleague wishing to attain market differentiation from its Packer-backed ARL rival. The British game as a corollary thus fell into line. Even more far-reaching plans from Australia emerged as the Superleague there, it was reported, had a contingency plan if it lost its court case with the ARL, with whom it was embroiled in a bitter struggle for dominance in Australia. This so called 'doomsday option', which included 11-a-side teams, forward passes and the abolition of scrums was designed to make the game unrecognizable from its original form. The plan was designed to bypass legal rulings that might have deemed the Australian Superleague unlawful (Hadfield, 1996).

Finally the revelation of the 'loyalty' clause in player contracts (Hadfield, 1995a) led to consternation over News Corporation control. This clause, 'you will not, amend or terminate your contract without News' prior consent' offered a large degree of control to News Corporation over where players would play. Despite denials of the implications of this clause, it threatened to fulfil a similar function as a 'draft' system, controlling the distribution of labour (players) amongst teams to ensure a commercially attractive product.

These examples are illustrative of the appropriation of the game by the Murdoch empire and wider commercial logic which rapidly permeated the stilted commercial status of British rugby league. The levels of control exerted by these commercial interests demonstrate the appropriation of the game at the structural level, irrespective of teams not merging and apparently maintaining their associations with local communities. Thus the proponents of market forces were ultimately pervasive in reorienting the game along commercial lines, irrespective of initial supporter resistance.

The commercial reorganization of the game can be summarized along four lines (Denham, 2000). First has been the overt and deliberate attempt to market the game to new audiences. Taking several guises, this has included razzmatazz, mascots and crowd orchestration. Second, new patterns of club ownership have emerged. Specifically new investor-owners have taken control of several clubs. Significantly such entrepreneurs are not tied to the game by any particular 'code loyalty', as was previously the case, but on the basis of financial returns. Examples include Richard Branson, owner of the Virgin 'empire', at the London Broncos, David Whelan, owner of the JJB sports retail chain, at Wigan, and leisure magnate, David Lloyd, at Hull. Third, a process of market-oriented rationalization has been evident. Examples include the implementation of a salary cap to control expenditure on labour and attempts at cartelization which included a three-year guarantee for teams promoted to Superleague. Fourth, there has been restructuring of the game through attempted expansion and franchising. In particular there have been attempts to spread beyond the game's traditional geographical boundaries. Significantly the application of the commercial logic associated with these changes has continued to conflict with the wider cultural positioning of the game.

Global commercial logic: fragmenting the local

One of the most evident influences of the Superleague has been the varying scheduling and playing of matches, which has implications for fan attachments and live spectating rituals at the local level. The protocols of television have resulted in the manipulation of start times to concur with broadcasting schedules, most often to maximize advertising revenue by coinciding with BSkyB's target audiences. Whereas a Sunday afternoon, 3pm kick-off used to be standard, the demands of television dictate that games are spread throughout the week. Such alterations contribute to the disruption of habit and leisure patterns, and the loss of routine of live attendance. This threat to live spectating rituals implicates the media-oriented Superleague in the fragmentation of local community identity through rugby league. The rise in admission prices as a result of the Superleague also threatened to place the game beyond financial means of many fans. The advent of the Premier League in soccer, a similar satellite TV-inspired league, as outlined in Chapter 2, without the levels of resistance which the Superleague provoked, led to a sharp rise in admission prices (see Nash, 2000). Similar moves in rugby league stand to further diminish live spectating rituals.

The Superleague also accelerated the propensity of historic teams to adopt commercially motivated nicknames, which in turn sever the symbolic links with local communities. Traditionally, rarely used team nicknames made reference to local industry, places, landmarks and historic team colours. Based firmly in the locality, these names were replaced by apparently more marketable monikers. Thus the Barrow club, formerly known as the Shipbuilders became the 'Braves', Whitehaven Colliers, the 'Warriors', and Halifax, known as the Thrum Hallers, became the 'Blue Sox' and so on. Additionally traditional club crests, based upon towns' historic coat of arms, were replaced by more marketable logos that lack local connections or significance. Further innovations have included razzmatazz, in the form of pre-match entertainment, cheerleaders, pyrotechnics and mascots that collectively have transformed the match day atmosphere.

Such strategies are illustrative of the commercial imperatives of the global promotional culture exerting pressures upon cultural attachments to the game. In the localized context of rugby league, however, not all the strategies have been successful. Kelner (1996: 9), for example, points out that the mascot, although 'designed to increase the game's appeal, leads to the reverse effect on those who have already pledged their allegiance [existing fans]'. Indeed financially motivated commercial imperatives, at points, conflicted with the cultural attachments embedded in notions of place pride and live spectating which traditionally contoured affiliations to the game.

Central to many of the criticisms of the imposed 'razzmatazz' was the manner in which it disrupted the traditions of live spectating and the terrace culture that was at the heart of that tradition. The fan comments[4] below illustrate this conflict:

> I find entertainment unnecessary. I like to savour the atmosphere and excitement of looking forward to a good contest. I like to listen to the banter, talk to the regulars who stand nearby ... Pre-match entertainment is pointless to me, people go to watch rugby and be entertained on the field, not off it. People just go early or have a pint or something to eat and maybe watch a curtain raiser ... on the terrace and talk rugby which is what the day is all about. (Feedback '95)

Such observations illustrate how commercial logics can affect traditional attachments and social networks associated with live attendance. Additional to transforming pre-existing cultural attachments of rugby league, the Superleague is implicated in the creation of new forms of attachment to the game.

These new attachments centre upon the attraction of a new audience for rugby league, that of the viewer and affluent consumer. The TV exposure given to the game on the BSkyB network, for example, is implicated in the creation of a new TV-fandom. Attempts at winning over this fandom were evident during BSkyB television broadcasts of the inaugural Superleague season. They were aimed at attracting a new fan base with vivid, spectacular match action, but also through educating and enticing the uninitiated viewer. Fan education was fulfilled with sections of programming that explained rules and terminology with the use of graphics. While fulfilling a function of 'converting' new spectators, such inclusions were more likely to stand as anathema to existing fans.

The intensive coverage and promotion are not in contraposition to the live gate. SKY TV was also actively involved in promoting live attendance at Superleague games. Commentator Eddie Hemmings, for example, urged the non-fan (particularly the new spectator), 'Don't forget ... There's nothing like being there at Superleague, if you haven't already tried it before, why not pay a visit to your local ground this week?' (Boots 'n' All *Sky Sports*, 9 May 1996). The motivations behind this policy are not in contradiction to TV coverage, but related to it. Thus Vic Wakeling, head of Sky Sports, candidly stated, 'if you haven't got bums on seats in the stadiums, we haven't got a good atmosphere, and sport without atmosphere is a loser for everyone' (quoted in Kelner, 1996: 154). This kind of 'plugging' on TV and promotion through pre-match entertainment is implicated in attracting a qualitatively different live fan from those traditional spectators to whom the new-found razzmatazz, mascots and nicknames may not be attractive.

Finally the Superleague has augmented the trend toward seeking 'corporate' support that had arisen along with the acceleration of commercial imperatives. The lucrative nature of corporate 'hospitality packages' was limited at rugby league matches prior to the Superleague. Heightened commercial concerns, however, accelerated the moves toward attracting this form of revenue. The qualitatively different kinds of live attendants, therefore, who are now being sought also signal a shift away from parochial localism. This shift has seen changes in spectator provision, with an increase in the amount of covered seating areas and corporate hospitality boxes in new stadium developments. Such moves are in contrast to the provision for the traditional fan who experienced the collectivity and ritualistic involvement that the concrete standing terrace offered.

The newer patterns of consumption represent the trend toward the dissolution of parochial community attachments to rugby league, as well as the fragmentation of live spectating rituals at the local level. The heightened commodification of rugby league of which the Superleague is emblematic heralded the creation of qualitatively different attachments to the game. Significantly these newer cultural attachments are more attuned to the global culture/ideology of consumerism.

The emergence of the Superleague was the result of the culmination of forces and interrelated trends, global in scope, which had profound influences at the local level. These changing forms of attachment to sport are located within broader processes, whereby the media industries and sports entrepreneurs have combined to facilitate a global sporting system, driven by transnational market forces. The Superleague is a good example of the results of these processes manifesting themselves in the reformulation of local sporting identities. The local–global nexus, however, is characterized by a two-way dialogue in the mediation of cultural meaning. Global processes, Lawrence and Rowe (1996: 11) remind us, 'however far-reaching must always negotiate local conditions'. The following section further outlines the reactions of fans to the changes that the Superleague represented for rugby league in Northern England, and considers the interaction between commercial processes and local cultural identities.

Fans' reactions to the reformulated game

As the protests and opposition to the initial Superleague plans detailed above demonstrate, fans have not been passive in the commercial transformation of the game. While initial movements to resist team mergers quickly receded, there have been examples of the way in which imposed commercial models may be subject to resistance and challenged in a variety of ways. Several examples illustrated the contested nature of changes associated with the Superleague. These range from sporadic and spontaneous responses to more sustained fan movements.

Examples of the former surrounded reactions to the introduction of mascots at games. As noted above, Disney-style figures have emerged as part of the 'entertainment package' of the marketing-led sporting event. Some reactions of fans were, however, considerably different from those intended. As *Open Rugby Magazine* documented, 'Hull, doing their bit to lighten up match days at the Boulevard, now have a lovely cuddly black and white mascot who goes by the name of Manda the Panda ... everything was sweet and nice until the Threepenny Stand crowd started singing to Manda 'you fat bastad ... you fat bastad [sic]' (*Open Rugby Magazine*, **178**, October 1995: 17). This example illustrates the potential for a commercially inspired innovation to be interpreted in a different manner from that intended. Hence the mascot is subject to playful resistance and ridicule by fans, rather than being an incentive for them to attend by adding to the appeal of 'the event'.

This potential was further illustrated at Oldham, where the mascot's meaning was 'recycled' and used by the crowd as entertainment within their own parameters. As *Open Rugby Magazine* explained, 'He had been on fine form during the first half, cavorting along the touchline to good effect ... during the half-time interval ... it began badly, a gentleman of an age to know better, sneaked onto the pitch on his blind side and floored him with a vicious tackle (**183**, March 1996: 15). While it would be folly to read too much into these fleeting incidents, they do demonstrate the scope for local reactions and resistance to the changes within the game occurring within traditional conceptions of terrace 'banter'. That is to say, while the presence of mascots is imposed by largely incontestable forces, their meaning and significance is open to resistance at the interpretive level. Such examples illustrate the scope for disjuncture between the logics of games being staged as 'entertainment packages' and traditions of fandom.

Similarly, when 'piped-in' 'crowd atmosphere' was played over the tannoy at Salford games, the supporters' fanzine commented:

> I couldn't believe what was happening ... I would suggest to whoever thought this would be a good idea – it is not – it is a shit idea that anyone who stands on the terraces would realise only serves to humiliate the club further. The best way to create atmosphere is ... genuine banter between opposing fans, we don't need someone with a mic telling us when we should be getting behind the team. (*The Scarlet Turkey*, issue 3, May/June, 1999)

In this manner, some fans are scathing about the new commercial logics that permeate the presentation of the game, and disrupt the terrace culture noted above. These illustrative examples, while largely anecdotal, represent the scope for local interpretations and resistance in the cultural 'reading' of global commercial innovations.

Alongside these fragmented, piecemeal forms of resistance, more sustained forms of engagement have emerged to contest, challenge and inform changes within the game. These have included the formation of fan lobby groups, independent supporters' associations, supporters' trusts, alternative 'media' in the form of fanzines, a multitude of Internet-based forums and interest groups, and movements to establish teams following loss or merger of existing ones. These examples of the reactivity and mobilization of fan communities illustrate the active nature of fandoms that hold the potential to play a role in those active, constitutive moments that can confound, resist and modify the impacts of the logics of accumulation.

A further outcome of the transformations within rugby league is the precipitation of alternative attachments for traditional fans to whom commercially driven impositions are distasteful. In this context there is scope for the 'relocalization' of supporter ties as fans may opt to watch local amateur teams in preference to the razzmatazz of the new professional game. Thus one fan commented, 'If the Superleague goes ahead, they will have lost me. I won't be buying a satellite dish, this week's replica jersey or even a Calder key ring. I'll be watching Ackworth'[5] (cited in Clayton *et al.*, 1995: 57). These amateur teams are still based on community representation in a non-commercial setting. Identities may then be maintained merely by finding a new medium following the alteration of the original. Thus the structural imposition of global commercial ideology is simply subject to evasion from fans who wish to maintain local traditional affiliations to rugby league. In this sense it may be possible to conceive of a 'relocalization' process contingent upon globalization.

The reformulated game presentation, then, is not necessarily accepted or adopted by traditional fans, but nevertheless still contours the nature of attachments at the local level. For example, mascots are not necessarily accepted as part of the game, but serve as a focus for the rejection of marketing-led practices. Despite this, the ethos of rugby league as a packaged entertainment event has become an imposed component of the game.

What's left after the media mogul's been to town? British rugby league post-1995

As I have detailed, British rugby league was rapidly incorporated within the global commercial logic of the emergent sport–corporate–media nexus. Notably, however, continuing disjunctures and friction with the wider cultural positioning of the game have stunted its subsequent commercial success. These developments reveal the need to understand the interplay between the logics of capital accumulation as an ever-present constraint and the cultural terrain and attachments of sport which shapes how that logic is experienced, understood and acted upon.

Despite intentions to the contrary, the post-1995 game has been characterized by reduced cultural and media prominence, financial difficulties and even geographical retraction within Britain. Specifically the development of the British game has continued to be entwined with wider media struggles, notably the ARL–SL imbroglio in Australia, which initially resulted in rival media-aligned rugby league competitions being played during 1997. Additionally internecine struggles within the British game have characterized the imposition of a heightened marketing-led model of the game. Such developments cast doubt over the inevitability of the success of these logics of global accumulation and marketing models in light of the cultural positioning of the game.

One post-1995 feature of the British game was its continued role within media struggles in Australia. An example of the way this has contoured the game was the generation of a 'World Club Challenge'. This competition featuring British and Australian Superleague sides was developed within the context of the Pay TV battle to secure ascendancy for Murdoch in Australia. The greater playing strength of the Australian sides, however, resulted in a series of one-sided games, leaving the competition with little sporting credibility. This sporting credibility was further undermined by the commercial logic of administrators who, desiring a breadth of markets to be represented in the latter stages, contrived to bias the competition in such a way that weaker British teams progressed at the expense of superior Australian ones, thereby securing 'wide market appeal'. This lack of credibility, however, alongside the resolution of the Pay TV struggle in Australia in late 1997, meant that the high-profile tournament was scrapped after only one year, amidst negative media coverage. Thus crude market logics and desire for 'globalism' were confounded by the playing imbalances between differing 'markets' of sporting competition.

Media struggles also contoured the playing of Australia versus Great Britain international games with a 1998 three match test-series played between only Superleague contracted players.[6] Hence a 100-year tradition of 'Ashes' test matches was played on the basis of media allegiances rather than national identities.

The development of the British game has also been characterized by internecine struggles for power and control. Shortly after the commencement of the Superleague a separate body was established by the elite clubs as a collective marketing and promotions arm. This was distinct from the existing governing body, the RFL, whose remit, in contrast, was the welfare of the entire game. This pseudo-governing body was further evidence of the de facto split between the elite and the remainder. Internal divisions within the game were reinforced when those clubs excluded from the summer Superleague made a decision to revert to a winter playing season in 1998, because of falling attendance figures. This move further reinforced the split between the game's lower levels and the elite that the Superleague had precipitated. Such divisions were entrenched by the refusal to allow Hunslet and Dewsbury, both small market clubs that had won promotion to the Superleague, to enter the competition. Alternatively Hull, Huddersfield, Wakefield and Widnes, with more favourable market features, were allowed into Superleague. Such moves were clear evidence of the pre-eminence of market dynamics in the composition of the Superleague.

With the Australian media imbroglio resolved, the British game, upon renegotiating television contracts with BSkyB, did so at a considerably reduced rate. A renegotiated five-year deal of £54 million, signed in 1998 represented a near 30 per cent cut in the level of the 1995 Superleague contract. The contract further reinforced the split of the game's elite from the lower levels. Under the new terms, the lower division clubs were gradually phased out of payment, so that ultimately all revenue was channelled to the elite clubs. Hence processes of commercialization have entrenched the polarization of elite clubs and the remainder.

Logics of market expansion were manifest, commencing in 1998, when Superleague clubs embarked on a series of 'on the road' games, played in areas beyond Northern England. Games took place in the east midlands, north-eastern and southern England, south Wales, southern France and Scotland. The games, however, played before paltry crowds in many cases, merely reinforced the lack of appeal of the sport beyond its traditional boundaries, both geographical and cultural. They yielded poor commercial returns and were scrapped. Hence desires for market expansion were limited by the games' cultural ties.

Further reflecting the new pressures to expand the market of the game, a Gateshead 'franchise' (situated in north-east England) was admitted to the Superleague in 1999. After only one season, however, in financial difficulties owing to poor crowds, the franchise was 'wound up' by means of a contrived merger with the Hull Sharks club. The subsequent 'amalgam', a team playing in Hull, in the historic black and white irregular hoops of the Hull team, at Hull's Boulevard stadium, and reverting to the Hull club's pre-Superleague title of 'Hull FC', left little doubt as to the dominant partner in this 'merger'. A similar 'merge-over' situation occurred between the Huddersfield Giants and Sheffield Eagles (towns over 30 miles apart). The two clubs joined to form the Sheffield–Huddersfield Giants, with home games split between the two cities during the 1999 season. The rhetoric of this merger, however, was revealed the following season, when the club reverted to the Huddersfield Giants name, playing all home games in Huddersfield. In reality both mergers had been designed to 'streamline' the league by jettisoning less profitable franchises. In turn, the remaining clubs received larger shares of television revenue.

The lack of association with the merged team in Sheffield led supporters to re-form the Eagles club, and commence playing within the lower divisions of the game. Similarly supporters in Gateshead, following the loss of their team, re-formed the club and entered a lower level of competition. The loss of Gateshead and Sheffield to these 'mergers', as well as the dissolution of the French Paris St Germain franchise after only two seasons of play, meant that the game at the elite level, despite expansionist rhetoric, underwent a geographical retraction.[7] The cases of the reformation of the Sheffield and Gateshead clubs, which had been lost to the new financial model, also demonstrate the scope for the resilience of local cultural identities within the game despite contrary economic logic. Indeed clubs in both Bramley and York were revived following their (economic) demise and departure from the professional leagues.

A World Cup tournament held in 2000 further illustrated the disjunctures associated with the imposition of expansionist commercial logic on the cultural terrain of rugby league. Specifically the lack of global diffusion confounded the holding of a global competition premised on media and corporate investment. Of the 16 competing teams, only five (Australia, England, France, Papua New Guinea and New Zealand) feature existing leagues. The remainder, including Lebanon, Russia, Scotland, the USA, South Africa and Morocco, largely constituted surplus Australian elite players based upon tenuous grandparent linkages. The result was a contrived tournament that lacked sporting credibility, and subsequently commercial return. Of the players representing the Scottish team, for example, none had been born within the country. Furthermore they were coached by an Australian. Similarly the Lebanese team was constituted of Australian players sharing ancestry. Yet no rugby league game had ever been played within the former country. Held across England, Ireland, France, Scotland and Wales, the tournament was characterized by poor crowds and a lack of competitive games in a series of locales having little cultural resonance with rugby league. The desire to be credible and commercially competitive within a global market in the guise of a world cup tournament was limited by the cultural confines of the sport. The consequence was large-scale financial losses.

These developments illustrate the way in which the imposition of commercial models and initiatives under the logics of 'globalism' has been confounded by the cultural positioning of the game. For example, hosting games in 'expansion' areas, underpinned by desires for market expansion, met a muted response because of the lack of resonance of the game with local people. Similarly the desire to host a World Cup event, thus reinforcing the credibility of the game within global sports marketplaces, was confounded by the lack of global diffusion and contrived attempts to overcome this. Additionally fans have been active in reforming clubs precluded by the economic logics of the commodified game. A further significant feature of these processes has been the reconfigured relationship with rugby union, which has historically been profound in the cultural positioning of the game.

The reconfiguration of the rugby union–rugby league relationship

As noted, the 1895 split from the RFU and the legacy of antipathy and acrimony between rugby codes was pivotal in historically defining the cultural character of rugby league. The processes noted above have been profound in reconfiguring the relationship between the two codes. Symptomatic of precisely the same pressures and processes reshaping rugby league, rugby union underwent profound transformation during the 1990s. Specifically the abandonment of 'shamateurism' in 1995 in favour of open professionalism in rugby union was both symptomatic and constitutive of heightened commercialism[8] (see Hutchins, 1999; Malcolm *et al.*, 2000). These transitions in rugby union have realigned the relationship between the two codes on a global scale. As a result, the relationship between the two codes in Britain, once characterized by mutual fear and loathing along class and regional lines, is now characterized by both the legacy of these cultural divides and a more overt commercial rivalry.

The result of the abandonment of 'shamateurism' has been new encounters and inter-code contact previously unseen. Symptomatic of the new relationship, 'cross-code' challenge matches between Bath (union) and Wigan (league) were played in 1996 with one game under the rules of each code. Similarly the Wigan (1996) and Bradford (2002) clubs participated in the union code's Middlesex sevens tournament. Additionally movements of playing, administrative and coaching personnel have characterized the new free gangway between the two codes. The bulk of the shift has been in the rugby union direction. Prominent league international players switching to union have included Jason Robinson (Wigan–Sale), Iestyn Harris (Leeds–Cardiff) and Henry Paul (Bradford–Gloucester), with persistent speculation surrounding others. The loss of these 'star' players raises question marks over the capability of rugby league to be sustainable commercially. As Whitson (1998) observes, the marketing of such 'marquee' players is pivotal to the ability to compete in the global sports marketplace.

The new 'terms' of the relationship between the two codes and the domination of rugby union in commercial terms has been countered by protectionist measures within rugby league. In reaction to the loss of elite players, for example, a 'club Great Britain' was established to protect national squad players from switching codes. Constituting payments from central funds to 'top-up' club wages, the measures were successful in keeping several key personnel within the game. Following the reconfiguration of the relationship between the two codes, and players' increasingly 'rational' approach to career opportunities, such economic incentives appear the chief means of protecting rugby league from the loss of personnel. The irony of this new interchange is that the 100-year-long discriminatory campaign of the RFU toward rugby league, had previously insulated the game from this loss of personnel.[9] Whereas the barrier had previously centred (notionally) upon the issue of amateurism, it is now based largely upon commercial logics, with union in a stronger position thanks to its national market, closer links with the corporate world and more lucrative international structure.

This new level of interaction has precipitated repeated speculation on the convergence of the elite levels of the game in some form of hybrid code, or even elite league clubs switching to union (see Wilson, 2001). Indeed the new entrepreneurs who have invested in rugby league appear less interested in the legacy of loyalty to the code than in commercial opportunities. For example, David Whelan, owner of the JJB sports retail chain and majority owner of Wigan, recently threatened to switch the historic and storied club to playing union (see Smith, 2001).[10] The commercial logic behind his threat was clear in his comment: 'Wigan get £600,000 a year for playing in Super League … if we make the premiership and Heineken Cup [play rugby union] we would get £2.4m a year' (cited in *The Guardian*, 16 December 2001). Thus the location of clubs within communities is integrally tied to the relative market worth of the club rather than culturally grounded affiliations. Hence historically grounded loyalties threaten to be broken down by new logics of accumulation.

Within the cultural space of the British sporting landscape, rugby league has arguably become more peripheral during the Superleague era. Specifically the shift to a summer playing season saw terrestrial coverage reduced, whilst that of rugby union has been cemented with the continued appearance of the six nations championships, on both the BBC and ITV. Additionally a European clubs competition is broadcast and promoted extensively by the BBC. The irony is that, aligning with global media interests and securing a lucrative deal with BSkyB, rugby league decreased the breadth of its exposure because of the nature of the UK satellite market, to which fewer people have access than have to terrestrial channels. Alternatively both association football and rugby union enjoyed the large revenues from BSkyB, but were also able to maintain a terrestrial presence, thereby securing and extending their prominent cultural status. In contrast, the Superleague saw rugby league terrestrial coverage reduced by half. These observations demonstrate the limits to the 'inevitability' of the success of the sports–media–corporate axis.

Summary: sport, commodification and the local–global nexus

This chapter has afforded the opportunity to reflect on the characteristics and complexities of the emergence of a sport–media–corporate nexus within the contexts of 'the global age' (Albrow, 1996). The acute transformation in structure, ethos and presentation of sport across a range of locales demonstrates the impacts of the tightening incorporation of sport within globally interconnected logics of capital accumulation. The case of British rugby league demonstrates the profound local impacts of these global processes.

Reformulations of the game must not be reified as operating inexorably. They are facilitated by the actions of media executives, entrepreneurial investors, corporate sponsors and administrators who find collective affinity in the remodelling of the game as a site for rationalized capital accumulation and a forum for stimulating consumption. Notwithstanding the profound impacts of these processes, they are not characterized by the untrammelled transformation of sport according to instrumentally rational market logics. Alternatively the transition is mediated, and indeed modified, by the historically contingent cultural terrain of sport. Furthermore, at points, it is contested, resisted and even confounded.

The economic rationalization of the game is subject to 'negotiations' with wider cultural forces in several ways. For example, the mobilization of supporters and resistance to proposed club mergers demonstrates that locals can and do contest these processes in significant ways. In this case, fans were successful in resisting the loss of club-oriented local identities that logics of 'market consolidation' would have precluded. There are also instances of more sustained, and potentially more significant, interventions.

For example, the re-formation of clubs by supporters in Sheffield, York, Gateshead and Bramley after they had been either excluded from the league on the basis of 'market rationalization' or made subject to merger signifies precisely those 'active constitutive moments' which Ingham *et al.* (1987) note as significant in limiting the determining nature of economic processes. For example, the re-formation of the Bramley club by supporters operating under the new title Bramley Rugby League *Community* Club in 2000 is symptomatic of resistance to or subversion of the control of entrepreneurial or corporate capital. Financed on a non-profit, cooperative basis by shareholding fans, the club subverts the model that leave clubs vulnerable to extinction dictated by investment and finances beyond fans' control. In this manner, elements of local cultures can maintain their own meanings, values and interpretations, thus retaining distinctiveness and identity, where the dictates of capital accumulation models would preclude them.

Furthermore the commercial failure of strategies of market expansion designed to seek credibility (and capital return) within the 'global sports marketplace' reinforces the significance of cultural factors. These failures are symptomatic, not of direct resistance, but of the limitations of logic of market expansion and desire for 'global brand' status to the historically informed cultural attachments and identification of sports. In the case of rugby league, the entrenched cultural ties and limited diffusion of the game have been significant in constraining the success of expansionist logics of accumulation. Thus the cultural affiliations of sport operate as mediators of economic logics. Indeed the April 2002 collapse of the £315m broadcast rights agreement between ITV-digital and the English football league, and downturns in several recent broadcast rights negotiations in Britain, reinforce the limitations of the sport–media axis. Clearly, within the emergent political economy of sport, some forms will be privileged as 'global media sports' over others.

Gauging this interplay is complex. As I have argued, initial resistance to team merger plans was less successful in terms of representing a negotiation between elements of local culture and global commercial interests at a structural level. Although it initially appeared significant that the format of the competition was altered owing to local resistance, seemingly a victory for local fans over global commercial pressures, subsequent evidence suggests that those aligned with market logics were ultimately successful in transforming the game. Furthermore marketers, investors and media executives are apt to incorporate and modify resistance. For example, both the Hull and Halifax clubs, facing opposition to their commercially motivated nicknames, have dropped the Sharks and Blue Sox monikers they had adopted. Yet the heightened commercial footing is undiminished. Furthermore nostalgia and discourses of 'community' are readily repackaged and commodified in marketing approaches.

Hence the shifts in the balance of power should not be underestimated. While levels of resistance are possible along certain indices, the new patterns of consumption associated with the Superleague hold long-term implications regarding the cultural attachments and meaning(s) of the game. The transitions have effected a qualitative transformation in the experience of attending games – traditionally at the core of fandom. Games now feature cheerleaders, mascots, musical cues, crowd orchestration and increased surveillance. Furthermore provision has shifted in the direction of all-seater stadiums or surveillance in terrace areas. Such alterations challenge and exert pressures on the historically constructed identities of fans and the traditional rituals of spectatorship. Furthermore the creation of a new live fandom to whom the new marketing gimmicks of mascots, cheerleaders and music are attractive, as well as corporate and business interests attending, represent the emergence of new affiliations to the game.

The transformation of British rugby league also offers the opportunity to reflect on questions concerning the local–global nexus. Notably the case demonstrates precisely the weakness of conceptions of the processes as necessarily global *versus* local; in the case of this chapter, global capital *versus* local game. Clearly global interconnectedness was, and continues to be, profound (as demonstrated, most notably, by the continuing Australian media struggle that Phillips, Hutchins and Stewart discuss in the following chapter). Yet the transitions were also shaped by struggles internal to the (local) game. At the local level, various 'agents' (investors, sponsors and administrators) are complicit and active in the changes. This was manifest in conflicts between a stratum of club owners and administrators who aligned themselves with the model advocated by Murdoch's media executives and traditionalist fans. Hence the local context itself is characterized by complex and fragmented social relations featuring negotiations and challenges, entwined with global processes. For example, the jettisoning of lower playing levels by the elite clubs from media revenue illustrates how local dynamics are significant. Such observations offer a corrective to simplistic conceptions of global *versus* local dynamics.

The chapter demonstrates the complex interplay between cultural legacy and attachments and the incorporation of sport within global commercial logic. The task for social scientists is to comprehend the full disjunctive complexity of these shifts. As Boyle and Haynes (2000) note, as globalization processes continue apace, sport remains an important cultural, political and commercial marker of boundaries, identities and markets. Cultural legacies and attachments remain significant as developments are contested and negotiated. Such observations reinforce the need for detailed case studies to shed light on the path between overly optimistic commentaries on the resurgence of local cultures or the alluring simplicity of deterministic homogenization theses.

Notes

1. This observation is echoed by Jackson and Andrews (1999) within the sporting literature.
2. Morley and Robins (1995) note that it is in fact erroneous to employ the term 'deregulation'. That is, market dynamics and imperatives impose their own

regulatory logic, just as regulation in the 'public interest' represented constraint on output.

3. Until 1995, the bourgeois-dominated RFU banned for life any player playing professional rugby league. Until 1973, even amateur rugby league players were banned. These formal bans were complemented by ostracism, discrimination in the armed forces (where the game was banned), the educational sector and media bias (see Hinchliffe, 2000).

4. These excerpts are taken from data from the Rugby League Supporters Association survey (carried out in 1995) entitled 'Feedback '95'.

5. Ackworth amateur RLFC play in the senior amateur league, Division 2.

6. Several British players had signed contracts with ARL clubs. Prominent examples include established international players Gary Connolly and Jason Robinson.

7. While developments in Britain are the central concern of this chapter, it is clear the impacts of these processes upon the French game, itself even more culturally marginal than in Britain (see Dine, 2001; Rylance, 1999), were profound and await documentation.

8. Notably the timing of the acceptance of open professionalism in rugby union was integrally entwined with the media struggle in rugby league (see Mirams, 2001; Fitzsimons, 1996).

9. Prior to open professionalism, the gangway had been one-way, as the RFU had banned those associated with rugby league.

10. His comment was made in the context of an imbroglio with Superleague authorities regarding the salary cap. At the following game Wigan fans made their feelings clear in no uncertain terms, singing 'stand up if you hate rugby union'.

References

Albrow, M. (1996), *The global age: state and society beyond modernity*, Cambridge: Polity.

Alger, D. (1998), *Megamedia: how giant corporations dominate mass media, distort competition and endanger democracy*, New York: Rowman & Littlefield.

Andrews, D., B. Carrington, S. Jackson and J. Mazur (1996), 'Jordanscapes: a preliminary analysis of the global popular', *Sociology of Sport Journal*, **13**, 428–57.

Boyle, R. and R. Haynes (2000), *Power play: sport, the media and popular culture*, London: Longman.

Clayton, I., I. Daley and B. Lewis (eds) (1995), *Merging on the ridiculous: the fans' response to the superleague*, vol. 1, Wakefield: Yorkshire Arts Circus.

Coleman, M. (1996), *Super League: the inside story*, Sydney: Ironbark.

Collins, T. (1998a), *Rugby's great split: class, culture and the origins of rugby league*, London: Frank Cass.

Collins, T. (1998b), 'Racial minorities in a marginalized sport: race, discrimination and integration in British rugby league football', in M. Cronin and D. Mayall (eds), *Sporting Nationalisms: identity, ethnicity, immigration, and assimilation*, London: Frank Cass, pp.151–69.

Conn, D. (1997), *The football business: fair game in the '90s?*, Edinburgh: Mainstream.

Delaney, T. (1993), *Rugby disunion: volume one – broken-time*, Keighley: Trevor Delaney.

Denham, D. (2000), 'Modernism and postmodernism in professional rugby league in England', *Sociology of Sport Journal*, **17**, 275–94.

Dine, P. (2001), *French rugby football: a cultural history*, Oxford: Berg.

European TV Sports Databook (1995), London: Kagan World Media Ltd.

Falcous, M. (1998), 'TV made it all a new game: not again! – rugby league and the case of the superleague', *Football Studies*, **1**(1), 4–21.

Featherstone, M. (1991), 'Global and local cultures', *Vrijetijd En Samenlevig*, **9** (3–4), 43–57.

Fitzsimons, P. (1996), *The rugby war*, Sydney: Harper Collins.

Gate, R. (1986), *Rugby league: an illustrated history*, London: Weidenfeld.

Hadfield, D. (1995a), 'Super leaguers shape up for the small screen', *The Independent on Sunday*, 20 August, p.22.

Hadfield, D. (1995b), 'Television threatens tyranny', *The Independent*, 20 December, p.21.

Hadfield, D. (1996), 'Superleague deny "doomsday option" ', *The Independent*, 3 January, p.19.

Hamil, S., J. Michie and C. Oughton (eds) (1999), *The business of football: a game of two halves?*, London: Mainstream.

Herman, E. and R. McChesney (1997), *The global media: the new missionaries of global capitalism*, London: Cassell.

Hinchliffe, D. (2000), *Rugby's class war: bans, boot money and parliamentary battles*, London: London League Publications.

Hutchins, B. (1999), 'Global processes and the rugby union World Cup', *Football Studies*, **2** (1), 34–54.

Ingham, A., J. Howell and T. Schilperoort (1987), 'Professional sports and community: a review and exegesis', *Exercise and Sport Sciences Review*, **75**, 427–65.

Jackson, S. and D. Andrews (1999), 'Between and beyond the global and the local', *International Review for the Sociology of Sport*, **43** (1), 31–42.

Kelner, S. (1996), *To Jerusalem and back*, London: Macmillan.

King, A. (1997), 'New directors, customers, and fans: the transformation of English football in the 1990s', *Sociology of Sport Journal*, **14** (3), 224–40.

King, A. (1998), *The end of the terraces: the transformation of English football in the 1990s*, London: Leicester University Press.

Lawrence, G. and D. Rowe (1996), 'Beyond national sport: sociology, history and postmodernity', *Sporting Traditions*, **12** (2), 3–16.

Malcolm, D., K. Sheard and A. White (2000), 'The changing structure and culture of English rugby union football', *Culture, Sport, Society*, **3** (3), 63–87.

McAllister, M. (2000), 'From flick to flack: the increased emphasis on marketing by media entertainment corporations', in R. Andersen and L. Strate (eds), *Critical studies in media commercialism*, London: Oxford University Press, pp.101–24.

McKay, J. and T. Miller (1991), 'From old boys to men and women of the corporation: the Americanization and commodification of Australian sport', *Sociology of Sport Journal*, **8**, 86–94.

Miller, T., G. Lawrence, J. McKay and D. Rowe (2001), *Globalization and sport*, London: Sage.

Mirams, C. (2001), *Beleaguered! The Warriors: from dream to nightmare*, Auckland: Hodder Moa Beckett.

Morley, D. and K. Robins (1995), *Spaces of identity: global media, electronic landscapes and cultural boundaries*, London: Routledge.

Nash, R. (2000), 'The sociology of British football in the 1990s: fandom, business and future research', *Football Studies*, **3** (1), 49–63.

Open Rugby Magazine (1995), 'Syd Scoop Supersnoop' column, **178** (October), 17.

Open Rugby Magazine (1996), 'Syd Scoop Supersnoop' column, **186** (March), 15.

Phillips, M. and B. Hutchins (1998), 'From independence to a reconstituted hegemony: rugby league in Australia', *Journal of Australian Studies*, **58**, 134–47.

Phillips, M. and B. Hutchins (2003), 'Losing control of the ball: the political economy of football and the media in Australia', *Journal of Sport and Social Issues*, **27** (3), 215–32.

Robertson, R. (1995), 'Glocalisation: time–space and homogeneity–heterogeneity', in M. Featherstone, S. Lash and R. Robertson (eds), *Global modernities*, London: Sage, pp.25–45.

Rowe, D. (1997), 'Rugby league in Australia: the super league saga', *Journal of Sport and Social Issues*, **21** (2), 221–6.

Rowe, D. and J. McKay (1999), 'Fields of soaps: Rupert v. Kerry as masculine melodrama', in R. Martin and T. Miller (eds), *SportCult*, Minneapolis: University of Minnesota, pp.191–210.

Rylance, M. (1999), *The forbidden game: the untold story of French rugby league*, Brighouse, West Yorkshire: League Publications Limited.

Smith, G. (2001), 'Saturday interview: Whelan peerless in Wigan', retrieved 16 April 2001 from the World Wide Web: http://www.sport.telegraph.co.uk/sport/main.jhtml?xml+/sport/2001

Spraklen, K. (2001), ' "Black pearl, black diamonds": exploring racial identities in rugby league', in B. Carrington and I. Mcdonald (eds), *'Race', sport and British society*, London: Routledge, pp.70–82.

The Scarlet Turkey: the independent Salford rugby league fanzine (1999), May/June, Issue 3, 'Let's Talk Turkey' – editorial, p.2.

Whannel, G. (2000), 'Sport and the media', in J. Coakley and E. Dunning (eds), *Handbook of sports studies*, London: Sage, pp.291–308.

Whitson, D. (1998), 'Circuits of promotion: media, marketing and the globalization of sport', in L. Wenner (ed.), *MediaSport*, London: Routledge, pp.57–72.

Wilson, A. (2001), 'Top Superleague clubs "set to switch codes" ', *The Guardian*, 18 July, p.30.

5

The Media Sport Cultural Complex: Football and Fan Resistance in Australia

Murray G. Phillips, Brett Hutchins and Bob Stewart

The control of spectator sports both in Australia and internationally increasingly has moved away from sports administrators and towards media executives. This shift in control can be illustrated most clearly by seeing spectator sport as part of a 'media sport cultural complex' (Rowe, 1999). Popular elite male sports such as Australian football and rugby league are not only linked to media organizations, marketing consultants and transnational corporations, but the influence of these agents can also consolidate and/or fracture traditional sporting cultural practices. The trend in Australia's two dominant football codes has been a fracturing, with competition structures, traditional club identities and fan loyalties all coming under significant challenge by ascendant corporate strategies and practices over the past two decades. The issue at hand is what happens when these sports are incorporated into the interests of media companies and their expansionist strategies. Instructive examples of this process are Australian rugby league and its radically reshaped competition and administration in the new millennium, and the popular Australian Football League (AFL) competition, which has undergone a national expansion programme and upheaval as club relocations and mergers have followed.

In this chapter we examine the changes outlined via a Marxist-influenced political economy paradigm. The use of traditional Marxist and liberal theories of political economy in the critique of the sport industry has recently been called into question. The apparent fragmentation and diversity of cultural politics, and the expansion and transformation of a transnational electronic media, have made it difficult to draw firm conclusions about the contours of sport production and consumption

(Andrews, 1998). Even given this, we concur with David Rowe (1995: 106) that value does remain in a Marxist-influenced political economy approach that emphasizes the production and reproduction of power relations under capitalism, particularly given the continuing inroads into the realm of culture made by global corporate capital. In our inquiry, investigation is centred on how these inroads have been made into Australia's most popular football codes, and the collective reactions that have resulted.

A political economy approach contextualizes the changing relations of domination, subordination and resistance over time in capitalist social and economic orders (Jarvie and Maguire, 1994) or, to put it simply, it helps us understand 'who gains, who loses and how' (Staniland, 1985: 2). Even given the 'hyperreal' character of the electronic media, the question remains as to who owns and controls the means and relations of economic production and political power. Political economy is at issue wherever ideology, economics and culture intertwine and enables us to see how these relationships are produced and reproduced.

The media sport cultural complex

Our analytical framework employs the concept of the media sport cultural complex (Rowe, 1999). This complex is an extension of previous work that has examined the relationship between sporting organizations, media and marketing organizations and commercial/transnational companies (Maguire, 1993, 1999; Wenner, 1998). Rowe (1999: 4) maintains the production element of Maguire's conceptualization of the media sport complex, but further stresses the 'two-way relationship between the sports media and the great cultural formation of which it is part':

> that is, the extent to which the great engine of signs and myths itself symbolizes and helps create out current 'being in the world'. By gaining a better knowledge and understanding of how media sports texts are produced and what they might mean, it is possible to learn more about societies in which 'grounded' and 'mediated' experience intermesh in even more insidious and seemingly seamless ways. (Rowe, 1999: 34)

This complex opens the way to examine the political economy of Australian football and rugby league, or any other major commercial sporting competition for that matter, via the interrelationships between key production processes, cultural change and patterns of resistance to this change. In attempting to understand fan resistance, Rowe's conceptualization is particularly useful as its emphasizes the signs, myths and codes that mediate and ground consumer culture, thereby providing an understanding of the discourses and meanings of supporter resistance. The media sports cultural complex provides a useful analytical framework that can account for both the social production of sports industries and their cultural consumption.

This chapter analyses media organizations, commercial companies and football administrations, and also draws attention to supporters' responses to changing football cultures. This represents an important contribution to the political economy of sport literature: a great deal is already known about globalizing processes and the considerable power wielded by companies such as Rupert Murdoch's News Corporation (Herman and McChesney, 1997; Westfield, 2000). Yet comparatively little has been written about fan movements and consumer cultures that attempt to challenge this power (Phillips and Nauright, 1999). Given the growing commodification of culture, will (or can) football fans provide a sustained challenge to the corporate power bloc controlling sport? Is there any expectation or possibility that sport will be used as a major site of anti-corporate and anti-globalization sentiment, as manifest in movements such as S11, the anti-Nike campaigns and the worldwide publishing phenomenon of Naomi Klein's *No Logo* (2001)? The evidence and arguments put forward in this chapter, through the case studies of rugby league and Australian football, state that the answer to these questions is a firm 'no'.

The football codes in Australia

Australia has four major football codes: Australian football, rugby league, rugby union and soccer. It may be surprising to some that soccer, or football as the rest of the world knows it, has a relatively small following in Australia. Soccer remains an underdeveloped sport that has been beset by administrative infighting, poor television coverage and small attendances, though it has the highest number of registered participants among the football codes (Mosely and Murray, 1994). The two most popular codes of football in terms of media and spectator interest are rugby league and Australian football. Rugby league has been the most popular professional football code in two of Australia's eastern states – New South Wales and Queensland – since the first decade of the twentieth century (see Table 5.1). A 13-person per team game featuring occasionally spectacular heavy body contact, the elite competition began in 1908 after splitting away from the amateur rugby union game over issues of 'broken-time' and match payments (Phillips, 1998). The recently

Table 5.1   Major football centres in Australia (2003)

City/state	Population (million)	Dominant football code
Adelaide, South Australia	1.1	Australian Football
Brisbane, Queensland	1.5	Rugby League
Hobart, Tasmania	0.2	Australian Football
Melbourne, Victoria	4.0	Australian Football
Perth, Western Australia	1.4	Australian Football
Sydney, New South Wales	4.3	Rugby League

professionalized rugby union could have served as a third pillar to this essay as many of the changes that have affected rugby league have also realigned rugby union globally (Hutchins, 1996; Hutchins and Phillips, 1999). As a professional sport, rugby league has always been associated with commodity value, but the acceleration of commercial involvement in the code over the past few decades has created massive disruption (Phillips, 1998). Australian football is by far the most watched game in every Australian state outside New South Wales and Queensland and has a growing audience within these locales. Indeed, in 2001 for the first time, the Brisbane Lions championship team in the AFL attracted more spectators than the vaunted Brisbane Broncos of rugby league. Historically Melbourne in Victoria has been the 'epicentre' of Australian football, with the code being 'born' there in 1858. By the beginning of the twentieth century the game had consolidated its presence in South Australia, Western Australia and Tasmania and was played in Queensland and southern border regions of New South Wales (Hess and Stewart, 1998). A free-flowing 18-person per team game, a defining feature of Australian football is that more people attend matches than any other sport in the nation (Australian Bureau of Statistics, 1999). As with rugby league, it has possessed a commercial character almost since its inception, when grounds were enclosed and spectators were charged for admission (Grow, 1998).

The media and football in Australia

There are both similarities and differences in the historical relationship between the media and Australian football and rugby league. Television was introduced in Australia to coincide with the 1956 Melbourne Olympic Games. In the same year, Australian football trialled the new medium on a closed circuit for a restricted audience, and by 1957 selected parts of the game were telecast. Fees were negotiated with television companies who were permitted to show parts of the games and other segments in a delayed format (Stewart, 1998). In a manner similar to Australian football, rugby league's first games were televised in 1961 with delayed coverage of sections of the game. Both sports were televised on monochrome screens with few camera angles and have been pejoratively described as nothing better than 'radio with pictures' (Phillips and Hutchins, 1998: 134–5).

This early period of broadcasting was typified by the ambivalence of both codes towards the new medium. Television companies were prepared to pay for the right to televise games, but rugby league and Australian football authorities, like many other sports in the United Kingdom and the United States (Gruneau and Whitson, 1993; Horne *et al.*, 1999), were concerned about the possible effects on gate receipts, their major source of income. For these reasons, games were partially covered, often in a delayed format and occasionally not televised at all. For instance, Australian football authorities, concerned by the decline in attendances, banned all live and direct telecasts after 1961, opting instead for delayed coverage (Stewart, 1998). A decade later, rugby league administrators could not reach an appropriate broadcast fee deal with any of the television companies, resulting in no regular game coverage for the season. These examples highlight several salient issues: gate receipts were still the main source of revenue, the potential financial windfall that television could provide was not fully comprehended, and the media sport cultural complex was in a very early stage of development (Phillips and Hutchins, 1998).

A key dynamic that transformed the relationship between Australian sport and the broadcast media was the introduction of colour television in 1975 (Goldlust, 1987). Colour television provided an unrealized appreciation of the game with the clarity of images enhancing viewers' experiences. The visual acuity of colour images attracted new viewers and produced increased advertising revenue and higher ratings that provided leverage in the negotiation of television rights (Stewart, 1980). By 1977, for instance, Australian football received close to $1 million from commercial and non-commercial television for annual broadcast fees (Stewart, 1984). Broadcast fees of this magnitude were unimaginable prior to the introduction of colour television.

Healthy ratings for televised football were the catalyst for the increased role of commercial companies in the sports industry. Companies have been involved in sport in Australia since the turn of the twentieth century, but this involvement was mostly irregular and minor in terms of overall contribution. Commercial involvement in the football codes began to increase in the 1960s, and the growth in audiences provided by colour television prompted commercial companies to invest heavily. The tobacco company, W.D. & H.O. Wills, paid $12,000 for signage and associated promotions during the 1968 final series in Australian football. Following the advent of colour television and the prohibition of direct cigarette advertising, the tobacco company had quadrupled their sponsorship by 1975 (Nadel, 1998). Similarly, in rugby league, tobacco sponsorship spread from pre-season competitions, player awards and partial competition rights to full sponsorship of all competitions by 1982, bringing in $850,000 over three years (Phillips, 1998). By the 1990s, commercial companies had purchased the rights to major competitions, individual clubs, referees' uniforms and playing fields to the point where commercial logos, announcements and deals had saturated both football codes.

The period between the mid-1970s and the very early 1980s highlights the development of distinctive features of the media sports cultural complex. Television networks used sporting events as high rating programmes that sold advertising time (Stewart, 1984). Football became an integral component of television programming and a highly prized commodity, as demonstrated by the competition between television networks to secure broadcasting rights. The codes were proven ratings successes thanks to their popularity with fans. Recognizing this, commercial companies increasingly invested in football in order to sell their goods and services to large and often selected audiences. In the active trading of their 'product' to television and commercial companies, the financial contribution to the football codes from these sources outstripped the contribution from gate receipts. The television industry, commercial companies and football administrators had come to realize that there were vast financial benefits in these synergies, leading to increasing levels of interdependency.

Organizational expansion

Australian football and rugby league underwent a number of structural changes that clearly demarcate the 1980s from the earlier history of both sports. There were large-scale television marketing campaigns, the introduction of night football competitions, modifications of game formats to suit television scheduling and programming, attempts to curb on-field violence through video surveillance and judiciaries, and the implementation and adaptation of predominantly American-style promotions (Hutchins and Phillips, 1997; Nadel, 1998a, 1998b; Phillips, 1998; Phillips and Hutchins, 1998). Many of these features were facilitated by changes to the administrative structures of both codes. In rugby league the administration was overhauled with a board of nine directors replacing the former 52-person committee (Heads, 1992). In Australian football, a five-person commission superseded the previous board of directors (Nadel, 1998a). These restructuring processes reduced the direct influence of individual clubs, centralized the control of the football codes into smaller management teams representing corporate, television and football interests, and involved the specialization of services and functions along the lines of corporations.

As Table 5.2 indicates, one of the most marked alterations to football in Australia between the 1980s and the mid-1990s was geographical expansion (Andrews, 2000; Phillips, 1998). This expansion in both Australian football and rugby league was characterized by the extension of competitions into cities in other states. For example, in Australian football expansion entailed relocating clubs such as South Melbourne to Sydney in 1982, while in rugby league new clubs were created in Canberra and Wollongong the same year. These trends continued as teams from cities in Queensland, Western Australia and South Australia were added to the premier Australian football competition, and cities in Queensland, Western Australia, South Australia, Victoria and New Zealand provided teams for the major rugby league competition. Competition expansion was pursued because it benefited the interests of all stakeholders (football administrators, television networks and commercial companies) and many football followers in areas previously

Table 5.2 Changing elite competition numbers in Australian football and rugby league

Year	Australian football	Rugby league
1982	12	14
1984	12	13
1987	14	13
1988	14	16
1991	15	16
1995	16	20
1997	16	22
1998	16	20
1999	16	17
2000	16	14
2002	16	15

without teams. Administrators discarded the traditional non-profit instrumental rationality that had guided strategic policies for half a century and fully embraced capital accumulation (Phillips and Hutchins, 2003). A national competition as opposed to a suburban based, single-city competition, generated larger broadcast rights, corporate funding and revenue from merchandising (Andrews, 2000). Television networks supported expansion because it offered larger viewing audiences and coincided with new satellite technology and nationally affiliated programming in the television industry (Smith and Stewart, 2000). Additionally, in cities that had not previously had a team, new clubs in the national competition provided 'home grown' local broadcasts featuring well known commentators, specific sports news and 'lifestyle' pieces on high-profile local players (Phillips and Hutchins, 1998). For commercial companies national competitions were perfectly suited to the promotion of products such as alcohol and tobacco. For football followers, this competition structure capitalized on pride built on geographical identity – an 'our town, our team' philosophy – and provided a stage for enacting historically ingrained inter-city and inter-state rivalries (Hutchins, 1997). There was resistance from football followers, particularly in local leagues already existing in Adelaide, Brisbane and Perth, which suffered as a result of these expanding elite competitions (Mulcahy, 1993). Overall, however, national football competitions flourished because they served the mutual and increasingly inseparable interests of football administrators, television networks, commercial companies and a large proportion of football communities.

While the expansion of the major competitions was widely supported, a growing tension emerged from these changes. The problem was that, while the competitions had expanded nationally, Australian football remained Melbourne-centred, with ten out of the 16 teams based in the city, while rugby league stayed Sydney-centred, with 11 out of the 20 teams based in the city (Linnell, 1995; Phillips, 1998). The older Melbourne and Sydney clubs competed in the same restricted market for sponsorship dollars, players and supporters, whereas single city teams had no immediate rivals and the support of a whole civic and business community upon which to draw. Many Sydney and Melbourne clubs suffered from declining crowds, reduced sponsorship and limited opportunities for marketing team merchandise. Administrators in both sports sought to reduce the number of clubs in Melbourne and Sydney by relocating clubs (as occurred in Australian football with South Melbourne's move to Sydney in 1982), by excluding clubs (as happened to Newtown in rugby league in 1983) or by encouraging the merging of existing clubs into new amalgamated identities (Phillips, 1998; Hess and Stewart, 1998). By 1995, Australian football fast-tracked the merging strategy by offering clubs an incentive bonus of four million dollars (Linnell, 1995). To the chagrin of many supporters, several clubs participated in merger talks during this period, with one struggling Melbourne club, Fitzroy, moving 2000 kilometres north to merge with the Brisbane club in 1997. The new identity received a six million dollar bonus (Nadel, 1998b).

In rugby league, pressure on the Sydney clubs produced incentives for teams to create merged identities. The key difference between rugby league and Australian football, however, was the introduction of pay television in 1995. For Australian football, pay television did not cause any major ructions, whereas in rugby league the new broadcast medium gave rise to a 'revolution' (Colman, 1996). Rugby league was a crucial commodity for rival pay television operators in capturing the key Sydney and Brisbane markets. The pay television operator, Optus Vision, had managed to secure the exclusive rights to rugby league. Their major competitor, Foxtel, also wanted to televise the games as part of a well-known strategy to attract subscribers through sports programming (Rowe, 1997). Foxtel's audacious solution, backed by its major commercial controller, Rupert Murdoch's News Limited (the Australian arm of News Corporation), was to start an entirely new competition by buying players, coaches and officials, purchasing and privatizing existing clubs and creating two new clubs. Two competing competitions existed for a year (1997), with neither being successful as supporters became disillusioned, crowds and television ratings fell, merchandise sales dropped away and a general malaise took hold. The ironic culmination of this situation was a merger between the two competitions. In the process, however, News Limited emerged as a clear victor in the pay television battle by gaining a majority stake in the new competition (the National Rugby League or NRL), part ownership of a number of clubs, pay television rights for a quarter of a century and sponsorship opportunities. Through its partial ownership of Foxtel and other businesses, News Limited assumed effective control of the sport and much of the media covering the sport (Phillips and Hutchins, 2003).

From this position of power, control and influence, News Limited initiated a rationalization of teams. The stated objective was to reduce the number of teams from 17 in 1999 to 14 for the following season. The criteria used to admit clubs for the 2000 season were crowd numbers, competition points, gate receipts, sponsorship (income), profitability and annual revenue, not unlike market conditions imposed on English rugby league teams. Historical significance within the game, attachments to the community and performance records in terms of premiership victories and past international representative players were not considered. Clubs who did not qualify for the top 14 positions would be forced to merge or be excluded. The result of this culling exercise was that four clubs decided to merge and one club was excluded.

In Australian football, similar pressures for rationalization existed, yet there were no financial criteria mandated by a transnational company or coercively directed by the administration. Instead incentives were provided to encourage mergers or relocations and, indeed, Fitzroy relocated and merged with the Brisbane team (Andrews, 2000). By contrast, in rugby league, the introduction of pay television, the ensuing corporate imbroglio and News Limited's control of the game's administration resulted in the creation of seven new clubs, the merger of six clubs and the exclusion of one club. In this short period, there was more structural upheaval in rugby league than in the previous 88 years.

Fan resistance

The relocation, merging and exclusion of clubs were part of a larger 'crisis' in the football codes. 'Crisis', as conceptualized by Ian Andrews (2000: 226), has three dimensions: a fateful phase or turning point that challenges the status quo, an unfolding phase where the old system is bound with the emergent system, and the final phase where the new is 'experienced and expressed through the medium of culture'. While there were certainly institutional differences in the development of the media sport cultural complex between the football codes, exemplified by their differing experiences upon the introduction of pay television, both Australian football and rugby league experienced crises that exposed the conflicting functions of sporting institutions. On the one hand, football competitions are economic entities maximizing their exchange value from gate receipts, commercial sponsorship, broadcasting rights and merchandizing. On the other hand, they are also social and cultural institutions inextricably enmeshed with individual and collective identities, as shown by the loyalties and involvement of supporters, officials and participants (Andrews, 2000). As economic imperatives increasingly force changes to competition structures, resistance from fans and administrators germinates.

Resistance to change from supporters and administrators took many forms. Adrian Budd (2001) argues there are two dominant forms of resistance, transformative and non-transformative, evident in sport. Transformative resistance, epitomized by examples such as the actions of Tommie Smith and John Carlos at the 1968 Olympic Games and Muhammad Ali's refusal to fight in the Vietnam War, involves sport being used to reshape or overthrow social conditions beyond the athletic arena. As will become apparent, the resistance expressed during the last two decades in football tended to target the influential role of corporate decision making, yet failed explicitly to challenge capitalist structures or to propose any political and economic alternatives to the organization of sport. Instead of fundamentally questioning the market-driven logic of the football codes, disillusioned supporters chose mainly to resist those individuals and organizations that they perceived were responsible for changes to football, ignoring broader social and political processes. Resistance was non-transformative, failing substantially to challenge social conditions. In other words, resistance in sport has prevailed, rather than political resistance via sport.

In Australian football, supporters fought against the relocation of South Melbourne to Sydney (1982) and Fitzroy to Brisbane (1997), as well as the ground rationalization programme that moved Melbourne teams from traditional fields to centralized venues (Andrews, 2000). Nevertheless fans continued to follow their clubs in their new forms at different locations. Similarly, in rugby league, supporter groups like 'Aussies for the ARL [Australian Rugby League]' and the 'Friends of Public Football Grounds' were explicit manifestations of resistance to Murdoch's News Limited and its agenda, but they did not represent a substantial challenge to the commercial philosophies underpinning the game's administration.

Clubs sometimes challenged rugby league and Australian football administrators in court. In selected instances they lost, as in South Melbourne , while in others they won, as with Western Suburbs in rugby league (1983) (Hess and Stewart, 1998; Heads, 1992). Legal challenges have often been mounted in conjunction with the formation of formal protest groups with emotive titles such as the 'Save the Bulldogs Committee' and 'SOS' ('Save Our Saints Committee') in Australian football and rugby league, respectively (Andrews, 2000; Phillips and Nauright, 1999). These groups held fund-raising functions to secure finances necessary for survival, lobbied local politicians as members of their constituencies, as well as launching public petitions and protests through media outlets. These protests included car stickers like the 'Up Yours Oakley' sticker, which expressed anger at a key administrator of Australian football, ceremonial rituals such as supporters wearing all black and carrying coffins at games, and cyber movements that have become prominent with the growth in personal computer access and use.

Resistance, both non-transformative and transformative, raises a number of questions. What is it about the institution of sport that arouses such passion and drives people to generate and participate in acts of resistance? What, if anything, does resistance in sport have to do with other social movements? Is this resistance based on an emotional attachment, does it have a geographical element, or is it a reaction to rapid changes to sport in a globalizing world? Is it a combination of these factors triggered by cultural, social and historical issues specific to the situation? Finally, how does individual resistance interact with the collective acts that have typified the reaction to the relocation, merging or exclusion of football clubs in Australia? Adequate response to these questions is well beyond the scope of this chapter, but we will briefly discuss one dominant discourse that has been commonly expressed in reactions to changes in the football codes. This discourse has centred on a perceived recent corporate takeover of sport and the devaluing of, or disregard for, social and cultural sporting traditions, as well as local community history.

The most prominent example of this discourse occurred in rugby league. The corporate control of rugby league was accelerated by the introduction of pay television into Australia, in addition to News Limited's control of the game and rationalization of the competition. When it was realized that several clubs would be merged or excluded in reducing the competition to 14 teams, resistance was commonly directed at News Limited. As a club administrator argued: 'We are told that rugby league is the people's game. It is not. It is Rupert Murdoch's game. News Limited has embarked on a strategy of attrition to destroy the clubs which remained loyal to the ARL' (Masters, 1999). Protest groups that represented supporters from different clubs, media personalities and trade unions forged alliances to fight rationalization, with News Limited as the target: 'we will not engage News [Limited] in the boardrooms and courtrooms as this is where News Limited has the advantage. The campaign will take place in the public arena. This is where the clubs have an advantage' (Weilder, 1999).

One of these 'public arena' protests attracted an estimated 30,000–50,000 people in the streets to Sydney. This protest, which was one of the largest Australian public protests since the Vietnam War (Moller, 2003), was focused specifically on saving the South Sydney club from exclusion. South Sydney is a special club in many ways: it is one of the foundation clubs of the competition, it has won more premierships (championships) than any other club, produced a multitude of international players and exemplifies the working-class origins of rugby league in inner-city Sydney. The club's recent history, however, has been typified by aging facilities, poor on-field performance, declining crowd attendances and financial troubles. Not surprisingly, many of the sentiments surrounding this club are enmeshed in nostalgic resistance that celebrates an idealized past in an uncertain and destabilized present (Nauright and White, 1996; Phillips and Nauright, 1999).

When South Sydney was excluded from the competition in late 1999, nostalgic representations were interwoven with resistance against corporatization and consumerism: 'Without Souths the game will be destroyed. League is a working-class game and Souths is a working-class team ... News Ltd seems to think we are like people in a shop and if we can't buy one thing, then we will choose something else' (Kennedy, 1999). In a rare display of bipartisan support in the Federal Parliament, all political parties backed a motion decrying the exclusion of South Sydney and urged their reinstatement. As one parliamentarian summarized: 'In excluding Souths, the NRL and its financier, News Ltd, are robbing the supporters of South Sydney of their property and investment in a sporting code that is nothing short of a way of life ... It is a grave day of shame that we start to see News Ltd, that powerful organisation, with too many fingers in too many pies, now destroying an Australian icon before our very eyes' (Murphy, 1999).

What emerges from these narratives is the realization that corporate capital has saturated football, controlling the management, organization and presentation of sport. Wenner (1998) argues that 'MediaSport' aptly describes the intermeshing of corporate cultural capitalism with those who deliver and create sports media outputs. Sport and the media have come to adhere to ideologies, structures and practices of corporate capitalism as they have satisfied each other's commercial needs. This integration has reduced the economic and social autonomy of sport over the last half-century as the media, and in particular television, have come to dominate its transmission and exposure, thereby regulating both audience and sponsor appeal (Whannel, 1992). That the lines between sport and the media have disappeared to become MediaSport is a corollary of this media-dominated power relationship. Whitson (1998: 71–2) stresses the increasing role of corporate capital in sport, but makes the point that this involvement has been relatively uncontested, to the point where commercial companies, sporting administrators and supporters see it as 'natural'. Consequently corporate logos adorn playing attire, fields and even balls, games are scheduled to suit television programming and advertising requirements, and a wide range of (sometimes very expensive) supporter merchandise is produced by the sports goods industry (Smith and Stewart, 2000).

What is particularly striking is that corporatization of Australian football and rugby league did not cause large-scale resistance until the localized dimensions of football support were placed under challenge. The closure of suburban, historic grounds and the relocation, amalgamation and extinction of clubs mobilized supporters. One supporter of the relocated and merged Melbourne club, Fitzroy, was devastated at the loss of a sense of community:

> My interest in footy was walking to the ground or catching a tram there, finding a spot inside the ground, watching the play and feeling a part of the whole scene ... then having a kick of the footy on the ground afterwards and a drink in the pub to talk about it all. The thing about barracking for Brisbane now is that the closest I generally get is to tape the game from television, watch it later while fast-forwarding through the ads and, if they are losing, pushing the stop button and doing something else. I am no longer part of it – I don't have that sense of belonging. I'm a consumer rather than a participant. (Stewart, 2001)

Rugby league experienced similar challenges to local cultures, but what emerges in these patterns of resistance is the centrality of globalizing forces. Many rugby league followers recognized that the challenges to their local culture were connected to a pay television industry funded by global capital and, more specifically, Rupert Murdoch's News Corporation. For example, there was open acknowledgment of News' strategy of purchasing sport for its global media outlets and the desire to position his companies for changes in the telecommunications industry (Stoddart, 1997). As Blain and O'Donnell (2000) found in their analysis of the 'unarmed armies' of football supporters in Northern England, rugby league protests represented local resistance to an increasingly globalized world, particularly the forms of globalization epitomized by transnational media corporations and their utilization of sport for corporate objectives. Rugby league supporters who have had their clubs merged, relocated or excluded are acutely aware of the role of global media corporations. As one supporter declared colourfully on hearing of South Sydney's exclusion: 'Rugby league is dead to me' (Micevski, 1999).

Conclusion

This chapter has focused on the media sport cultural complex in Australia by taking both an historical and a broad political perspective, and taking into account the sources and potential power of fan resistance. An historical perspective outlines the similarities and differences between the political economies of rugby league and Australian football, and alludes to the relevance of understanding specific social and cultural contexts in the formation of the media–sport–culture interdependencies and interactions. In both rugby league and Australian football, the media drove the national expansion programme from the 1980s, as well as the subsequent rationalization agenda that has characterized the last decade. A key dividing dimension of rugby league and Australian football, however, has been the relative impact of pay television and this media platform's utilization of sport as a commodity to attract viewer subscriptions.

By taking a broad view of the media sport cultural complex, we have also been able to highlight the resistance of supporters to rationalization processes in Australia's football codes. The resistance offered by fans to prospective club mergers or relocation in both codes has largely been conservative or, to use Budd's terminology, non-transformative. Club supporter groups in Australian football and organizations such as 'Aussies for the ARL' and the 'Friends of Public Football Grounds' have quite specific targets in mind. They wish to lessen the influence of media moguls and transnational companies such as Rupert Murdoch and News Limited, and they also want their club to remain in a particular geographical area or to maintain a specific identity. Activists in the football community may argue that adopting non-transformative approaches has been successful in challenging corporate control and ownership of sport. Such a 'victory' was the readmission of the South Sydney club for the 2002 rugby league season after a long series of public protests and court battles against News Limited. South Sydney supporters have their club back in the premier competition and there is a resulting regeneration and/or rearticulation of many local, cultural and historical traditions.

Despite South Sydney's readmission, their case does not necessarily exemplify a community victory over the corporate media. Rather it is better read as an example of the way media and commercial corporations coopt and reintegrate community sentiment. News Limited stands to benefit from the marketing and media exposure that South Sydney provides. South Sydney is the lucrative media sign that stands for, in the Australian lexicon, the 'battler', 'the ordinary man or woman in the street' and the 'working class hero'. As prominent South Sydney supporter Andrew Denton explains:

> Tradition in sport is a very, very powerful thing ... It's the brand that sells itself, as indeed at Souths because you don't have to create the

hype, you don't have to create the sizzle. They are their own story. It's a marketer's dream. (Australian Story, 1999)

The sense of identity typified by South Sydney runs the risk of becoming just another 'branded experience' (Klein, 2001: 152) that has been successfully sold back to pay television subscribers, free-to-air viewers and advertisers, and those who pay at the turnstiles. News Limited and the NRL may have been embarrassed for a limited period by the protests against South Sydney's exclusion, but they stand to gain a great deal in the coming season via television ratings, merchandising and crowds. For example, South Sydney's first regular season game in 2002 was an almost unprecedented sell-out and the club led merchandise sales for the year. As heartening to supporters as South Sydney's 'victory' is, and as other attempts to block mergers in Australian football are, we concur with Andrews (2000) that the economically driven trajectory of the football codes has not been altered. Resistance to relocations, mergers and exclusions, as symbolically important as it is to individual and collective identities, is a temporary barrier to the profit maximization and consumerist agenda that underpins many components of the media sports cultural complex.

What many supporters fail to realize and articulate is that their feelings, desires and actions are implicated in much larger and pervasive political and economic structures, institutions and processes. Indeed those wanting proactively to stave off the rumoured relocation of their club in the future would be better off lobbying governments to regulate media ownership and influence, developing community strategies that negotiate the local outcomes of globalization processes, and opposing the dismantling of the welfare state and an untrammelled individualist ethos that undercuts community sentiment and action. In other words, supporters could benefit from taking their eyes off the ball for a moment and instead adapting some of the developing strategies of the anti-globalization movement, as characterized by S11, the Reclaim the Streets Movement, the Fairwear campaign, *Adbusters* and the Critical Mass bicycle rides. Just as with those fighting to save their clubs, these movements are contesting the ownership of public space, thought and identity with the aim being to increase community influence in government and corporate decision making. Instead of focusing on particular business decisions, individual club relocations, mergers or exclusions, what is required is a better articulated, more broadly focused and sustained agenda, of active and continuing allegiance within and between specific communities, which at least holds out the potential of giving supporters some say in the destinies and identities of their teams.

References

Andrews, D. (1998), 'Excavating Michael Jordan: notes on a critical pedagogy of sporting representation', in G. Rail (ed.), *Sport and postmodern times*, Albany: State University of New York, pp.185–219.

Andrews, I. (2000), 'From a club to a corporate game: the changing face of Australian football', in J.A. Mangan and J. Nauright (eds), *Sport in Australasian society: past and present*, London: Frank Cass, pp.225–54.

Australian Bureau of Statistics (1999), 'Media Release', 20 December.

Australian Story (1999), *Mission impossible*, Australian Broadcasting Corporation, 23 September.

Blain, N. and H. O'Donnel (2000), 'Current developments in media sport, and the politics of local identities: a 'postmodern' debate?', *Culture, Sport, Society*, 3 (2), 1–22.

Budd, A. (2001), 'Capitalism, sport and resistance: reflections', *Culture, Sport, Society*, 4 (1), 1–18.

Colman, M. (1996), *Super league: the inside story*, Sydney: Pan Macmillan.

Goldlust, J. (1987), *Playing for keeps: sport, the media and society*, Melbourne: Longman Cheshire.

Grow, R. (1998), 'From gum trees to goalposts, 1858–1876', in R. Hess and B. Stewart (eds), *More than a game: an unauthorised history of Australian Rules Football*, Melbourne: Melbourne University Press, pp.4–44.

Gruneau, R. and D. Whitson (1993), *Hockey night in Canada: sport, identities and cultural politics*, Toronto: Garamond.

Heads, I. (1992), *True blue: the story of the NSW Rugby League*, Sydney: Ironbark.

Herman, E.S. and R.W. McChesney (1997), *The global media: the new missionaries of corporate capitalism*, London: Cassell.

Hess, R. and B. Stewart (eds) (1998), *More than a game: an unauthorised history of Australian Rules Football*, Melbourne: Melbourne University Press.

Horne, J., A. Tomlinson and G. Whannel (1999), *Understanding sport: an introduction to the sociological and cultural analysis of sport*, London: Spon.

Hutchins, B. (1996), 'Rugby wars: the changing face of football', *Sporting Traditions*, 13 (1), 151–62.

Hutchins, B. (1997), 'Mediated violence: the case of State of Origin rugby league', *Sporting Traditions*, 13 (2), 19–39.

Hutchins, B. and M. Phillips (1997), 'Selling permissible violence: the commodification of Australian rugby league 1970–1995', *International Review for the Sociology of Sport*, 32 (2), 161–76.

Hutchins, B. and M. Phillips (1999), 'The global union: globalization and the Rugby World Cup', in T.J.L. Chandler and J. Nauright (eds), *Making the rugby world: race, gender, commerce*, London: Frank Cass, pp.149–64.

Jarvie, G. and J. Maguire (1994), *Sport and leisure in social thought*, London: Routledge.

Kennedy, A. (1999), 'Legalise Bugs Bunny fans as Souths fight on', *Sydney Morning Herald*, 30 November.

Klein, N. (2001), *No logo*, London: Flamingo.

Linnell, G. (1995), *Football Ltd: the inside story of the AFL*, Sydney: Pan Macmillan Australia.

Maguire, J.A. (1993), 'Globalization, sport development, and the media/sport production complex', *Sport Sciences Review*, 2, 29–47.

Maguire, J.A. (1999), *Global sport: identities, societies, civilizations*, Cambridge: Polity.

Masters, R. (1999), 'Rebellious Rabbitohs won't go quietly', *Sydney Morning Herald*, 29 September.

Micevski, R. (1999), 'All I ever wanted was to watch my team play', www.groups.yahoo.com/groups/rabbitohs/message/9106, 9 December.

Moller, M. (2003), 'Grassroots ethics: the case of Souths versus News Corporation', in C. Lumby and E. Probyn (eds), *Remote control: new media, new ethics*, Melbourne: Cambridge University, pp.216–29.

Mosely, P. and B. Murray (1994), 'Soccer', in W. Vamplew and B. Stoddart (eds), *Sport in Australia: a social history*, Melbourne: Cambridge University Press, pp.213–30.

Mulcahy, D. (1993), *Them and us: a national league?*, Northbridge: Access.

Murphy, D. (1999), 'MPs unite in supporting exiled Souths', *Sydney Morning Herald*, 23 November.

Nadel, D. (1998a), 'Colour, corporations and commissioners, 1976–1985', in R. Hess and B. Stewart (eds), *More than a game*, Melbourne: Melbourne University Press, pp.200–24.

Nadel, D. (1998b), 'The league goes national, 1986–1997', 'in R. Hess and B. Stewart (eds), *More than a game*, Melbourne: Melbourne University Press, pp.225–55.

Nauright, J. and P. White (1996), ' "Save Our Jets": Nostalgia, Community, Professional Sport and Nation in Contemporary Canada', *AVANTE*, **2** (4), 24–41.

Phillips, M.G. (1998), 'From suburban football to international spectacle: the commodification of rugby league in Australia, 1907–1995', *Australian Historical Studies*, **29** (110), 27–48.

Phillips, M.G. and B. Hutchins (1998), 'From independence to a reconstituted hegemony: rugby league and television in Australia', *Journal of Australian Studies*, **58**, 134–47.

Phillips, M.G. and B. Hutchins (2003), 'Losing control of the ball: the political economy of football and the media in Australia', *Journal of Sport and Social Issues*, **27** (3), 215–32.

Phillips, M.G. and J. Nauright (1999), 'Sports fan movements to save surburban-based football teams threatened with amalgamation in different football codes in Australia', *International Sports Studies*, **21** (1), 23–38.

Rowe, D. (1995), *Popular cultures: rock music, sport and the politics of pleasure*, London: Sage.

Rowe, D. (1997), 'Rugby league in Australia: the Super League saga', *Journal of Sport and Social Issues*, **21** (2), 221–6.

Rowe, D. (1999), *Sport, culture and the media*, Buckingham: Open University Press.

Smith, A. and B. Stewart (2000), 'Australian sport in a postmodern age', in J.A. Mangan and J. Nauright (eds), *Sport in Australasian society*, London: Frank Cass, pp.278–304.

Staniland, M. (1985), *What is political economy? A study of social theory and underdevelopment*, New Haven, CT: Yale University.

Stewart, B. (1984), 'The economic development of the Victorian Football League 1960–1984', *Sporting Traditions*, **2** (1), 2–26.

Stewart, B. (1998), 'Boom-time football, 1946–1975', in R. Hess and B. Stewart (eds), *More than a game*, Melbourne: Melbourne University Press, pp.165–99.

Stewart, C. (2001), 'The game is not the same', *Australian Magazine*, 24–5 March.

Stoddart, B. (1997), 'Convergence: sport on the information superhighway', *Journal of Sport and Social Issues*, **21** (1), 93–102.

Weilder, D. (1999), 'Stars protest to save clubs', *Sydney Morning Herald*, 29 August.

Wenner, L.A. (1998), 'Playing the mediasport game', in L.A. Wenner (ed.), *Mediasport*, London: Routledge, pp.3–13.

Westfield, M. (2000), *The gatekeepers: the global media battle to control Australia's pay TV*, Annandale, Sydney: Pluto.

Whannel, G. (1992), *Fields in vision: television sport and cultural transformation, communication and society*, London: Routledge.

White, P., P. Donnelly and J. Nauright (1997), 'Citizens, cities and sports teams', *Policy Options*, **18** (3), 9–12.

Whitson, D. (1998), 'Circuits of promotion: media, marketing and the globalization of sport', in L.A. Wenner (ed.), *Mediasport*, London: Routledge, pp.57–72.

Yeates, H. (1995), 'The league of men: masculinity, the media and rugby league football', *Media Information Australia*, **75**, 35–45.

6
Paradoxes of Material Culture: The Political Economy of Surfing

Douglas Booth

Back in the early 1950s, when I started surfing, the main comment from parents and non-surfing peers was: 'When you grow up, you'll realise you were wasting your time when you could have been doing something useful.' I could never figure out why golf, tennis, baseball, football or being a cheerleader was 'useful' and surfing wasn't. What became a 'lifestyle' later was just how we lived without giving it much thought. We knew we had to live by the ocean and needed to figure out a way to make a living there. Hobie made surfboards, Gordon Clark made foam blanks, John Severson started *Surfer* magazine, I started making movies. Whatever we did, the main focus was how it would affect our surf time. Getting rich wasn't important. What was important was having the freedom to do what we wanted. (Bruce Brown, producer and director of *The Endless Summer*, Kampion, 1997: 21)

As a production, marketing and consumption system, [culture] exhibits many peculiarities in the form its labour process takes, and in the manner of linkage between production and consumption. The one thing that cannot be said of it is that the circulation of capital is absent, and that the practitioners and agents at work within it are unaware of the laws and rules of capital accumulation. And it is certainly not democratically controlled and organised, even though consumers are highly dispersed and have more than a little say in what is produced and what aesthetic values shall be conveyed. (David Harvey, 1990: 346–7)

Surfing is far more than a physical recreation. For millions of people surfing defines their way of life, their manner of living, in short, their culture [Jenks, 1993a: 5; Jenks, 1993b: 156, 157]. Surfers organize their lives around the rhythms of the tide and the seasons that determine when, and where, the surf is running; they follow their own fashions, and speak their own language. Yet, irrespective of its social, artistic or spiritual content, surfing, like all cultures, has material dimensions. Cultures involve separating, combining, transforming and presenting material objects; they involve technologies of reproduction and circulation, the organization of markets for trading, expansion and profit; and they involve a range of social relations between those who give and those who receive, between those who produce and those who consume, and between those for whom the culture is their livelihood and those for whom the culture is a religious experience. Tensions invariably arise in these social relations as different groups compete for ownership of, and access to, resources, or as they seek to control technologies or the diffusion of ideas. (Williams, 1995: 87, 89–118)

This chapter analyses the material bases of surfing culture (including surfboards, wetsuits, clothing, accessories, magazines, books, memorabilia, videos, competitions, tourism and surfing schools),[1] which is worth an estimated US$4 billion each year (Gliddon, 2002: 20). In particular, it investigates the paradoxes of a culture that celebrates social freedom, escape from drudgery and a harmonious interaction with the natural world, and which simultaneously propagates capitalist accumulation, competition and exploitation in its modes of economic and political organization.[2] Most surfers are only too well aware of the paradox; but how do they reconcile the contradictions?

Accumulation, appropriation, acculturation

The surfing industry began as a series of backyard operations in the early 1950s, concomitant with the invention of lightweight fibreglass Malibu surfboards.[3] Jack O'Neill, the founder of O'Neill wetsuits, conducted a surf business from his San Francisco garage where he shaped surfboards, sold accessories like paraffin wax (rubbed on boards to prevent slipping) and glued strips of neoprene rubber into wetsuit vests (to insulate surfers against extreme water and air temperatures) (Kampion, 2001). When Brian Singer and Doug Warbrick decided to manufacture Rip Curl surfboards, they converted a home garage at Torquay (Victoria, Australia) into a shaping bay and glassing room and then put up a sign (Jarratt, 1998b: 67). Champion surfer Terry Fitzgerald established Hot Buttered Surfboards in a two-bedroom weatherboard cottage in Sydney.

He turned one of the bedrooms into a shaping bay and went into business (Jarratt, 1998a: 43–4).

Some surfers stumbled into the industry. Greg Noll, a member of the American lifeguard team that introduced Malibu surfboards to Australia during a tour in 1956, took a movie camera on the trip 'to show everybody back home what Australian surf looked like'. Returning to California, he discovered eager viewers willing to pay a dollar each to watch his film. By showing the film in high school auditoriums, Noll earned enough money to finance his surfing travels. In 1958, he spent several months at Mazatlán (Mexico) and repeated the filming exercise (Noll and Gabbard, 1989: 71, 85). John Severson began his career as a surf film cinematographer in the late 1950s when the army posted him to Hawaii. He made 16mm movies with a Keystone camera and spliced several bits of film together under the title *Surf*. In 1960, Severson produced a black and white booklet, *The Surfer*, to promote the films he was by then producing regularly. It proved so popular that Severson developed the booklet into a quarterly magazine called *Surfer*. A decade later *Surfer* was a monthly magazine with a circulation of 100,000 (Severson, 1985: 110–13; Lueras, 1984: 133).

Early technology was simple, often crude. Film enthusiasts, for example, watched the movies produced by Noll, Severson and others in church, school and public halls. The producers had little equipment. Bud Browne introduced his films from the stage, rushed 'to the projection room to join the operator of an arc projector', and watched the screen holding a microphone over the tape machine that played music. He recalls advertising his early films by nailing 'handmade posters ... to telephone poles near popular surf spots' (McClelland, 1995: 36). Greg Noll never bothered to adjust the lens setting on his camera: 'the guy at the store where I bought the camera set it up for me and I just left it there' (Noll and Gabbard, 1989: 89). Surfboard and wetsuit manufacturing technologies were equally primitive. Brian Singer admits that Rip Curl's 'first boards were pretty rough. I graduated from fin sanding to glassing but we didn't have a room clean enough for finish coating, so we used marine varnish and told everyone it was the new thing' (cited in Jarratt, 1998b: 67). Allan Green, who made the first wetsuits in Australia under the Rip Curl label in the late 1960s, described the first batches as totally inadequate (ibid.: 72).

Backyard industries were critical to the growth and diffusion of surfing culture. (Anthropologist John Irwin [1973] estimates that the surfboard riding population of Southern California grew from 5,000 in 1956 to 100,000 in 1962 [p.144].) Manufacturers opened retail shops that make boards readily accessible and thus increased participation; films and magazines directed riders to new wave locations, board designs, riding styles and general trends in fashion and taste. Cultural expansion opened new doors for budding entrepreneurs. In Australia, Bob Evans, and Alby Falzon and David Elfick, followed the path of cinematographer and magazine publisher John Severson. They began showing imported surf films before producing their own and then launching magazines (*Surfing World* and *Tracks*, respectively) as vehicles to promote their films. Wetsuit pioneer Allan Green diversified into sheepskin Ug boots and boardshorts. Meanwhile, Rip Curl shifted to mass production of its wetsuits. Brian Singer recalls the 'defining moment': 'We had one hundred orders to meet one week with ten bucks profit in every suit ... I suddenly thought, shit, we could make a bit of money out of this' (cited in Jarratt 1998b: 72).

Today the leading manufacturers produce hardware and clothing for surfing and its first cousins snowboarding and skateboarding (Humphreys, 1997: 150–53), and they sit atop a rapidly expanding, and intensely competitive and secretive, multi-billion dollar industry (Ernest, 1999a, Gliddon, 2002: 23, Noll and Gabbard, 1989: 123, 133). Surfboard manufacturing is virtually the last vestige of the early backyard operations. The sport's governing body in Australia estimated that 600 surfboard manufacturing facilities produced approximately 85,000 boards for the domestic and export market in 1992. Of these facilities, 75 per cent employed fewer than five people and 50 per cent were one or two-person operations (Stranger, 2001: 211, n. 84). Small-scale board shapers and manufacturers face crippling pressure from larger manufacturers, wholesalers and retailers that sell boards at near cost price, in some cases even at a loss. Small manufacturer Graham Carse, owner of Quarry Beach (Dunedin, New Zealand) claims that the retail cost of surfboards would be nearly 33 per cent higher were it not for pressure exerted by large-scale manufacturers, although he hastens to add that 'there has never been much profit in boards' (Carse, 2003). Among retailers, surf-board sales are of minor importance: their primary income derives from surfclothing (estimated to be worth US$3.5 billion annually) (Barilotti, 2003: 104). Small-scale board manufacturers also face free trade agree-ments that allow larger dedicated manufacturers effectively to dump products in some markets. Australian board manufacturers such as DHD and Darcy sell shortboards in New Zealand for around NZ$600, prices which small local manufacturers (who pay twice as much just for their foam blanks) simply cannot match (Carse, 2003). Even the handful of small-scale shapers and manufacturers fortunate enough to produce for leading professional surfers confront competitive hurdles. The large companies appropriate surfboards as their advertising space; they contractually oblige their sponsored surfers to display clothing, wetsuit and accessory logos prominently on surfboards while refusing shapers and manufacturers reciprocal advertising space on their products (Dahlberg, 2002; Gliddon, 2002: 24).

Apart from failing economically, options for small board manufacturers and independent retail outlets are limited. They can hope that the overall market, and their niche within this market, continues to grow, or they can form purchasing groups to improve their buying power and negotiate discounts from wholesalers. In New Zealand, for example, 11 independents recently formed a composite retail group that is also selling its own clothing range, Coastlines. One particular motive of this group is to claw back sales that surf industry retailers have lost to mainstream department stores (Carse, 2003).

The industry that once catered for an exclusively male clientele now also looks to women. Quiksilver led the way in 1995, launching the Roxy label for girls and women (Booth, 2001b: 13; Baker, 2002: 99). Since entering this market, Roxy has diversified far beyond board sports. It now produces fragrances, bedroom accessories and luggage (Checkwood and Stouffer, 1999; Jones, 1999; Bold, 1999) and books (Levine, 2003), while Quiksilver moots plans to open travel agencies catering for the adventure market (Ernest, 1999b). Mambo, which began as a surf t-shirt company, now produces swimwear, sunglasses, bags, wallets, watches, jewellery, ceramics and posters (Mambo, 1999). Expanding ranges of products means additional revenue for the previously 'pure' surfing culture. But 'Butch' Barr, a former accountant at Rip Curl and who now holds the Australian licence for Reef footwear, insists that the industry leaders have not traded their lifestyles for pursuit of wealth. He describes Singer and Warbrick still following their basic nomadic surfing instincts: they are forever 'dipping into [the till] and then pissing off somewhere' (cited in Jarratt, 1998b: 74).

If tight-fisted accountancy and diversification into fragrances, bedroom accessories and travel agencies support Karl Marx's contention that 'accumulation for the sake of accumulation' and 'production for the sake of production' are the motors of bourgeois ambition (Marx, 1976: 742), surfing's refusal to embrace big capital and its resistance to institutionalization remind us that surfers still privilege culture.

In the late 1950s, Hollywood movie houses, the Southern California music industry and a plethora of advertising and marketing companies seized on surfing as a potential source of profit. Columbia Pictures initiated the Hollywood genre of surf film when it recreated Frederick Kohner's *Gidget* stories. Columbia's *Gidget* (1959) reproduced the idyllic fantasy lifestyle of California surfers and contributed to the diffusion of surfing into popular culture. Columbia followed with three more surf films including two Gidget sequels; American International Pictures produced five surf films, and Twentieth Century Fox, Paramount and American Academy one each (Booth, 2001a: 91–3). Hollywood surf movies and California-based surf music were 'commercial monsters' (Lueras, 1984: 119). American International Pictures' *Muscle Beach Party* (1964) grossed US$3.5 million and set box office records nationwide; *Surfer's Choice*, the first album produced by Dale and the Del-Tones, sold 75,000 copies in Southern California in three months (Wardlaw, 1991: 48).

In order to ensure financial viability, Hollywood, with its elaborate sets, specialized labour systems, multiple cameras, expensive developing techniques, sophisticated advertising and complex distribution networks, had to appeal to universal audiences. Thus Hollywood surf films focused on beach life that the industry correctly saw as more encompassing, including women as well as men, and more accessible to a wider age range. But in broadening the appeal of its films, Hollywood alienated surfing aficionados who spurned the genre. Screen writer Marc Rubel, for example, denounced Hollywood's philosophy which he said reduced surfing to a 'total adolescent pastime'. Among the stalwart 'older generation' surfing was much more. It was a vital activity and 'something that kept us sane,' Rubel said (cited in Gillogly, 1982: 58).

On the other hand, while surfers recoiled at Hollywood's interpretations of their culture, the cinematographers who issued from surfing culture, as opposed to the established film industry, sought access to the distribution networks of the latter. *The Endless Summer* enjoyed enormous popularity among surfers and its producer Bruce Brown approached several Hollywood companies with a view to distributing it on the commercial circuit. They refused, claiming that it 'would wipe out in any city further than ten miles from a beach'. To prove them wrong, Brown screened the film in Wichita, Kansas, in mid-winter. For two weeks more people filed through the doors in Wichita to watch *The Endless Summer* than to see either *The Great Race* or *My Fair Lady*. Brown enlarged the film to 35mm and sold it worldwide. It grossed US$8 million (Wardlaw, 1991: 45). The commercial cinemas learned their lesson; 30 years later they snatched up Brown's *The Endless Summer II*.

Surf film cinematographers may have been prepared to travel along corporate pathways, but grassroots surfers would not accept organized competitive surfing. Surfers view themselves as communing with nature and organized competition constitutes an unpalatable form of institu-tionalization. Renowned big wave rider Australian Bob Pike articulated the sentiments of many when he said, 'I don't like to compete and I don't think any of the top board riders do. It takes too much of the pleasure out of the sport and creates too many jealousies. Competitions are all against the spirit of surfing' (*Australia's Surfing Life*, 1992: 88).

Anti-competition advocates faced their first challenge in the early 1960s. Surfers with a competitive bent wanted a system that would bestow formal peer recognition and status, and endear them to the broader public. They established new regional and national associations, and organized competitions to take surfing into the mainstream sporting world. Initially they appeared to have succeeded. Big capital and vested political interests flocked to surfing (Barilotti, 2003: 105–6).[4] Sponsors of the first official world surfing championships at Manly Beach, Sydney, in May 1964 included Manly Council, Ampol (Petroleum) and TAA (Trans Australian Airlines). They were blunt about their motives: 'Manly will get a lot of publicity from international television coverage of the event,' said Mayor Bill Nicholas, while a senior representative of Ampol described surfing as 'the fastest growing sport in Australia' and pledged his company's continuing support (*Manly Daily*, 1964a, 1964b). But cele-brations and congratulations proved premature. Organized competition required formal rules, and codification was no simple matter with surfing styles reflecting regional variations, particularly between California and Australia: Australians wanted to slash and conquer waves, Californians sought waves for artistic expression. Debate over style fuelled dissension over judging methods and scoring, and led to accusations of corruption, cronyism and nepotism. The result was a significant decline in competitive surfing in the late 1960s (Booth, 2001a: 100–106).

Not all the political pressures emanated from within surfing culture. The counterculture also influenced the development of surfing and its subsequent modes of economic and political organization, although the full extent of that influence is open to debate.

New trends in the competitive marketplace

An amalgam of alternative, typically utopian lifestyles and political activism, the counterculture contained its own logic and direction. David Harvey (1990: 38) states:

> Antagonistic to the oppressive qualities of scientifically grounded technical–bureaucraic rationality as purveyed though monolithic

corporate, state and other forms of institutionalised power ... the counter-cultures explored the realms of individualised self-realisation through a distinctive 'new left' politics, through the embrace of anti-authoritarian gestures, iconoclastic habits (in music, dress, language and lifestyle), and in the critique of everyday life.

Soul-surfing (riding waves for 'the good of one's soul') articulated this new politics and critique, and conjoined surfing with the counter-culture. Soul-surfers scorned organized sport as a form of institutionalized power. They applied increasingly esoteric interpretations to surfing: waves became dreams, playgrounds, podia and even asylums, and the search for perfect waves became an endless pursuit. Surfing signified self-expression, escape and freedom (Booth, 2001a: 100–106).

Yet, as pervasive as it was, soul-surfing never totally subsumed surfing. Not all surfers embraced its alternative philosophies. Fred Hemmings, the 1968 world surfing champion, denounced soul-surfers for impairing surfing and society (*Surfer*, 1968: 68) while an acerbic indigenous Hawaiian accused 'long-haired, hippie-type, drug-taking surfers' of 'infest[ing] our best and most beautiful surfing spots with their repulsiveness' (Haas and Resurrection, 1976: 77–8). Moreover the idealistic tenets of soul-surfing made absolute subscription impossible. An attempt by surf clothing manufacturer Golden Breed (founded by Duke Boyd after he sold his pioneering Hang Ten surf label to the Richton Corporation for US$3.5 million) to promote an egalitarian anti-competition ethos collapsed under the weight of petty jealousies and material realities. Golden Breed's infamous 'expression session' – the best surfers, on the best waves, with the performers deciding when, and where, to hold the event (within a two-week window) and with all invitees receiving a US$200 appearance fee (enough to survive a winter on the North Shore of Hawaii) – was a noble concept. It also proved threadbare: a group of non-invitees protested their exclusion by violently gate-crashing the formal launch, recreational surfers refused to leave the water during the session, making it impossible for spectators and television to identify the invitees, and as the two-week window wound down many of the invited cast withdrew to prepare for a financially lucrative orthodox competition (Jarratt, 1997: 86–91).

Big capital also proved highly adaptive to soul-surfing. Even at the height of soul-surfing, it continued to boost, incorporate and exploit surfing's clean, refreshing and sporting images (Booth, 2001a: 117). Surfing 'naturally' complemented products concerned with body, health and lifestyle, and appeared in advertisers' messages in magazines and newspapers, and on radio, television, neon signs, billboards and posters. Advertising agencies inverted many negative images, such as the casual indifference associated with soul-surfing. Surfer 'Jimmy Peterson' (*Blo-Clear* medicated cream) symbolized the ideal middle-class Australian youth of the early 1970s. His tanned skin, lengthy blond streaked hair and casual form (nestling with his girlfriend) conveyed an image of simplicity and innocence rather than the scruffy untidy indifference of the itinerant soul-surfer.

Some scholars identify the counterculture as a turning point in capitalist modes of consumption, production and distribution.[5] John Clarke and his colleagues note that 'in many aspects, the revolutions in lifestyle were a pure, simple, raging, commercial success. In clothes, and styles, the counterculture explored shifts in taste which the mass consumption chain-stores were too cumbersome, inflexible and over-capitalised to exploit' (Clarke *et al.*, 1976: 67; see also Harvey, 1990: 63). Surfing suggests that the revolution in consumption, production and distribution predated the counterculture by 20 years. Surfing youth were an integral part of a consumer reaction in the 1950s to the blandness and conformity imposed by standardized mass production. They demanded new fashions, new styles and new products that would enable them to express their individuality and distinctiveness. Their demands had a major impact on production processes, which, in turn, led to new modes of political and economic organization, although these demands also posed new constraints. Attempts by prominent surfing brands 'to break into the mainstream market' and 'sell the surfer style through popular [department] stores' proved to be a 'fairly short term affair': selling to mainstream shops threatened surfing's cultural credibility (Stranger, 2001: 214, 221; see also Gliddon, 2002: 23).

Modern consumers have insatiable appetites for novelty, perpetual stimulation and authentic, sophisticated and design-conscious products. Meeting their demands means continual innovation and fast production methods. Rip Curl, for example, launched itself into the international wetsuit market during the 1970 world titles held in Torquay. It appropriated different designs worn by foreign surfers who arrived for the competition; before the contest ended it had begun producing a full-body wetsuit with an underarm gusset to relieve chafing. The new wetsuits were an instant success and several foreign surfers took the Rip Curl product home (Jarratt, 1998b: 72).

Demands for novelty also led producers to focus on aesthetic qualities and to repackage and rename products constantly. In the case of surfing this frequently means provocative labels with an anti-social innuendo.

Parawax, Waxmate, Dr Zog's Sex Wax, Mrs Palmer's Five Daughters and Big Pecker Surf Wax are just some of the names given to the humble board wax. Do aesthetics and packaging sell products? Dare Jennings, founder of Mambo, and Jim Jannard, CEO of leading sunglass manufacturer and retailer Oakley, both believe so: 'Almost any idiot [can] make a few dollars by sticking a picture on the back of a t-shirt,' boasts Jennings (cited in Mambo, 1999). 'Consumers recognise us', Jannard claims, 'for wrapping our superior technology in artistically distinct styling' (cited in Smith, 1999). Oakley is renowned for aggressively pursuing competitors who steal its patents. More recently the demand for novelty has shifted attention from the production of goods to the production of events that have an almost instantaneous consumption time (Harvey, 1990: 157). Illustrating this trend in surfing is the flood of speciality events organized and sponsored by surf companies: OP Pro Boat Trip Challenge, Reef Big Wave World Championships, Quiksilver Mavericks Big Wave Event, Rip Curl World Heli Challenge, Billabong Challenge, Quiksilver Airshow and Vans Airshow.

'The maelstrom of ephemerality', as David Harvey (1990) describes the increasing pace of turnover in consumption and production, kindled unforeseen consequences. Among these is the current highly fashionable 'search for historical roots' as individuals look for 'more secure moorings and longer-lasting values in a shifting world' (p.292). Surfing, too, has been caught up in this nostalgic drive, as demonstrated by the rush of museums, memorabilia collections, books, videos and magazines devoted to the history of surfing. The annual Noosa Festival of Surfing – 'Waves, Raves & Wall to Wall Legends' – specializes in bringing surfing legends to Noosa Heads (Queensland, Australia); the 1999 festival even scheduled a rematch of the 1964 world championship title featuring the five living finalists.

Consumer demands for instant satisfaction have created volatile markets that make long-term planning exceedingly difficult for producers of goods. The latter, however, are not completely powerless. Advertising and other forms of image building (sponsorships, direct marketing) enable them to manipulate taste and opinion (Harvey, 1990: 287). In 1986, Quiksilver sponsored the amateur world titles at Newquay (England). The sponsorship cost more than US$100,000 but the company's directors estimated that creating brand awareness was worth ten times that amount (Jarratt, 1997: 164).

Advertisers have also changed their approaches to deal with volatile markets. When Rip Curl put its first full-page advertisement – the dawning of Rip Curl surfboards – into *Surfing World* in 1969, the company's objective was simply to inform surfers of a new brand (Jarratt, 1998b: 69). Today 'advertising is no longer built around the idea of informing or promoting in the ordinary sense'; instead it is 'geared to manipulating desires and tastes that may or may not have anything to do with the product to be sold' (Harvey, 1990: 287). 'The Search' is the fulcrum of Rip Curl's current marketing strategy. As the company's co-founder and co-owner Doug Warbrick explains, 'The Search' expounds a philosophy of discovery (in its broadest sense) that Rip Curl has successfully tagged to its brand:

> The Rip Curl philosophy ... started as The Search for the uncrowded perfect wave. But it goes beyond that. In the mountains we Search for the perfect untracked powder bowl. Silent. Still. No people. Same thing – perfection with no crowds and no hassles. So physically and spiritually I think that's the kind of Search a surfer or rider or free skier is into, but it can go much further. There's always adventure when you travel the world and some of the culture you become involved with is amazing. It goes on and on. There's also the inner Search we go through in trying to find deep inside what we're really achieving in life, and what our true values are. (Rip Curl, 1999)[6]

'The Search' label now appears on all Rip Curl products.

As well as a tool for producers and retailers to manipulate desire, advertising helps ensure company and brand recognition in competitive markets. Surfing advertisements highlight reputations for reliable and innovative products. Again 'The Search' is a good example:

> If you're going to travel around the world, and get into travel and adventure, and be right out on the edge, you need product that is functional. Stuff that really works for a surfer, or works for a rider, or works for a skier. And that is definitely one of our other quests – The Search for the best materials and technology to make products that really work when you're on the edge. It's a driving force for anyone who seeks the ultimate expression of time and place – the perfect wave hitting an uncharted reef or the eerie silence of an untracked powder bowl over the next ridge. (Rip Curl, 1999)

Even when surf companies win conspicuous market advantages with superior products, such as Quiksilver with its hip-hugging, yoke-style scalloped-leg boardshorts (Jarratt, 1997: 137), the need to invest in image building never ceases. As Rip Curl and Quiksilver can both testify, market advantages are sometimes lost faster than they are won. Poor quality control at its new factory in California cost Rip Curl market share in the late 1970s; nearly two decades later, poor production by an outsourced manufacturer (consumers returned 90–95 per cent of one wetsuit style) almost destroyed consumer and retailer confidence in Quiksilver wetsuits (Jarratt, 1998b: 74; O'Brien, 1999). However, at least one industry insider doubts whether quality overly concerns the big surf companies: 'hard core surfers only buy 10 per cent of wetsuits'. Ninety per cent are 'worn only a few times, probably to go water-skiing, and spend most of their life hanging in garages' (Carse, 2003).

Workers, aristocrats, moguls

Carcinogenic dust, chemicals and glues make the production of surfboards and wetsuits dangerous occupations (Renneker *et al.*, 1993: 345–7). While occupation and safety legislation in developed countries removes some of the risks, ultimately the health of workers depends on the relations of production. And these are purely capitalist. The big movie houses had no qualms exploiting surfers. Screen writer Marc Rubel charged Hollywood producers with 'treat[ing] surfers about as well as ... the American Indian' (Gillogly, 1982: 58). Mickey Dora, who worked as a double in two Hollywood surf films was equally scathing, with comments that raised the spectre of anti-semitism: 'The jews came down to the beach, they shoot their movie, sell it to the kikes and they all make a pile of money. I didn't [get paid]' (cited in Jarratt, 1975: 13). Nor do surfers baulk at taking advantage of their surfing comrades. Joe Larkin allowed Terry Fitzgerald to shape just three boards for the rack at his Gold Coast (Queensland) shop. Fitzgerald could only resume working after the shop sold one board. At A$10 each he needed to sell at least four boards a week to survive. 'My shaping had to improve or I'd starve', Fitzgerald recalls (Jarratt, 1998a: 41).

The professional surfing circuit is a hive of exploitation. In the 1970s, a group of surfers established the pro-tour in the belief that it would offer them an economic avenue to eternal hedonism (Booth, 2001a: 125–33). The reality is somewhat different. Professional surfers earn a mere fraction of that commanded by golfers, boxers and tennis players. Rarely do winners of major surfing events take home more than US$25,000. For those outside the regular place-getters the circuit means hard labour and perpetual struggle. In 1985, Terry Richardson, then ranked thirteenth, left his family for a three-month tour:

> I left a week's grocery money, paid the bills for that month ... every tournament I went in I sent two thirds of the money back home and

half of that was to be kept for groceries and the other half for bills if there was enough for bills. The other third I was living on. I got lucky in California, I got a third and that made it all worthwhile ... believe it or not I got back with all my bills paid. Well, my wife was a bit thinner and my kids were just that little bit thinner but they weren't starving, that's the main thing. (Cited in Baker, 1986: 25)

The tour also takes a heavy toll on social relationships. Richardson doubted whether he could ever 'make up for the lonely months' that he inflicted on his wife and two sons. Iain Buchanan is more forthright. You simply 'can't have a steady relationship' when you tour, he says: it puts too much 'mental strain' on the surfer and those she or he leaves at home (ibid.).

At the dawn of the professional era, Mickey Dora predicted that professionalism would force surfers into 'total subservience to the few in control' (Kampion, 1997: 144). (Dora made his own protest against professionalism during the 1967 Malibu Invitational Surf Classic when he dropped his boardshorts and gave the crowd of 4,000 a browneye – a view of his anus – while riding a wave.) Many examples confirm Dora's prognosis. A few months after finishing second on the 1983 tour, Wayne Batholomew's principal sponsor demanded he retire from competition, relocate to the company's headquarters in Torquay and contribute to the company's corporate development. He refused and Quiksilver withdrew his A$25,000 annual sponsorship. Other sponsors were unwilling to step into the breach. According to Bartholomew (1996), Rip Curl, which gave him A$10,000 per annum, kept saying, ' "Don't worry. She'll be right. We'll look after you." But all they did was dwindle me down to such negligible money and I became so disgusted that I just had to walk away. After 17 years with Rip Curl, I just got faded out the back door' (pp.273–4).[7]

Interestingly the big surfing manufacturers and retailers keep their financial support for the professional tour to a minimum. While they sponsor individual competitions and surfers, and happily invest substantial sums in potential champions,[8] the big companies steadfastly refuse to underwrite the world surfing championship grand prix circuit. The reasons are not hard to find. The manicured images portrayed by professional surfers to win broad public appeal simply do not resonate with a culture that marches to a different beat and that shuns institutionalism in all its guises.[9] Many of the corporate elite in the modern surfing industry helped lay the foundations of that culture with which they still identify. Rip Curl's Brian Singer, for example, still recalls the event that led him to abandon university. 'I left Torquay', he said, and was 'halfway to Melbourne [100 kilometres away] to sit an exam when I noticed the wind had changed. I pulled over and got out and a hot northerly hit me in the office, so I turned around and drove straight back' to the surf (Jarratt, 1998b: 68, see also Gliddon, 2002: 24). But even the less idealistic corporate contingent has sound reasons for maintaining its distance from professional surfing. Loud enthusiasm for professionalism exposes their companies' credibility to the grassroots surfers who buy the products and generate the profits, and who are vitriolic in their opposition. 'As soon as those assholes in the seventies tried to turn "surfing the artform" into "surfing the sport" surf culture suffered', complains Kit, a correspondent whose words echo the sentiments of thousands (*TransWorld Surf*, 1999; see also *Tracks*, 1991).

Like most industries, surfing supports an aristocratic class of worker. In surfing's case these are the editorial surfers. Leading editorial surfers earn between US$60,000 and $80,000 per annum to travel to the world's best and most exotic breaks where they are variously photographed and/or filmed wearing/riding/using their sponsors' products. Most editorial surfers begin their careers on the professional circuit that remains the principal means of exposure to potential sponsors. (Paradoxically the surfers most in demand for editorial work are the top echelon of professional competitors, but scheduling conflicts, exclusive contracts and high asking prices often exclude them from participating in pure photographic or filming trips.) Once recruited, and having established the 'right image', editorial surfers lead charmed lives. Donovan Frankenreiter boasts that he is 'the luckiest person in the world'. 'My life is killer', he says, 'I get to surf all the time [and] I'm saving money.' The only 'work' (what he called the 'bullshit') Frankenreiter did on his first few trips to Indonesia was to pose for 'photos next to a tree' and ride 'crummy waves' to take advantage of optimal lighting conditions (cited in Taylor, 1999).

Editorial surfers illustrate a key feature of the political economy of surfing: wealth derives, not from ownership of the means of production and control over wage labour, but from ownership of aesthetic ingenuity and the ability to create and mobilize cultural authenticity. As Hollywood's failure to appropriate surf culture illustrates, the market for surfing culture is sophisticated and discerning.[10] The ability to read the market is a prerequisite for financial success. In the late 1960s, most observers predicted that the commercial value of Jeff Hakman would plummet following his arrest for illegally importing marijuana into Hawaii. But Duke Boyd recognized Hakman's real aesthetic worth: his uniquely smooth surfing. He recruited Hakman into the Golden Breed stable to give the fledgling company credibility. The strategy worked. Irrespective of his social standing in the wider community, Hakman remained a respected cult figure (Jarratt, 1997: 84).

Quiksilver's foray into Western Europe in the mid-1980s is a classic example of the creation and mobilization of cultural authenticity. At the time, southwest France was the only place in Europe with a vibrant surf culture. There seemed little prospect of developing a market for print t-shirts and boardshorts among people who wear three layers of wool nine months of the year. But Harry Hodge, the one-time surf film cinematographer who headed the consortium that bought Quiksilver's Western European licence, 'realised that the difference between a small company selling surf products to parts of Europe and a big company supplying the lifestyle needs of the entire region, was simply a matter of lateral thinking'. Hodge and his senior partner, the ubiquitous Jeff Hakman, headed to the mountains: 'we looked at what [people] were wearing, and we saw how we could make Europe work for us. We would take surf clothes to the mountains.' Within two years of arriving in France, Quiksilver's net sales rose to US$6 million; within six years they reached US$26 million and within a decade over US$70 million. In 1998, net sales exceeded US$113 million. Quiksilver's success derived from the fact that opposition companies had no sense of cultural authenticity. 'When we saw the [businessmen wearing grey] suits [at the trade fairs], we knew we had a big chance of making it in Europe', Hodge said, adding that 'the people running it up to then were just businessmen. They didn't understand the lifestyle' (cited in Jarratt, 1997: 159–62, 168, 174; *TransWorld Surf Business Magazine*, 1999).

In 1990, Quiksilver USA bought 100 per cent of Quiksilver Europe and Hodge and Hakman became multi-millionaires (Jarratt, 1997: 174). The mongrels were now moguls. *Bulletin* journalist Joshua Gliddon (2002: 23) puts the personal fortunes of Rip Curl's Brian Singer and Billabong's Gordon Merchant at A$241 million and A$580 million, respectively. Financial affluence raises questions about the nature of money and its role in determining individual liberty and class-consciousness. Neither Hodge nor Hakman retired. The former moved into an executive position, while the latter accepted a brief to explore the marketplace and 'bring back the knowledge' (ibid.). What effect does money have on class-consciousness? According to at least one cultural insider, wealth generated by surfing has not changed social relationships: 'If you go down to the pub [at Torquay], you'll still see [Quiksilver's Allan Green] having a beer with the plumber, or [Rip Curl's] Brian [Singer] having one with the gardener, who probably used to be the dope dealer ten years ago. We're like family' ('Butch' Barr, cited in Jarratt 1998b: 76). Fashion, style, taste, language and localism contribute to cultural identity and it is not unreasonable to expect cultural practices to conjoin producers and consumers and workers and capitalists in a relatively passive form of symbolic order (Harvey, 1990: 347–8). Nonetheless even harmonious social relationships cannot conceal material realities. Flexible work practices in the surfing industry may give workers access to the surf and, by extension, a semblance of command over the conditions of work.[11] But, as the experiences of Terry Richardson and Terry Fitzgerald testify, flexibility does not equate to control over job security, wages, insurance coverage or pension rights (ibid. 151). Workers and capitalists in the surfing industry may ride the same waves; however only a minority of workers enjoy material prosperity and real independence.

Conclusion: the political economy of irreverence

All cultures, even irreverent ones like surfing, comprise material elements critical to their diffusion. Like the culture on which it feeds, the surfing industry continues to grow and prosper; today the surfing industry even has its own association – SIMA (Surf Industry Manufacturers Association). In this growth one finds numerous examples of both industrial imperialism and cultural hegemony.

In Australia small surf-shops complain about being bullied into stocking certain companies' products (Stranger, 2001: 213), forcing them to 'lift sales by an average of 10 percent every year to qualify for volume discounts', and threatening to remove their accounts if they 'discount outside traditional end-of-season sales' (Gliddon, 2002: 24). Magazine editors grumble about manufacturers influencing editorial policy and effectively silencing critical commentary. Mark Stranger observed an unusual silence in the surfing media after the courts convicted Quiksilver for false labelling (their wetsuits carrying 'made in Australia' tickets were actually produced in China):

> The editor of one of the top magazines at the time said that the company had 'strenuously' put it to him that there was nothing to be gained by publicising the case, and while there had been no threat of withdrawing advertising he didn't want to let it get to that stage and agreed with their request. [In the words of the editor] 'we walk a fine line between trying to maintain our independence and not upsetting these companies'. (Stranger, 2001: 214; see also Gliddon, 2002: 24)

Such imperialism extends beyond the immediate confines of the industry. By the mid-1980s, less than 20 years after Brian Singer and Doug Warbrick hung the Rip Curl sign outside their garage in Torquay, the surfing industry had economic control over the one-time family summer holiday resort and farming community. Based on Rip Curl, Quiksilver, Oakley, Full Bore, No Fear, Strapper, Hughes Surf Craft, Gash Surfboards, Moonlight Laminating, Watercooled, Rojo Australia and Propaganda, the surf industry is the second largest employer in the Surf Coast Shire, behind tourism–hospitality, and generates more than A$15 million each year in wages, salaries and other operating expenses (Surf Coast Shire, no date: 8, 12).[12] Leading players in the industry have not been shy to exert their newfound power. Quiksilver, for example, threatened to move inter-state to Burleigh Heads when a bureaucratic delay in rezoning land for commercial purposes stalled its plans to build new international headquarters in Torquay (Dorling, 1999).

Concomitant with the economic and political power of the manufacturers, surfing culture has also strengthened its hegemony in Torquay (and elsewhere; see Barilotti, 2003: 107). When McDonald's applied to the Surf Coast Shire to open a restaurant in the town, a group of local residents formed an action group, SCRAM (Surf Coast Residents Against McDonald's), to oppose the project. SCRAM claimed that McDonald's would sully Torquay's cultural identity. When the Shire approved the application, SCRAM appealed to the Victorian Civil and Administrative Tribunal. Among its submissions was a letter from former world surfing champion Nat Young. 'McDonald's have nothing to do with surfing and never have,' he wrote. 'They are simply a multinational franchise outlet who understands the value of peddling their second rate food to kids on TV' (*The Age*, 1999). The Tribunal upheld the Shire's decision, noting that the proposed site 'will not jeopardise the surfing industry'. But it did impose a number of modifications on the building plan, including an order prohibiting illumination of the red background on the main neon sign. According to the Tribunal, the traditional McDonald's neon sign contrasted too sharply with the colours and designs used by the Shire to promote its coastal theme (Groundswell, 1999). At least one surfer recognized the hypocrisy in the Tribunal's decision. 'I've never seen such a gaudy and ugly town', wrote G.L.D. in *Tracks*, 'from the mega-sized surf shops with two story signs to the ugly high-density housing' (Tracks, 1999).

Some insiders believe that its prominence in the youth market for adventure and irreverence offers surfing unlimited economic potential. Bob Hurley is one believer. He recently left Billabong, whose target market is the 18 to 24-year-old male surfer, to start a new company,

Hurley, which aims to capture more of the Generation Y market. Bob Hurley identifies the latter as 'sixteen-year-old boys and girls who like surfing, skateboarding, snowboarding, punk-rock music, hip-hop music, Lawrence Welk, Spaghetti-O's' (Marcus, 1999). Bob McKnight, CEO of Quiksilver International, is another believer. While admitting that less than 10 per cent of those who identify with surfing, skating or snowboarding actually participate, McKnight insists that the image is strong enough to capture millions within its orbit: 'while this Generation Y customer might go to the coast for a week during the year, he wants to look like a surfer while he's there. And so he goes back to Des Moines [Iowa], and to him, he's a surfer – and you're not going to tell him any different' (Checkwood and Stouffer, 1999; see also Gliddon, 2002: 24). Others are more cautious, the memories of earlier failed forays into mainstream markets still fresh. But the optimists reign in a seemingly inexhaustible sea of surf consumers. 'Hurley's got a lot of mojo [momentum]', reports Eric John, who owns five surf shops in Los Angeles: 'Kids come in and just have to have it' (Ernest, 1999a).

Paradoxically established market sages, marketing gurus, hypemasters and creative agents may be sowing the seeds of a reversal in the fortunes of the surfing industry. Wearing its emblems and fashions is not tantamount to understanding the spirit of a culture, or even being able to interpret its nuances, much less living by its tenets. The following quotation by Vipe Desai, former accounts director of The Shop (a marketing and creative agency) and currently marketing director for SMP (surf, snow, skate, motorcross and BMX clothing), reveals an industry on the verge of losing touch with its market.

> A lot of parents grew up in a culture of surf, skate and snowboarding. Now they ... want their kids to do those activities [and] to dress as hip as they did. Parents are willing to buy brand-name goods for their eight-year-olds, which helps establish consumer brand allegiance at an earlier age. (Jones, 1999)

Living differently and displaying irreverence are the essence of surf culture. The new generation of surf wear manufacturers, with names such as Lost 'dysfunctional clothing' and Vermin 'untamed surfwear', understand this only too well. In their hunger for a share of the market they beseech the young to cast off their parents clothes with their staid styles. 'Be unpredictable, your parents won't understand', implores Loose Unit while the Umgawa International label carries a warning: 'wearing the same tired old brands as your father can lead to loneliness and isolation'.

Notes

1. Stranger (2001) offers a particularly useful configuration of the surfing culture industry as an inverse pyramid resting on the subjective experience of surfing. 'The first level supplies functional commodities to surfers, such as surfboards, wetsuits, wax, legropes and a few other minor and non-essential accessories. The next level up – one step removed from the experience – supplies surfers with lifestyle commodities such as magazines, videos, travel packages and the clothing and accessories which provide the tokens of identification, and the means for communication beyond the local community. These signs are also marketed in the final level where the surfing image is sold to the mainstream as surf fashion' (p.217).

2. In *Capital*, Karl Marx (1976) demonstrated that three conditions, and three only, determine the capitalist mode of production. Firstly, there must be continuous economic growth. Secondly, the quest for accumulation by the owners of the means of production (capitalists) leads them to extort maximum surplus-value from those who own only their labour power (workers). Thirdly, accumulation of capital fuels competition between capitalists, and leads them to seek new technology and new ways of organizing and controlling labour.

3. So named after the place where they were first ridden. Technology prevented surfing from becoming a popular pastime earlier in the twentieth century. The first surfboards were made of wood and were heavy and cumbersome; thus they were difficult to transport and impossible for all but the highly skilled to ride (Booth, 2001a: 206, n.9).

4. Barilotti (2003) examines the infatuation of modern mainstream industry and advertising with surfing culture and the increasing number of conflicts between cultural insiders and outsiders as the latter attempt to appropriate surfing culture.

5. The counterculture coincided with what the regulationist school of political economy refers to as a crisis in the regime of accumulation and the transition from Fordism to flexible accumulation (Harvey, 1990: 125–72).

6. Quiksilver replied to 'The Search' with 'The Crossing', a two year boating expedition in search of perfect waves. 'The Crossing' launched a new line of products (Ernest, 1999b).

7. In 1999, the Association of Surfing Professionals appointed Bartholomew president and CEO.

8. Quiksilver aims to have at least one surfer in the top five (Bartholomew, 1996: 272, 274) and it paid rising star Kelly Slater – who went on to win six world titles – US$1 million to wear its products before he even turned professional.

9. For insider views of the ideal images expected of professional surfers, see Hemmings (1969: 64–5), Jarratt (1977a: 13, 1977b: 17), Latronic (1992: 90).

10. Hollywood is not the only example of failed imitation. In the 1960s, several surfboard manufacturers experimented with automated assembly-line technology. Using moulds, shaping machines, chopped-glass appliers and other techniques, they mass-produced 'pop-out' surfboards. The experiment failed: 'kooks' – novices – were more sensitive and aware of their culture than even manufacturers realized (Kampion, 1997: 97).

11. Evidence as to the existence of flexible work patterns in the surfing industry is contradictory. Tak Kawahara, co-founder of T & C Surf Designs, reports that the days of surfers simply bunking work when the surf is up are long gone and that today 'you have to work' irrespective of surf conditions (Noll and Gabbard, 1989: 114). On the other hand, an employee of a surfing company told Stranger that, when he was hired, 'the executive director [said] he expected to see me in the surf when it was good and not in the office' (Stranger, 2001: 216). Stranger interpreted this as part of the company's efforts to preserve its links with the foundational culture.

12. Torquay is the capital of the Surf Coast Shire. In the early 1990s, the Victorian state government amalgamated urban councils and rural shires. The Surf Coast Shire – The Place of Well Being – conjoined the former Barrabool and Winchelsea Shires and a part of the City of South Barwon.

References

Australia's Surfing Life (1992), 'Australia's fifty most influential surfers', November, pp.70–123.

Baker, T. (1986), 'The other side: a look at the not so glamorous world of pro surfing', *Tracks*, July, pp.25–7, 51.

Baker, T. (2002), 'The women's rev-illusion', *Australia's Surfing Life*, April, pp.92–102.

Barilotti, S. (2003), 'Surfin' USA redux', *Surfer*, February, pp.102–7.

Bartholomew, W. with T. Baker (1996), *Bustin' down the door*, Sydney: HarperSports.

Bold, K. (1999), 'A big wave in bedding design', *Los Angeles Times*, 5 August.

Booth, D. (2001a), *Australian beach cultures: the history of sun, sand and surf*, London: Frank Cass.

Booth, D. (2001b), 'From bikinis to boardshorts: wahines and the paradoxes of surfing culture', *Journal of Sport History*, 28 (1), 3–22.

Carse, G. (2003), 'Personal interview', 26 September.

Checkwood, A. and J. Stouffer (1999), 'Chairman of the boards: Bob McKnight believes in surfing', *TransWorld Surf Business Magazine*, 1 (2); retrieved 5 November 1999 from World Wide Web: http://www.transworldsurf.com.

Dahlberg, R. (2002), 'Industry opinions', *Australia's Surfing Life*, June, p.104.

Dorling, P. (1999), 'Personal correspondence with Peter Dorling, Strategic Planner, Surf Coast Shire', 16 December.

Ernest, L. (1999a), 'Many catching surf wear's wave', *Los Angeles Times*, 19 October.

Ernest, L. (1999b), 'Quiksilver's truly endless summer', *Los Angeles Times*, 29 October.

Gillogly, B. (1982), 'Surfing Sunset and Vine', *Surfer*, September, pp.56–9.

Gliddon, J. (2002), 'Mad wax', *Bulletin* (Australia), 13 August, pp.20–4.

Groundswell (*The Surf Coast Shire Community Newsletter*) (1999), 'Tribunal allows McDonald's in Torquay', November.

Haas, M. and P. Resurrection (1976), *Politics and prejudice in contemporary Hawaii*, Honolulu: Coventry Press.

Harvey, D. (1990), *The condition of postmodernity*, Oxford: Blackwell.

Hemmings, F. (1969), 'Professionalism is white', *Surfer*, November, pp.64–5.

Humphreys, D. (1997), 'Shredheads go mainstream? Snowboarding and alternative youth', *International Review for the Sociology of Sport*, **32** (2), 147–60.
Jarratt, P. (1975), 'A conversation with Mickey Dora', *Tracks*, October, p.13.
Jarratt, P. (1977a), 'Ego's not a dirty word', *Tracks*, April, p.13.
Jarratt, P. (1977b), 'A profile of Graham Cassidy', *Tracks*, December, pp.16–17.
Jarratt, P. (1997), *Mr Sunset: the Jeff Hakman story*, London: Gen X.
Jarratt, P. (1998a), 'The sultan of speed', *The Australian Surfer's Journal*, Autumn, pp.28–45.
Jarratt, P. (1998b), 'Boys town: Torquay', *The Australian Surfer's Journal*, Autumn, pp.62–77.
Jenks, C. (1993a), 'Introduction: the analytical bases of cultural reproduction theory', in C. Jenks (ed.), *Cultural Reproduction*, London: Routledge, pp. x–xx.
Jenks, C. (1993b), *Culture*, London: Routledge.
Jones, R. (1999), 'Girls surf market overview', *TransWorld Surf Business Magazine*, **1** (2); retrieved 5 November from World Wide Web: http://www.transworldsurf.com.
Kampion, D. (1997), *Stoked: a history of surf culture*, Los Angeles: General Publishing Group.
Kampion, D. (2001), 'History of Jack O'Neill', retrieved 15 January from the World Wide Web: http://www.oneill.com.
Latronic, M. (1992), 'Kelly Slater: lovin' it', *The Surfer's Journal*, **1** (2), 90–5.
Levine, B. (2003), 'The next wave in literature', *Los Angeles Times*, 5 April.
Lueras, L. (1984), *Surfing: the ultimate pleasure*, New York: Workman.
Mambo (1999), retrieved 8 August from World Wide Web: http://www.mambo.com.
Manly Daily (1964a), 'World surfboard titles at Manly', 16 April, 16–17 May.
Manly Daily (1964b), 'Manly's record sporting crowd sees Farrelly's board win', 19 May.
Marcus, B. (1999), 'Hurley burly: Bob Hurley looks backward and forward', *TransWorld Surf Business Magazine*, **1** (2), retrieved 18 August from World Wide Web: http://www.transworldsurf.com.
Marx, K. (1976), *Capital*, vol. 1, Harmondsworth: Penguin.
McClelland, G. (1995), 'Scenes from the life and times of Bud Browne', *The Surfer's Journal*, Fall, 30–51.
Noll, J. and A. Gabbard (1989), *Da bull: life over the edge*, Berkeley, CA: North Atlantic Books.
O'Brien, S. (1999), 'Quiksilver brings its wetsuit program in-house', *Trans World Surf Business Magazine* (Business news archive), retrieved 10 October from World Wide Web: http://www.transworldsurf.com.
Renneker, M., K. Starr and G. Booth (1993), *Sick surfers ask the surf docs and Dr. Geoff*, Palo Alto: Bull.
Rip Curl (1999), '1999 Heli-Challenge', retrieved 10 August 1999 from World Wide Web: http://www.heli-challenge.co.nz/ripcurl.htm.
Severson, J. (1985), 'In the beginning', *Surfer*, January, pp.110–13.
Smith, S. (1999), 'Oakley raids counterfeiter', *TransWorld Surf Business Magazine* (Business news archive), retrieved 20 November from World Wide Web: http://www.transworldsurf.com.
Stranger, M. (2001), 'Risk-taking and postmodernity: commodification and the ecstatic in leisure lifestyles: the case of surfing', unpublished PhD thesis, University of Tasmania.

Surf Coast Shire (no date), 'A business profile', brochure, Surf Coast Shire.

Surfer (1968), 'Hemmings is hot', November, pp.64–9.

Taylor, G. (1999), 'Dream job: how to get paid to surf the world's best waves without grovelling in contests', *TransWorld Surf*, 1 (3), retrieved 15 July from World Wide Web: http://www.transworldsurf.com.

The Age (Melbourne) (1999), 'Big Mac hit by a wave of anger', 13 August.

Tracks (1991), 'Surfers on pro surfing', October, pp.90–1.

Tracks (1999), 'Letter', December, p.20.

TransWorld Surf (1999), 'Forum: Derek Hynd's new tour', retrieved 20 August from World Wide Web: http://www.transworldsurf.com.

TransWorld Surf Business Magazine (1999), 'Chairman of the boards: quick facts', 1 (2), retrieved 18 August from World Wide Web: http://www. transworldsurf.com.

Wardlaw, L. (1991), *Cowabunga*, New York: Avon Books.

Williams, R. (1995), *The sociology of culture*, Chicago, IL: University of Chicago Press.

Part III

Place Competition: Sport Mega-Events and Urban Development

7
Selling Places: Hallmark Events and the Reimaging of Sydney and Toronto

C. Michael Hall

Whether it is to attract a new car factory or the Olympic Games, they go as supplicants. And, even as supplicants, they go in competition with each other: cities and localities are now fiercely struggling against each other to attract footloose and predatory investors to their particular patch. Of course, some localities are able successfully to 'switch' themselves in to the global networks, but others will remain 'unswitched' or even 'plugged'. And, in a world characterized by the increasing mobility of capital and the rapid recycling of space, even those that manage to become connected in to the global system are always vulnerable to the abrupt withdrawal of investment and to [partial] disconnection from the global system. (Robins, 1991: 35–6).

Image

Image is a key concept of the twenty-first century. Whether one is restructuring, reimaging, deconstructing, reconstructing, promoting, advertising or just being a dedicated follower of fashion, the role of image is highly important. Sports, tourism and urban development are three areas of human endeavour in which the image has assumed vital importance. With all three we are concerned with issues of commodification, identity and the development of products to be sold in the marketplace. All three are also intimately interrelated. This chapter examines the nature of these relationships and the implications for urban regeneration, communities and the hosting of sports events, with special reference to the hosting of large-scale sports events such as the Olympic Games, especially the Sydney 2000 Games. However the chapter notes that, while mega sports events may be glamorous to cities and spectators, their hosting may not come without a price.

Urban centres, tourism and reimaging

Although urban centres have long attracted visitors, it is only in recent years that cities have consciously sought to develop image and promote themselves in order to increase the influx of tourists (for example, Burns *et al.*, 1986; Law, 1993; Page, 1995; Murphy, 1997; Essex and Chalkley, 1998; Judd and Fainstein, 1999; Page and Hall, 2003). Following the economic restructuring of many regions and the subsequent loss of heavy industry in many industrial and waterfront areas in the 1970s and 1980s, tourism has been perceived as a mechanism to regenerate urban areas through the creation of leisure, retail and tourism space. This process appears almost universal in the developed world. Such a situation led Harvey (1988, cited in Urry, 1990: 128) to ask, 'How many museums, cultural centres, convention and exhibition halls, hotels, marinas, shopping malls, waterfront developments can we stand?' Similarly Zukin (1992: 221) observed that the city is a site of spectacle, a 'dreamscape of visual consumption'.

One of the primary justifications for the redevelopment of inner city areas for sports and events is the perceived economic benefits of tourism (for example, Hall, 1992; Law, 1993; Page, 1995). For example, in Australia the 1986/7 America's Cup Defence was used to develop Fremantle in Western Australia, a Commonwealth Games bid from Victoria was used as a justification for the further redevelopment of the Melbourne Docklands, while Sydney utilized the 2000 Olympic Games to the same effect (Hall, 1998a). However such redevelopments are not without their social and economic costs (Olds, 1998). As Essex and Chalkley (1998: 195) cautioned with respect to the Atlanta Olympics experience, 'As a result of the traffic congestion, administrative problems, security breaches and overcommercialization, Atlanta did not receive the kind of media attention it would ideally have liked. Its experience highlights the dangers as well as the benefits of being under the international Olympic spotlight.'

Urban imaging processes are clearly significant for urban planning and development. The ramifications of such an approach are far-reaching, particularly in the way in which cities are now perceived as products to be sold with the focus on the supposed economic benefits of sport and tourism reinforcing 'the idea of the city as a kind of commodity to be marketed' (Mommaas and van der Poel, 1989: 264). Modern urban imaging strategies are typically policy responses to the social and economic problems associated with deindustrialization and associated economic restructuring, urban renewal, multi-culturalism, social integration and control (Roche, 1992, 1994; Page and Hall, 2003). The principal aims of urban imaging strategies are (a) to attract tourism expenditure, (b) to generate employment in the tourist industry, (c) to foster positive images for potential investors in the region, often by 'reimaging' previous negative perceptions, and (d) to provide an urban environment which will attract and retain the interest of professionals and white-collar workers, particularly in 'clean' service industries such as tourism and communications (Hall, 1992).

Urban imaging processes are characterized by some or all of the following:

1. the development of a critical mass of visitor attractions and facilities, including new buildings/prestige/flagship centres (for example, shopping centres, stadiums, sports complexes and indoor arenas, convention centres, casino development);
2. the hosting of hallmark events (for example, Olympic Games, Commonwealth Games, the America's Cup and the hosting of Grand Prix) and/or hosting major league sports teams;
3. development of urban tourism strategies and policies often associated with new or renewed organization and development of city marketing (for example, 'Absolutely, Positively Wellington', Sheffield City of Steel, Cutlery and Sport); and
4. development of leisure and cultural services and projects to support the marketing and tourism effort (for example, the creation and renewal of museums and art galleries and the hosting of art festivals, often as part of a comprehensive cultural tourism strategy for a region or city).

Reimaging is intimately connected to the competition between places in a time of intense global competition for capital. According to Kotler *et al.* (1993) we are living in a time of 'place wars' in which places are competing for their economic survival with other places and regions, not only in their own country, but throughout the world. 'All places are in trouble now, or will be in the near future. The globalization of the world's economy and the accelerating pace of technological changes are two forces that require all places to learn how to compete. Places must learn how to think more like businesses, developing products, markets and customers' (ibid.: 346). Tourism is inseparable from the place marketing process because of the way in which it is often used as a focus by government for regional redevelopment, revitalization and promotion strategies. For example, Hughes (1993: 157, 159) observed that 'the Olympics may be of particular significance in relation to the "inner city" problems that beset many urban areas of Europe and N[orth] America' and noted that Manchester's bid for the 2000 Summer Olympics was 'seen as a possible contribution to solving some of' the city's 'inner city problems'. Indeed it is the inherent belief that the Olympics or other mega-events will attract tourism and investment because of the improved image and promotion of a place that serves to justify redevelopment, often with large investments of public funds and with the suspension of normal planning practice (Roche, 2000).

Place competition occurs at international, national and regional levels and may reinforce previous competition within existing political systems, particularly federal systems. For example, of considerable significance to urban tourism and reimaging strategies in Australia has been the degree of rivalry between the New South Wales and Victorian State governments for increasingly mobile international capital (Hall, 2004). This rivalry is typically concentrated on attracting investment to the two state capitals of Sydney and Melbourne and is illustrated by the aggressive competition that exists for the hosting of events and the urban redevelopment and reimaging programmes that have been established for both cities. For example, Melbourne's unsuccessful bid for the 1996 Olympic Games was followed by Sydney's successful bid for the 2000 Summer Olympics. In the case of Melbourne, the bid was tied to the redevelopment of the Melbourne Dockland area, while the key feature of the Sydney bid was the redevelopment of the former industrial site and waste dump at Homebush Bay on Sydney Harbour as the main Games stadium complex. Waitt details environmental issues related to Homebush in the final chapter of this volume. In both Melbourne and Sydney the bidding for events by state governments has been integrated into the development of new cultural, leisure and tourism policies which focus on attracting visitors to the city and broader urban redevelopment programmes that seek to develop cultural, housing, leisure and entertainment complexes in waterfront areas (Hall and Hamon, 1996).

Event tourism

Short-term staged attractions or hallmark events have been a major component of the growth of tourism in Australia in the past decade. Hallmark tourist events, otherwise referred to as mega (Ritchie and

Yangzhou, 1987) or special events (Burns *et al.*, 1986) are major festivals, expositions, cultural and sporting events that are held on either a regular or a one-off basis. Hallmark events have assumed a key role in international, national and regional tourism marketing strategies, their primary function being to provide the host community with an opportunity to secure high prominence in the tourism marketplace for a short, well-defined, period of time (Ritchie, 1984; Hall, 1992).

The hallmark event is different in its appeal from the attractions normally promoted by the tourist industry as it is not a continuous or seasonal phenomenon. Indeed, in many cases, the hallmark event is a strategic response to the problems that seasonal variations in demand pose for the tourist industry. Although the ability of an event 'to achieve this objective depends on the uniqueness of the event, the status of the event, and the extent to which it is successfully marketed within tourism generated regions' (Ritchie, 1984: 2).

If successful, events can help construct a positive image and help build commercial and public awareness of a destination through the media coverage that they generate. For example, Victoria has been aggressively promoting itself as the event state, with Tourism Victoria (1997a, 1997b) reporting that its research indicates that Melbourne is now recognized as the Australian city which hosts major international sporting and cultural events, ahead of Sydney, Adelaide, Brisbane and Perth.

The positive image which events are able to portray to the public, and the media exposure they offer, probably explains the lengths to which governments and politicians will compete to host major national and international events. For example, in Australia, cities and state governments competed for the right to host the 1996 and 2000 Olympic Games, Victoria and New South Wales competed to host the Australian Motorcycling Grand Prix, while Victoria aggressively outbid South Australia for the rights to host the Australian Formula One Grand Prix. Such is the extent of inter-state rivalry that nearly all state governments have now established specific event units to assist in the bidding for major sporting and cultural events.

Given the large sums of money involved and the potential for high media profile it is therefore not surprising that the analysis of the impact of events is also often highly political, not only between government parties but between the government and public interest groups. For example, there has been substantial debate over the economic benefits of the Qantas Australian Formula One Grand Prix. According to Tourism Victoria (1997a: 24), the 1996 Grand Prix 'was watched by an estimated overseas audience of more than 300 million people, Total attendance at the race was 289,000 over the four days ... An independent assessment of the 1996 ... Grand Prix indicated that it provided a gross economic benefit to the Victorian economy of $95.6 million and created 2,270 full year equivalent jobs'. In contrast, a thorough evaluation of the 1996 Grand Prix by Economists at Large and Associates (1997) for the Save the Albert Park Group concluded that the claim of $95.6 million of extra expenditure was a misrepresentation of the size of the economic benefit; claimed gross benefits are overstated or non-existent; and, ironically, compared to what might have been achieved, Victorians are poorer where they could have been wealthier, if the government had chosen a more 'boring' investment than the Grand Prix (ibid.: 8).

The amount of local involvement and the actions of government in the planning of events appear to be crucial to deriving the maximum benefit from hosting an event for the host community. The more an event is seen by the public as emerging from the local community, rather than being imposed on them, the greater will be that community's acceptance of the event. However the international dimension of many events will often mean that national and regional governments will assume responsibility for the event's planning. Because of the interests and stakeholders that influence upper levels of government, local concerns may well be lost in the search for the national or regional good, with special legislation often being enacted to minimize disturbance to the hosting of an event. The short timeframe in which governments and industry have to react to the hosting of events may lead to 'fast track planning', where proposals are pushed through the planning process without the normal economic, social and environmental assessment procedures being applied.

A classic example of the failure of governments to give adequate attention to the broad impacts of hallmark events was Sydney's hosting of the 2000 Summer Olympics. The bid for the games had as much to do with Sydney and state (New South Wales) politics than a rational assessment of the economic and tourism benefits of hosting the games. As research on large-scale events such as the Olympics or World Fairs has indicated, the net costs of the event often tend to far outweigh any net benefits, except in terms of potential political and economic benefits for urban elites (Hall, 1992; Roche, 1994, 2000). The Sydney Games was designed more to assist with urban redevelopment and imaging than with concern over the spread of social, economic and environmental impacts (Hall and Hodges, 1996; Waitt, 1999). Furthermore there is a possibility that the hosting of the Olympic Games may actually have served to dissuade rather than encourage some visitor arrivals. As Leiper and Hall (1993: 2) observed in their submission to the House of Representatives' Standing Committee on Industry, Science and Technology Inquiry into Implications for Australian Industry Arising from the Year 2000 Olympics:

> A major outcome could be that the 'tourist boom' imagined by many commentators might be just that – imagination. The Olympics will attract certain types of tourists, but it will certainly repel other tourists who, in normal circumstances, would have visited Sydney and other regions of Australia ... Moreover, there is no certainty that publicity around the Olympics, broadcast internationally about Australia, will lead to any significant increase in inbound tourism in the months and years afterwards.

While these arguments were dismissed by the Australian Tourist Commission as being 'rather light' and 'unsubstantiated', it is interesting to note that Tony Thirlwell, Chief Executive Offices of Tourism New South Wales, confirmed that there was a need for some 'reality checks' to be brought home to New South Wales in the light of the Atlanta Olympics experience:

> The simple fact that people travel to Olympic Games for sports events cannot be overstated. ... Zoo Atlanta, Six Flags Over Georgia and other attractions ... suffered adversely because of the Olympic Games. Revenue losses were caused by Olympic distortion of attractions' usual visitation patterns and by costs of their attempts to leverage off the Olympics. (Thirlwell, 1997: 5)

Nevertheless the long-term expectations for the Olympics are high. According to Tourism New South Wales (1997a: 1), 'an extra 2.1 million overseas tourists [were] expected between 1994 and 2004 – A $4 billion tourism boost', while the games are also regarded as important in increasing the exposure of Sydney in the international media and contributing to the ability of the Sydney Convention and Visitors Bureau to win major international conferences. In addition Tourism New South Wales (1997b: 9) reported the results of a survey which showed that, outside Sydney, '39% of respondents said they would definitely or probably travel to Sydney for the event' with the survey also finding 'that 73% of Sydneysiders were interested in attending Games events'. Unfortunately for the games organizers, initial ticket sales were not as great as they had expected and many events did not sell out. And, even though regarded as a great success from a promotional standpoint, the official figures for the tourism impact of the games had been downgraded by 2001 with the number of Olympic-induced visitors for 1997–2004 being forecast at 1.6 million (Australian Tourist Commission, 2001). Nevertheless, despite both the overt and 'hidden' costs of hosting events, substantial gains can be made through event tourism if strategies are carefully considered, appropriate strategies are developed and there is meaningful consultation with affected stakeholders. However, unfortunately, this is rarely the case.

The Sydney 2000 Games

Until the recent confirmation (Simson and Jennings, 1992) of long alleged corruption and scandal within the International Olympic Committee (Evans, 1999; Magnay, 1999; Stevens and Lehmann, 1999; Washington, 1999), the success of the Sydney 2000 Olympic bid was highly regarded by much of the Australian media and certain quarters of government and industry as having the potential to provide a major economic boost to the New South Wales and Sydney economy. The initial economic impact study undertaken for the New South Wales (NSW) government by KPMG Peat Marwick suggested that the net economic impacts as a result of hosting the games would be between $4.093 billion and $4.790 billion, and between $3.221 billion and $3.747 billion for Sydney (KPMG Peat Marwick, 1993). More recently, a report by the accounting firm Arthur Andersen undertaken in conjunction with the Centre for Regional Economic Analysis at the University of Tasmania, stated that the Olympics would generate a total of $6.5 billion in extra economic activity in Australia from 1994–5 to 2005–6, with $5.1 billion of this activity occurring in NSW. The report also indicated that the NSW government would collect about $250 million in extra tax revenue, against official government estimates of $602 million. The state treasurer, Michael Egan, described the significance of the gap as 'an academic exercise' that would not affect the NSW budgetary position (Power, 1999: 9). In addition, in January 1999, the NSW auditor-general, Tony Harris, calculated the readily quantifiable cost to the state government of hosting the Olympics at $2.3 billion, which was approximately $700 million above the $1.6 billion figure included in the 1998 state budget. Presumably the greatest benefit of the Olympics was seen in terms of employment, with the Arthur Andersen report noted earlier stating that the Olympics would create 5,300 jobs in NSW and

7,500 jobs Australia-wide over a 12-year period (Power, 1999). However this still ranks as an expensive job creation exercise.

From its earliest stages the political nature of planning and decision making associated with the Sydney Olympics was quite clear (political in the sense that politics is about who gets what, where, why and how). As with any mega-event, many, if not all, of these planning decisions will have substantial implications for the longer-term economic and social development of the city and the region. For example, the state government passed legislation in 1995 with respect to the Sydney Olympics to assist in the development and regeneration of projects associated with the games. This was achieved at the cost of the people of Sydney losing their rights of appeal to initiate a court appeal under environment and planning legislation against the proposed Olympic projects. The location and dealings of the amendment were far from being open and honest. As Wayne Johnston of the Environmental Defenders' Office commented, 'this amendment is buried on page 163 of the threatened species legislation ... not a bill where you would find such a change, and you have to wonder why they put it there' (Totaro, 1995: 1).

Further legislation passed under the New South Wales Government's Olympic Co-ordination Authority Act allows, somewhat ironically, given the green image which was an integral part of the games bid (Sydney Organising Committee for the Olympic Games [SOCOG], 1996), all projects linked with the games to be suspended from the usual Environmental Impact Statements requirements (Totaro, 1995). Unfortunately, however, the same reasons which propel cities to stage large-scale tourist events (such as redevelopment, dramatic urban development) and also to fast-track the planning process, 'are also some of the very factors which result in an adverse effect on residents in cities in which they are held' (Wilkinson, 1994: 28).

In the case of the Sydney Olympics at least the need to consider the environmental dimensions of the games did receive attention. In contrast, the socio cultural dimensions of the games were not an issue in the bidding process, except to the extent that the different cultures of Australia could be used to promote an image that might see the bid attempt succeed. According to the Sydney Olympics 2000 Bid Limited (SOB) (1992: 19), 'With the dawn of the new millennium, the peoples of the earth will look to the Olympic Movement for renewed inspiration. Sydney's cultural program for the 2000 Olympic Games will celebrate, above all, our shared humanity and the eternal goals of peace, harmony and understanding so sought amongst the peoples of the world.' Indeed one of the objectives of the cultural programme was to 'foster awareness and international understanding of the world's indigenous cultures, some of which have survived from earliest times, and to promote especially, a knowledge and appreciation of the unique culture of the Australian Aboriginal peoples' (ibid.). It is therefore ironic that the Australian federal government has been trying to alter native title legislation in order to extinguish some Aboriginal claims to pastoral leases, an action which led to suggestions that some Australian Aboriginal groups would call on some African and South Pacific nations to boycott the games in order to attempt to improve the human and land rights position of Aborigines (Sydney 2000 Olympic Games News, 1997). Although such a boycott did not happen, Aboriginal rights did feature in the games through the sporting achievements of Cathy Freeman in the 400 metres race and through rock band Midnight Oil's wearing of T-shirts with 'sorry' written on them while singing 'Beds are Burning'. The song is a direct reference to Aboriginal land rights and the T-shirt referred to the Australian Commonwealth government's refusal under Prime Minister John Howard to apologize for Aboriginal injustices created by successive governments until the 1970s. Although the potential the Olympics provided to highlight Aboriginal issues was significant, other social dimensions of the hosting of mega-events may have more immediate impacts on certain sections of the host community.

The housing and real estate dimensions of mega-events

Mega-events which involve substantial infrastructure development may have a considerable impact on housing and real estate values, particularly with respect to their 'tendency to displace groups of citizens located in the poorer sections of cities' (Wilkinson, 1994: 29). The people who are often most affected by hallmark events are typically those who are least able to form community groups and protect their interests. At worst, this tends to lead to a situation in which residents are forced to relocate because of their economic circumstances (Hall, 1994; Olds, 1998).

In a study of the potential impacts of the Sydney Olympics on low-income housing, Cox *et al.* (1994) concluded that previous mega-events often had a detrimental effect on low-income people who are disadvantaged by a localized boom in rent and real estate prices, thereby creating dislocation in extreme cases. The same rise in prices is considered beneficial to homeowners and developers. Past events have also shown that this has led to public and private lower-cost housing developments being pushed out of preferred areas as a result of increased land

and construction costs (for example, see Cox *et al.*, 1994; Olds, 1998). In the case of the Barcelona Games, 'the market price of old and new housing rose between 1986 and 1992 by 240% and 287% respectively' (Brunet, 1993, in Wilkinson, 1994: 23). A further 59,000 residents left Barcelona to live elsewhere between 1984 and 1992 (Brunet, 1993, in Cox *et al.*, 1994).

In relation to Australia, past mega-events have lead to increased rentals, increased conversion of boarding houses to tourist accommodation, accelerating gentrification of certain suburbs near where major events are held, and a tendency for low-income renters to be forced out of their homes (Hall and Hodges, 1996).

Studies of previous events also indicate that an inadequate level of prevention policies and measures was developed to ameliorate the effects of hosting mega-events on the low-income and poor sectors of the community. The pattern that had occurred in past events therefore had very real and serious implications for the hosting of the 2000 Games. Nevertheless, despite the increasing concern and attention being given to resulting social impacts caused by hosting mega-events such as the Olympics (Olds, 1988, 1989, 1998; Cox *et al.*, 1994), and the undertaking of such a study with the previous Melbourne bid to host the 1996 Summer Games (Olympic Games Social Impact Assessment Steering Committee, 1989), no social impact study was undertaken by the Sydney bid team during the bidding process. This may be considered somewhat surprising given the potential impact of the Sydney 2000 Olympics and associated site development on housing and real estate values in the Sydney region. After the bid was won, a comprehensive housing and social impact study was carried out by Cox *et al.* (1994). The housing report also presented a number of recommendations that could be implemented as a positive strategy to improve such impacts in relation to the preparation and hosting of the Sydney Games. However this study was undertaken for low-income housing interests, not the state government or the Sydney Olympic organization.

Since the announcement in September 1993 that Sydney would be the Olympic 2000 host city, an increased number of developments commenced in the traditional inner west industrial suburbs near the main games site at Homebush Bay, while the Olympics also assisted in giving new impetus to the Darling Harbour development (Hall, 1998b). In the municipalities of Leichhardt, Ashfield, Drummoyne, Burwood, Concord and Strathfield an increased number of apartment projects were built in an area known as the 'Olympic corridor'. The increase of residential activity had a significant effect on the housing areas located through the

Olympic corridor, with one of the main outcomes sought by real estate interests being to 'raise the profile of this area and create demand for residential accommodation' (Ujdur, 1993: 1).

Recent housing developments have indicated a movement towards the 'gentrification' of many of the inner western suburbs of Sydney by white-collar professionals and a move away by lower-income earners from the traditional low-income areas as higher-income households are sought. The Olympics, therefore, greatly accelerated existing socioeconomic processes. As a result, the cost of private housing is increasing in the inner west region in particular and throughout the metropolitan area in general. The potential for problems to occur is heightened by the fact that many of the tenants in these areas are on Commonwealth (federal government) benefits for unemployment, sickness, disability and aged persons, and more often than not are single people (Coles, 1994). It is these people who will suffer as the prices of houses and rentals increase in their 'traditional' cheaper housing areas, forcing them to relocate in extreme cases.

Approximately 20 per cent of Sydney residents rent accommodation, yet Sydney was already facing a 'rental squeeze' as the shortage of rental properties continued to increase, along with a rise in rentals. The situation worsened significantly throughout 1995, and church leaders and welfare groups expected the situation to get more desperate as the Olympics approached (Russel, 1995). Although the Sydney Olympics was four years away, by early 1996 housing impacts, such as increasing rental and real estate prices, had clearly begun to emerge in specific areas of Sydney. Indeed, as has been stated in the Sydney media: 'As the revitalization of the inner city continues and is hastened by the Olympics, it is expected that the problem of homelessness will be exacerbated' (Coles, 1994: 15). The Homeless Centre predicted that 'the greatest potential negative impact of the Sydney 2000 Olympics will be those living in low cost accommodation' (Coles, 1994: 2).

A number of means were available for protecting and monitoring the effect of the games on low-income residents (Hall, 1992; Cox *et al.*, 1994). The main options included the establishment of a housing impact monitoring committee, development of an Olympics accommodation strategy, tougher legislation to protect tenants and prevent arbitrary evictions, provision of public housing and emergency accommodation for disabled people, and a form of rent control.

Despite intensive lobbying from housing, welfare and social groups, the state and Commonwealth governments failed to act on the significant housing and community issues which emerged. One likely reason for this is that the Olympic concerns of government were concentrated more on the development of Olympic facilities and infrastructure and the potential implications of IOC scandals for both the image of the games and any possible effect on the ability of the Sydney Games to raise commercial sponsorship (Riley, 1999). Furthermore a change in government at the federal level in 1996 from the middle-ground Labor Party to the right-wing Liberal–National Party coalition meant that national financial assistance to the New South Wales government for low-income housing and urban redevelopment and infrastructure projects all but dried up (Hall and Hodges, 1996). However the political reality of the Olympics was that the social impacts of the games are not an issue. As Waitt (1999: 1056) observed, 'city marketing demonstrates government policies informed by entrepreneurial rather than welfare goals to address deindustrialisation. Bidding for the Olympics demonstrates local politics' transformation from a bureaucratic to an entrepreneurial role'.

Share the spirit: and the winner is ...?

Despite claims to the contrary from the Olympic movement as to the social value of the 'Olympic spirit', the games are more about the spirit of corporatism than about the spirit of a community. The Olympics are not symbolic of a public life or culture that is accessible to all local citizens. The Sydney Olympics, along with the increasingly event and casino-driven economy of the State of Victoria and the other Australian states, are representative of the growth of corporatist politics in Australia and the subsequent treatment of a city as a product to be packaged, marketed and sold, and in which opinion polls are a substitute for public participation in the decision-making process. Nevertheless, as Smyth (1994: 258) has recognized, 'for sustenance of the urban economy and future livelihoods, it may also be necessary to first promote the project to the local population'. A tentative conclusion of this analysis is that local authorities and initiators fear local reactions, and so try to avoid them. This begins to induce two consequences:

1. an inability to listen, understand and respond to local needs, in other words, reinforcing the move away from serving towards political and economic control and power; and
2. an open invitation to move further towards governance and away from government, in other words, away from accountability and towards implicit secrecy.

In the case of the Sydney Olympic bid the former premier and key member of the bid team, Nick Greiner, argued that 'The secret of the success was undoubtedly the creation of a community of interest, not only in Sydney, but across the nation, unprecedented in our peacetime history' (1994: 13). The description of a 'community of interest' is extremely apt, as such a phrase indicates the role of the interests of growth coalitions in mega-event proposals (Hall, 1997; Jenkins, 2001). The Sydney media played a critical role in creating the climate for the bid. As Greiner stated:

> Early in 1991, I invited senior media representatives to the premier's office, told them frankly that a bid could not succeed if the media played their normal 'knocking role' and that I was not prepared to commit the taxpayers' money unless I had their support. Both News Ltd and Fairfax subsequently went out of their way to ensure the bid received fair, perhaps even favourable, treatment. The electronic media also joined in the sense of community purpose. (Greiner, 1994: 13)

Greiner's statement begs the question of 'which community?' Certainly the lack of adequate social and housing impact assessment prior to the games' bid and after 'winning' the games, indicates the failure of growth coalitions to recognize that there may well be negative impacts on some sections of the community. Furthermore, in terms of the real estate constituency of growth coalitions, such considerations are not in their economic interest. Those that are most affected are clearly the ones least able to affect the policy making and planning processes surrounding the Games (Hall, 1997). The perceived 'need' by some interests for the tourism and associated economic developments of hosting an Olympic Games creates 'a political and economic context within which the hallmark event is used as an excuse to overrule planning legislation and participatory planning processes, and to sacrifice local places along the way' (Dovey, 1989: 79–80). For example, it took the NSW government and the Australian Olympic Committee eight years to release one of the major confidential documents outlining the terms and conditions under which NSW taxpayers through the government were responsible for funding Sydney's bid, building venues and meeting all costs associated with the Games (Moore, 1999). It was only when the IOC scandal with respect to the bribing of Olympic delegates had broken that the Australian commercial media began investigating the bidding process (for example, Moore *et al.*, 1999), but by then it was too late. The released contract noted (above) stated: 'The State and the city will not permit the [organising committee] to cancel the staging of the Games for any reason whatsoever, including *force majeure'* (Moore, 1999: 7).

With the focus on one narrow set of commercial, economic and political interests in the pursuit of major sporting events such as the Olympics, other community and social interests, particularly those of inner-city residents, are increasingly neglected (Hall, 1992, 1994). However, this is something that has been known for a relatively long time; but do we learn from it?

Toronto: 'The Biggest and Most Costly Mega-Project in the History of Toronto'

Toronto made a bid to host the 2008 Summer Olympic Games. Toronto's bid, as with its previously unsuccessful bid for the 1996 Games, was built on a waterfront redevelopment strategy that sought to revitalize the harbour area through the development of an integrated sports, leisure, retail and housing complex. However, as in the case of Sydney, or in any other mega-event with substantial infrastructure requirements, critical questions can be asked about the process by which the event is developed and who actually benefits from hosting the event.

One of the most striking features of the new Toronto bid was the extent to which information on the bid was either unavailable or provided only limited detail on the costs associated with hosting the event. However, unlike the Sydney Olympic bid, Toronto was fortunate to have a non-profit public interest coalition, Bread Not Circuses (BNC), actively campaign for more information on the bid proposal and for government to address social concerns.

BNC argued that, given the cost of both bidding for and hosting the Olympics, the bidding process must be subject to public scrutiny: 'Any Olympic bid worth its salt will not only withstand public scrutiny, but will be improved by a rigorous and open public process' (Bread Not Circuses, 1998a) and also argued that Toronto City Council should make its support for an Olympic bid conditional on the following:

1. The development and execution of a suitable process that addresses financial, social and environmental concerns, ensures an effective public participation process (including intervenor funding) and includes a commitment to the development of a detailed series of Olympic standards. A time-frame of one year from the date of the vote to support the bid should be set to ensure that the plans for the participation process are taken seriously.

2. A full and open independent accounting of the financial costs of bidding and staging the games.
3. A full and open independent social impact assessment of the games.

The other key elements of a public participation process promoted by BNC included the following:

1. A full, fair and democratic process to involve all of the people of Toronto in the development and review of the Olympic bid.
2. An Olympic Intervenor Fund, similar to the fund established by the City of Toronto in 1989, to allow interested groups to participate effectively in the public scrutiny of the Toronto bid.
3. An independent environmental assessment of the 2008 Games; and strategies should be developed to resolve specific concerns.
4. The development of a series of financial, social and environmental standards governing the 2008 Games, similar to the Toronto Olympic Commitment adopted by City Council in September 1989 (ibid.).

In addition to the factors identified by BNC it should also be noted that the city's previous experiences with stadiums and events raised substantial questions about the public liability for any development. For example, in 1982, the then Metropolitan Toronto Chairman Paul Godfrey promised that Toronto's SkyDome, a multi-purpose sports complex used for baseball and Canadian football, could be built for Can.$75 million, with no public debt. However the final price of the development was over Can.$600 million, with taxpayers having to pay more than half. BNC also noted that even the previous Toronto bid costs were 60 per cent over budget, 'with a great deal of spending coming in the final, overheated days of the bidding war leading up to the International Olympic Committee (IOC) Congress. There was no public control, and little public accountability, over the '96 bid', while 'There was virtually no assessment of the social, environmental and financial impact of the games until Bread Not Circuses began to raise critical questions. By then, it was too late to influence the bid' (Bread Not Circuses, 1998c).

BNC lobbied various city councillors in terms of their decision of whether or not to support a bid. However only one councillor out of 55 voted against the Olympic bid proposal, even though they only had a 20-page background document to the proposal in terms of information. When city councillors voted on the project, they did not have an estimate of the cost of bidding for the games, a list of the names of the backers of 'BidCo', the private corporation that is heading the Olympic bid, a reliable estimate of the cost of staging the games, a plan for the public participation process, the environmental review process or the social impact assessment process, or a detailed financial strategy for the games.

Such a situation clearly had public interest organizations, such has BNC, very worried as to the economic, environmental and social costs of a successful bid. Clearly the history of mega-events such as the Olympic Games indicates that such a situation was not new (Olds, 1998). As regards the International Olympic Committee (IOC), they have already sought to ensure that the games are environmentally friendly. Perhaps it is now time to see that they are socially and economically friendly and build wider assessment of the social impacts of the games into the planning process as a mandatory component of the bidding process. In this vein BNC, in a letter to the IOC president requested 'that the IOC, which sets the rules for the bidding process, take an active responsibility in ensuring that the local processes in the bidding stage are effective and democratic' and specifically address concerns regarding the 'financial and social costs of the Olympic Games', and proposed the following:

1. an international network to be created that includes COHRE, the HIC Housing Rights Subcommittee, academics, NGOs (including local groups in cities that have bid for and/or hosted the games);
2. a set of standards regarding forced evictions and so on would be developed and adopted by the network;
3. a plan to build international support for the standards, including identification of sympathetic IOC, NOC and other sports officials, would be developed and implemented;
4. the IOC would be approached with the request that the standards be incorporated into the Olympic Charter, Host City Contracts and other documents of the IOC (Bread Not Circuses, 1998b).

Such a social charter for the Olympics would undoubtedly greatly assist in making the games more 'place friendly' and perhaps even improve the image of the IOC. However, in 2004, at the time of concluding this chapter, the books of the Toronto bid had not been fully opened for public scrutiny. Neither had there been any response to the proposal for creation of a set of social standards for the Olympics. Toronto was unsuccessful in its bid, while the IOC continues to try and repair its tarnished image in the aftermath of questions about the means by which it selects host cities and runs its own activities. In the meantime another Canadian city, Vancouver, has won the right to host the 2010 Winter

Olympics over Pyeongchang in South Korea and Salzburg in Austria. Yet, even here, questions are being asked about the benefits of hosting the event. As *The Economist* reports, 'Nor do many Vancouverites, except hotel and restaurant owners, imagine the games will do them good. In opponents' minds, the Olympics mean mostly debt and higher taxes; Montreal, after all, has only just paid off its debt from the games it hosted in 1976' (*The Economist*, 2003: 37).

A new basis for mega-events and imaging strategies?

Undoubtedly there will be some positive benefits arising from the hosting of the Olympics. Any event of an Olympic size with its associated spending on infrastructure must have some trickle-down and flow-on effects (Australian Tourist Commission, 2001). However, broader issues over the most appropriate long-term economic, social, environmental and tourism strategies have not been adequately considered, while the most effective distribution of costs and benefits through the community is all but ignored. In the aftermath of the images of Sydney broadcast around the world, of the final Olympic parade, the Sydney Harbour firework show, and the medals won by Australia's successful athletes, all of which cast Sydney and Australia in a positive light, few think about counting the cost. Indeed a substantial case could be put forward that the Olympics has in fact deflected Sydney's planners and developers away from the longer term to concentrate on the target year 2000 (Hall, 1997). The irony is that government, which is meant to be serving the public interest, is instead concentrating its interests on entrepreneurial and corporate rather than broader social goals (Hall, 1999; Jenkins, 2001). As Waitt (1999: 1057) observed, 'As a political device, the bid was employed to imbue social consensus in an era distinguished by a sense of alienation, anomie and increasing social inequalities within cities by income, ethnic identity and life opportunities. During the 1990s, Sydney was not exempt from these problematic features of city living.'

The revitalization of place requires more than just the development of product and image. The recreation of a sense of place is a process that involves the formulation of urban design strategies based on conceptual models of the city which are, in turn, founded on notions of civic life and the public realm and the idea of planning as debate and argument (Bianchini and Schwengel, 1991). As Smyth (1994: 254) recognized:

This needs to be undertaken in a frank way and in a forum where different understandings can be shared, inducing mutual respect, leading to developing trust, and finally conceiving a development which meets mutual needs as well as stewarding resources for future generations ... This proposes a serious challenge to the public sector as well as to the private sector, for authorities have undermined the well-being of their local populations by transferring money away from services to pay for flagship developments.

Unfortunately such ideas have only limited visibility within the place marketing and tourism realms, as tourism and place planning are often poorly conceptualized with respect to participatory procedures, while the institutional arrangements for many of the public–private partnerships for urban redevelopment actually exclude community participation in decision-making procedures (Hall, 1999, 2000). If there are no lasting benefits and no identifiable economic opportunity costs from selling the city through the hosting of hallmark events, then we are left with the proposition of Bourdieu: 'the most successful ideological effects are those which have no words' (quoted in Harvey, 1989a: 78). The function of a flagship development is then 'reduced to inducing social stability, assuming the generated experience is sustainable for enough people over a long period and is targeted towards those who are potentially the harbingers of disruption ... what is the purpose of marketing the city?' (Smyth, 1994: 7).

Policy visions for Olympic cities, whether they be for places, sport or tourism, typically fail to be developed in the light of oppositional or critical viewpoints. Place visions tend to be developed through the activities of industry experts rather than the broad populace, perhaps because the vision of the wider public for a place may not be the same as those of civic boosters who have most to gain from the hosting of hallmark events. Unfortunately it is likely that in this situation we are not only seeing the selling of a city but we are also witnessing the local people being sold short.

Acknowledgement

Sections of this chapter are based on a paper originally presented at the Sport in the City Conference, Sheffield Hallam University, Sheffield, July 1998.

References

Australian Tourist Commission (2001), *Tourism reaps rewards of the Games*. Sydney: ATC, retrieved 6 May 2001 from the World Wide Web: http://www. atc.net.au/news/olympic/olympic2.htm.

Bianchini, F. and H. Schwengel (1991), 'Re-imagining the city', in J. Corner and S.Harvey (eds), *Enterprise and heritage: crosscurrents of national culture*, London: Routledge, pp.212–34.

Bread Not Circuses (1998a), *Bread alert!* (E-mail edition), **2** (2), 20 February.

Bread Not Circuses (1998b), *Bread alert!* (E-mail edition), **2** (3), 26 February.

Bread Not Circuses (1998c), *Bread alert!* (E-mail edition), **2** (8), 8 April.

Burns, J.P.A., J.H. Hatch and F.J. Mules, (eds) (1986), *The Adelaide Grand Prix: the impact of a special event*, Adelaide: The Centre for South Australian Economic Studies.

Coles, S. (1994), *Submission to the preliminary social impact assessment of the Sydney Olympics*, Sydney: The Homeless Persons Information Centre.

Cox, G., M. Darcy and M. Bounds (1994), *The Olympics and housing: a study of six international events and analysis of potential impacts*, Sydney: University of Western Sydney.

Dovey, K. (1989), 'Old Scabs/new scares: the hallmark event and the everyday environment', in B.J. Shaw, D.M. Fenton and W.S. Muller (eds), *The planning and evaluation of hallmark events*, Aldershot: Avebury, pp.73–88.

Economists At Large (1997), *Grand Prixtensions: the economics of the magic pudding*, prepared for the Save Albert Park Group, Melbourne: Economists At Large.

Essex, S.J. and B.S. Chalkley (1998), The Olympics as a catalyst of urban renewal: a review, *Leisure Studies* **17** (3), 187–206.

Evans, M. (1999), 'Sydney linked to IOC crisis', *Sydney Morning Herald*, 22 January, pp.1, 9.

Greiner, N. (1994), 'Inside running on Olympic bid', *The Australian*, 19 September, p.13.

Hall, C.M. (1992), *Hallmark tourist events: impacts, management and planning*, Chichester: John Wiley.

Hall, C.M. (1994), *Tourism and politics: policy, power and place*, Chichester: John Wiley.

Hall, C.M. (1997), 'Mega-events and their legacies', in P. Murphy (ed.), *Quality management in urban tourism*, Chichester: John Wiley, pp.75–87.

Hall, C.M. (1998a), *Introduction to tourism: development, dimensions and issues*, South Melbourne: Addison-Wesley Longman.

Hall, C.M. (1998b), 'The politics of decision-making and top-down planning: Darling Harbour, Sydney', in D. Tyler, M. Robertson and Y. Guerrier (eds), *Tourism management in cities: policy, process and practice*, Chichester: John Wiley, pp.9–24.

Hall, C.M. (1999), 'Rethinking collaboration and partnership: a public policy perspective', *Journal of Sustainable Tourism*, **7** (3/4), 274–89.

Hall, C.M. (2000), *Tourism planning: policies, processes and relationships*, Harlow: Prentice-Hall.

Hall, C.M. (2004), 'Seducing global capital: reimaging and the creation of seductive space in Melbourne and Sydney', in C. Cartier and A. Lew (eds), *Seductions of place: geographies of touristed landscapes* (2004), New York: Routledge.

Hall, C.M. and C. Hamon, (1996), 'Casinos and urban redevelopment in Australia', *Journal of Travel Research*, **34** (3), 30–36.

Hall, C.M. and J. Hodges, (1996), 'The party's great, but what about the hangover?: the housing and social impacts of mega-events with special reference to the Sydney 2000 Olympics', *Festival Management and Event Tourism*, **4** (1/2), 13–20.

Harvey, D. (1989a), *The condition of postmodernity*, Oxford: Blackwell.

Hughes, H.L. (1993), 'Olympic tourism and urban regeneration', *Festival Management and Event Tourism*, **1** (4), 157–9.

Jenkins, J. (2001), 'Statutory authorities in whose interests? The case of Tourism New South Wales, the bed tax, and "the Games" ', *Pacific Tourism Review*, **4** (4), 201–18.

Judd, D. and S. Fainstein, (eds) (1999), *The tourist city*, New Haven, CT: Yale University.

KPMG Peat Marwick (1993), *Sydney Olympics 2000 Economic Impact Study*, 2 vols, Sydney Olympics 2000 Bid Ltd, Sydney, NSW, in association with Centre for South Australian Economic Studies, Sydney: Sydney Olympics 2000 Bid.

Kotler, P., D.H Haider and I. Rein, (1993), *Marketing places: attracting investment, industry, and tourism to cities, states, and nations*, New York: The Free Press.

Law, C.M. (1993), *Urban tourism: attracting visitors to large cities*, London: Mansell.

Leiper, N. and C.M. Hall, (1993), 'The 2000 Olympics and Australia's tourism industries', submission to House of Representatives' Standing Committee on Industry, Science and Technology Inquiry into Implications for Australian Industry Arising from the Year 2000 Olympics, Southern Cross University/ University of Canberra, Lismore/Canberra.

Magnay, J. (1999), 'Games scandals hit Melbourne 2006 bid', *The Age*, 21 January, pp.1, 2.

Mommaas, H. and H. van der Poel (1989), 'Changes in economy, politics and lifestyles: an essay on the restructuring of urban leisure', in P. Bramham, I. Henry, H. Mommaas and H. van der Poel (eds), *Leisure and urban processes: critical studies of leisure policy in Western European cities*, London: Routledge, pp.254–76.

Moore, M. (1999), 'Contract puts burden on taxpayers', *Sydney Morning Herald*, 23 January, p.7.

Moore, M., M. Evans and G. Korporall (1999), 'Sydney 2000 chiefs told: lift the lid', *Sydney Morning Herald*, 6 February, pp.1, 7.

Murphy, P.E. (ed.) (1997), *Quality management in urban tourism*, International Western Geographical Series, Chichester: John Wiley.

Olds, K. (1988), 'Planning for the housing impacts of a hallmark event: a case study of Expo 1986', unpublished MA thesis, Vancouver: School of Community and Regional Planning, University of British Columbia.

Olds, K. (1989), 'Mass evictions in Vancouver: the human toll of Expo '86', *Canadian Housing*, **6** (1), 49–53.

Olds, K. (1998), 'The housing impacts of mega-events', *Current Issues in Tourism*, **1** (1), 2–46.

Olympic Games Social Impact Assessment Steering Committee (1989), *Social impact assessment, Olympic Games bid Melbourne 1996*, report to the Victorian government and the city of Melbourne, Melbourne: Olympic Games Social Impact Assessment Steering Committee.

Page, S. (1995), *Urban tourism*, London: Routledge.

Page, S. and C.M. Hall (2003) *Urban tourism management*, Harlow: Prentice-Hall.

Power, B. (1999), '$35.0m tax jolt just "academic" says Egan', *Sydney Morning Herald*, 22 January, p.9.

Riley, M. (1999), 'Scandal a costly blow to funding for Games', *Sydney Morning Herald*, 23 January, p.7.

Ritchie, J.B.R. (1984), 'Assessing the impact of hallmark events: conceptual and research issues', *Journal of Travel Research*, **23** (1), 2–11.

Ritchie, J.B.R. and H. Yangzhou (1987), 'The role and impact of mega-events and attractions on national and regional tourism: a conceptual and methodological overview', paper prepared for presentation at the 37th Annual Congress of the International Association of Scientific Experts in Tourism (AIEST), Calgary, Canada.

Robins, K. (1991), 'Tradition and translation: national culture in its global context', in J. Corner and S. Harvey (eds), *Enterprise and heritage: crosscurrents of national culture*, London: Routledge, pp.21–44.

Roche, M. (1992), 'Mega-events and micro-modernization: on the sociology of the new urban tourism', *British Journal of Sociology*, **43** (4), 563–600.

Roche, M. (1994), 'Mega-events and urban policy', *Annals of Tourism Research*, **21** (1), 1–19.

Roche, M. (2000), *Mega-events and modernity: Olympics and expos in the growth of global culture*, London: Routledge.

Russel, M. (1995), 'Plea for action as rent squeeze tightens', *Sydney Morning Herald*, 20 September, p.2.

Simson, V. and A. Jennings (1992), *The lords of the rings: power, money and drugs in the modern Olympics*, London: Simon & Schuster.

Smyth, H. (1994), *Marketing the city: the role of flagship developments in urban regeneration*, London: E and FN Spon.

Stevens, M. and J. Lehmann (1999), 'IOC purge starts race for reform', *The Australian*, 26 December, p.1.

Sydney 2000 Olympic Games News (1997), 'Aboriginal activist Michael Mansell suggests that some nations could boycott the games', *Sydney 2000 Olympic Games News*, 8 February, retrieved 9 February 1997 from the World Wide Web: http://www.gwb.au/gwb/news/olympic/080927.html.

Sydney Olympics 2000 Bid Limited (1992), *Fact sheets: a presentation of the bid by the City of Sydney to host the games of the XXVII Olympiad in the year 2000*, Sydney: Sydney Olympics 2000 Bid Limited.

Sydney Organising Committee for the Olympic Games (SOCOG) (1996), *Environmental guidelines*, Sydney: SOCOG.

The Economist (2003), 'Vancouver and the Winter Olympics: Somewhat cool. Will the 2010 games do British Columbia any good?', *The Economist*, 5 July, p.37.

Thirlwell, T. (1997), 'Atlanta revisited', *Tourism Now*, **25** (April), 5.

Totaro, P. (1995), 'Olympic opponents denied sporting chance', *Sydney Morning Herald*,16 December, p.1.

Tourism New South Wales (1997a), *Sydney 2000: tourism and the 2000 Games fact sheet*, Sydney: Tourism New South Wales.

Tourism New South Wales (1997b), 'Olympic visitor boost', *News*, Spring, p.9.

Tourism Victoria (1997a), *Annual Report 1996–97*, Melbourne: Tourism Victoria.

Tourism Victoria (1997b), *Strategic business plan 1997–2001: building partnerships*, Melbourne: Tourism Victoria.

Ujdur, G. (1993), *Sydney Olympics 2000: impact on property*, Sydney: Hooker Research Limited.

Urry, J. (1990), *The tourist gaze: leisure and travel in contemporary societies*, London: Sage.

Waitt, G. (1999), 'Playing games with Sydney: marketing Sydney for the 2000 Olympics', *Urban Studies*, **36** (7), 1055–77.

Washington, S. (1999), 'IOC allegations may affect funding', *Australian Financial Review*, 19 January, p.5.

Wilkinson, J. (1994), *The Olympic Games: past history and present expectations*, Sydney: New South Wales Parliamentary Library.

Zukin, S. (1992), *Landscapes of power*, Berkeley, CA: University of California.

8
Public Policy, Sports Investments and Regional Development Initiatives in Japan

Wolfram Manzenreiter and John Horne

Japan is the world's greatest repository of wealth, its 'high savings and under-consumption' has supported 'the US's low-savings, high-debt regime' for the past decade and more (McCormack, 2002: 5). Yet, since the beginning of the 1990s, the Japanese economy has been stuck in the doldrums. A loose monetary policy, delayed reorientation of the production and service sectors, and over-generous spending by central government has generated a heavy burden on Japanese corporations, small and medium-sized businesses, municipalities and individuals throughout the country. Far from being evenly balanced, the distributional patterns of the crisis are strongly bound to long-established regional disparities of productivity and prosperity. Towns, cities and rural districts of the Northeast, the South and other localities of the Japanese peripheries that always struggled to keep pace with the move towards an information- and services-based, post-Fordist, society have continued to fall behind the metropolitan areas and industrial zones of Central Honshū. Gradual industrial decline and steady population migration into the over-crowded capital and major cities have inflicted severe repercussions on the vitality of regions confronted with a rapidly aging population and a diminishing income tax base. Within this scenario, sport and leisure have been recently assigned special importance to counterbalance the widening gap between the centre and peripheries in Japan.

The argument that sport-related capital investment carries with it an 'economic multiplier' that will benefit an entire city or region (Baade and Dye, 1990) has been prominent in North America, Western Europe and Australia, where construction of sport facilities has become likened to both job 'engines' and economic development 'magnets' (Schimmel, 2001). It is asserted by growth coalitions and sport boosters that tangible economic benefits will be generated by the 'big time' image that a professional sport franchise and a 'world class' facility presents to global capital (Chapin, 1996). Yet there is insufficient evidence supporting many of the claims made about sport's role in economic regeneration, as the psychological benefits of living in a 'World Cup venue' or 'major league' city cannot be summed up accurately in dollars, yen or in the number of jobs created, and studies on the sport economy often fall short of identifying total benefits of new sports stadiums and arenas (Rosentraub, 1996). In fact, most academic studies agree that the economic effects of new stadiums are minimal. Sport economists provide evidence that the economic benefits that do accrue for sport-related development is centred around low-wage, seasonal employment (Baade and Dyc, 1990; Baade, 1996). Furthermore economic activity generated by sport facilities is not captured in the local area; it spills over to other jurisdictions (Nunn and Rosentraub, 1995) putting municipalities that finance stadiums into financial jeopardy. Furthermore scholars in the sociology of sport provide evidence that the sociospatial consequences of this type of urban growth have regressive effects on the local population (see Schimmel, 2001).

The Japanese discourse on sport and development began during the 1970s, when leisure and sports were considered important elements that enhanced the quality of life and overall social development. Since that time, the role of sport in Japanese society has changed considerably, particularly since 1990 (cf. Nakayama, 2000; Harada, 2002). Local policy planners now envision two general benefits emerging from the promotion of sports (Koiwai, 1994; Kubotani, 1994; Ōnishi, 1994). On the one hand, sport is viewed as an income generator. Since about 1995, numerous cities and municipalities of various population sizes have been enthusiastic about the prospects of economic growth fuelled by investment in new sport facilities and theme parks, the subsequent increase in tourism and the anticipated improved image of the region. Forging partnerships with other beneficiaries of regional development, particularly private enterprises, local governments assumed a leading role in paving the way for business expansion and new kinds of public–private partnerships. On the other hand, a modern and enlarged sports infrastructure would still have a positive impact on the quality of life of local inhabitants of the region. Similarly staging sports events on a major scale, or being the hometown to a team competing in one of the professional leagues, could provide ample sources of regional pride, thereby fostering feelings of community belonging and local identification. Such intangible benefits were also considered to help prevent younger members of the population from moving away from smaller or less desirable regions, thus helping to stablize internal migration while promoting regional development across Japan.

The following analysis of sports policy and sport infrastructure in modern Japan is set within this broader concern with Japanese public policy, regional development programmes and private sector initiatives. Drawing on the major trends of the past two decades, with particular reference to the establishment of the J.League, Japan's professional association football (soccer) league, and the 2002 FIFA World Cup finals, we will outline the changing role of public policy, the new faces of public–private partnerships and the impact of global sports on Japan.

History and trajectories of sports investment

Until the rise of the consumer society in the 1960s, for most members of the Japanese population, sports involvement was primarily associated with physical education in school. Prior to the Second World War, national sports policy was concerned with building up physical strength and disciplined bodies prescribed by the needs of the military's expansionist policy. Schools and national youth organizations trained their students and recent graduates in gymnastics and the Japanese martial arts that were deemed to be most suited to achieving national goals. Access to modern/Western sports, such as track and field or team sports, was limited almost exclusively to an elite group of higher education institutions and a few employees at some of the large *zaibatsu* (large conglomerates or corporations). It was only after the Second World War that broad-based sports participation became a major objective of national policy. Policy makers, under the heavy influence of American occupation forces, developed sports as a training tool for the promotion of democratic values (Kishino and Kyūzō, 1959).

National Athletic Meetings (*kokumin taiiku taikai*; or Kokutai), that initially also served as national championships, were held as early as 1946. Each year the Kokutai opened in a different prefecture (province), until in 1992 every prefecture had been provided with stadiums and sport facilities needed to host large-scale sports events. One result of building these new facilities was the capability of Japan to host major international sporting events beginning with the judo world championship in 1956 (staged in the newly built Budokan), the Tokyo Olympics of 1964 and the Sapporo Winter Olympics of 1972. The Tokyo Olympics especially acted as a showcase of Japanese economic and technological achievement whereby a world audience witnessed Japan's full return to the international community of nation states. The games, at the same time, united the nation and bridged remaining cleavages between conservative and progressive political blocs.

The national governing body for sport, the Japan Amateur Sports Association (JASA), was formally established as a non-governmental, non-profit organization during this time. Owing to its financial dependence on the federal budget, the close personal relationships between its own officials, mostly former high-ranking bureaucrats or retired world-class athletes and people from the world of politics and business, and because of its internal divisions into national sports federations and prefectural sports associations, JASA willingly embraced the national goal of improving international competitive levels of Japanese athletes. Mass sports continued to be promoted by educational institutions and corporate welfare, however. From the time of the Tokyo Olympics, private sector business funded sports began to replace the former elite sports run by university amateurs. The sports boom set off by the Games led to the establishment of national leagues for soccer (1965), volleyball, ice hockey and basketball (1966). Teams, as well as facilities and stadiums, were maintained by Japan's leading industrial corporations. They used the leagues as opportunities for displaying their strength and competitiveness. Although these were strictly amateur affairs, companies vied with each other by hiring the most successful members of high school or university teams in a range of sports. These athletes, in turn, were allowed to concentrate solely on enhancing the fame of the company, increasing its advertising impact and encouraging a sense of loyalty and unity among employees (Sugimoto, 1995: 186–7; Tamaki, 2001: 66–74).

The enactment of the Sports Promotion Law (Supōtsu Shinkō Hō) in 1961, even though permissive rather than mandatory in nature, was directly linked with preparing the nation for the Tokyo Olympics. Under the influence of European national wellness programmes, such as Germany's 'Golden Plan' of the 1960s, Japan's national and local governments started to move away from a sole emphasis on competitive sports. Following the revision of the post-war Social Education Law (Shakai Kyōiku Hō) in 1964, sport was officially acknowledged as a public good for the first time. Guidelines for administration were issued in order to guarantee sport opportunities for all, and particularly for those who were denied access to sport facilities owing to the lack of formal membership of either school teams or company clubs. A Parliamentary Commission for Health and Physical Fitness was established in order to develop concrete programmes adjusted to the needs of the people. According to the final report (*Taiiku, supōtsu no fukyū shinkō ni kansuru kihon hōsaku ni tsuite*) issued in 1972, coping with the lack of public sport facilities was the most urgent task facing local administration. As part of an emerging social welfare state in the 1970s, Japan's sports infrastructure was considerably extended. In 1969, the total number of public sports facilities was 10,193; this amount almost tripled over the ensuing decade and doubled during the next (Nagazumi, 1999: 160). The Ministry of Education, which is formally in charge of sport policy, operated a very broad definition of sport facilities and these included anything from mountain paths, swimming pools, sports arenas and multiplex stadiums, to gateball pitches (gateball is a variant of croquet particularly popular amongst Japanese senior citizens). The apex of the boom in construction activities was reached in 1985. However the ratio of roughly one facility per 2,000 people that was finally achieved was well below the Commission's original stated expectations.

Both the readjustment of the Japanese economy following the oil crises of the 1970s and mounting social security expenses exerted strong pressure on government budgets. Following the recommendations of the Second Committee for Structural Administrative Reform, spearheaded by Nakasone Yasuhiro (later to become prime minister), the reduction of direct state support for sports began in the early 1980s. The policy shift in general aimed at easing the financial burden on government while opening up the supply of sports to market forces and private enterprise initiatives, or public–private partnerships. School sports facilities that in earlier reports were considered to be the most valuable resource for local residents became central pillars of mass sports. Although by the mid-1990s about 90 per cent of compulsory school sport facilities and 50 per cent of high school sport facilities were open to the public, only 16.4 per cent of mass sport participants used these resources, compared to alternatives such as public (18.2 per cent) or private (23.8 per cent) facilities. Only a third of scholastic sports facilities opened their doors to the public more than once a week, and less than 50 per cent could be used after dark (SSF, 1997: 102–4).

Investments in public facility building started to decrease after 1982, notwithstanding the concomitant rising demand and surge of interest in sports and leisure in general. In order to cope with the budgetary deficit, the government aimed at the reduction of public involvement while encouraging private sector investment as much as possible (see Figure 8.1). Accordingly the Second Committee for Structural Administrative Reform suggested a reduction in public spending for public sports facilities and the handing over of public facilities to private business. MITI's (Ministry

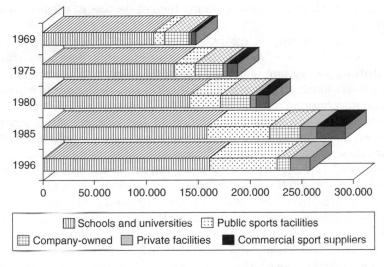

Note: No number available for commercial sports suppliers in 1996.
Source: Ministry of Education, Japan: *Waga kuni no taiiku supōtsu shisetu*, various years.

Figure 8.1 Ownership of sport facilities in Japan, 1969–96

of International Trade and Industry) report, *Sports Vision 21*, published in 1990, designated sport as a key industry and growth market of the twenty-first century but it strongly recommended that the management of it should be left to the private sector. Even the Ministry of Education, supposed to be the public's advocate for sports participation, was subjugated to the laws of the market and international competition. The Basic Plan for the Promotion of Sports in the Twenty-first Century (1989) (which was partly born out of the disappointing results of Japanese athletes at the Seoul Olympics in 1988, when they obtained less than half the number of medals achieved in Los Angeles in 1984 and finished fourteenth overall) was more concerned with quality management of elite sports than with social education issues. In this regard, the plan delegated the responsibility for sports supply and participation opportunities to the local level, where public governments should secure funding for the basic supply, administered by local educational boards, and commercial providers should enrich the sports market (Seki, 1997: 482–7). During the 1980s, municipalities such as Tokyo supported the establishment of commercial sport suppliers and even handed over the management and maintenance of sport facilities to private business. Not surprisingly, private ownership became the only viable growth segment of sports facility management during the last decades of the twentieth century.

A second objective of the policy shift towards more market-based economic principles was to counter the mounting Japan–US trade imbalance. Recreation, sports and tourism were explicitly named in the Fourth National Development Plan of 1987 as viable options to expand domestic consumption and to revive the peripheral regions. All these ambitions became most clearly visible in the Comprehensive Resort Region Provision Law (known as the 'Resort Law') passed in 1987. Prefectures were invited to submit development plans for regions to be designated as resort areas. Public input was meant to come either from freeing public assets, especially from privatisation and land sales, or from tax incentives, low-interest loans, relaxed land use regulations and supporting development programmes of the surrounding infrastructure. The execution of the construction projects and the management of resort areas and leisure sites were to be left to private businesses or public–private partnerships.

The Resort Law (1987) triggered not only a scramble for 'resort area' status by towns, villages and prefectures, but also a mini-construction boom extending over the whole archipelago. By the end of 1989, more than 850 applications for designated resort projects had been submitted that, if completed, would have seen nearly 20 per cent of the Japanese landscape being rebuilt and refashioned for the leisure industry (Satō, 1990: 98). In fact, although most of the projects were approved within a short time, many were never realized. Few schemes ever went beyond the planning stage as the bursting of the bubble economy, which had also been inflated by mounting land prices, destroyed these assets as well as the dreams of many speculators. The devaluation of the assets that served as collateral to the credit-financed projects threatened to crush banks under the burden of non-performing loans. This made many companies bankrupt or forced them to withdraw from their partnerships, leaving local governments to explain where all the taxpayers' money had gone (Funck, 1999: 336ff). The large-scale resort planning itself was seriously criticized and in most places became impossible to implement (McCormack, 1996: 86).

Nonetheless the 'Resort Strategy' did contribute to a measurable nation-wide construction and facility maintenance boom. Since the mid-1980s, this has continued to absorb the largest part of sports-related federal expenses, ranging from 65 to 80 per cent. About 35 per cent were immediately assigned to the former Ministry of Construction, but also the Ministry of Education (20 per cent) and the Ministry of Health and

Welfare (15 per cent) invested part of their allocation in facility management. Until the structural reform of the national government and ministries implemented in early 2001, no fewer than 12 ministries were competing for shares of the sports budget. Over the past 15 years, sports-related expenses of the central government were quite stable in relation to GDP (about 0.08 per cent), and so too was the composition of the budget, which indicates how well the arrangement between the ministries was established. Yet compared to the state, local governments had to invest quite large amounts, despite having hardly any direct income. The composition of the sports administration budget for 1990 (¥754.2 billion) showed central government contributing 43.8 per cent, prefectures 10.3 per cent and local municipalities 45.9 per cent (Ikeda *et al.*, 2001: 16). Under conditions of 'one-third autonomy' – local governments' share of direct tax income – prefectures and local government were forced to rely on direct funds allocated by the central government. The composition of the total sports budget indicates that, both at the local level of the cities, towns and villages, where the impact of economic change is most drastically felt, and at the central level of national policy planning, belief in the social and economic benefits of sport and the economic merits of sports facility construction is prominent in equal measure. Based on our reading of the current 10-Year Plan for the Promotion of Sport (MEXT, 2000), it seems that this view will continue to influence policy well into the twenty-first century.

The J.League as a 'public–private partnership'

In 2002, the first football (soccer) World Cup Finals ever to take place in Asia were co-hosted by Japan and Korea. The staging of the World Cup in two countries which, until recently, were considered peripheral to the game, further demonstrates that, over the past two decades, football has truly become the 'people's game'. The broader background and key social issues involved in the 2002 World Cup (Horne and Manzenreiter, 2002) as well as the Japanese Professional Football League or 'J.League', formed in 1991 and officially launched in 1993, is a subject of our earlier research (Horne, 1996, 1999, 2001; Manzenreiter, 2002; Horne and Manzenreiter, 2004). Elsewhere we have considered the influence of the 'people's game' on business and culture in other East Asian economies (Manzenreiter and Horne, 2004). Here, however, we look more closely at the impacts of the J.League and the World Cup on regional development in Japan. An increasing number of studies have examined the role played by sports 'mega-events' (for example, Roche, 2000) in social, economic and urban regeneration, the promotion of sports tourism and their role in the development of urban communities. This research, based solely on European, US and Australian case studies, indicates that the highly touted potential benefits of sport-related urban development have not yet been clearly demonstrated (Gratton and Henry, 2001). The 2002 World Cup in Japan and Korea, which some observers described as the world's largest sporting event ever, offered a unique opportunity to carry out equivalent study into the impact of a sporting event in Asian societies (cf. Manzenreiter, 2003).

Developments in the J.League provide an excellent case study, indicating what can happen when sport as a form of social policy, and sport as a tool for regional revitalization and urban development plans, intersects with market forces and national prestige thinking. The grand design of the incorporated professional football league was indebted both to the European club sports system and to the American business model of professional team sports. Member clubs were expected to link closely to a local entity (a hometown) thereby raising local pride and fostering community feeling among residents. Rather than relying on subsidies and the management decisions of owner companies, as is the case in Japan's professional baseball leagues, clubs were envisioned to work as autonomous and economically viable corporations. In addition the establishment of the J.League was also closely linked to three national objectives: strengthening the national team, improving the international achievements of Japanese football squads and securing the World Cup Finals for Japan. When Joao Havelange, long-time president of world football's governing body FIFA, declared in the late 1980s his intention to award the 2002 World Cup to an Asian host, Japan only had one specialized football stadium of considerable size (Nishigaoka) and no more than three stadiums matching the FIFA standard of providing space for 40,000 spectators. Constructing the required infrastructure of a minimum of eight stadiums would not have been possible without broadened interest in football and the support of the public in Japan.

The J.League (the consumer product) was introduced to the prospective market in a very sophisticated and gradual way, which stretched over a period of almost four years. During the first phase, the general concept of the new league and the brand name 'J.League' itself were presented to the public. In the background, the market potential was analysed, prospective sponsors were approached and the first franchise partners were selected. The originally sceptical Japanese media were finally won over at a 1991 press conference where the founding ten club teams and their playing strips were first unveiled. Sony Creative Products (SCP), which secured the exclusive merchandising rights for the entire J.League until 1998, had been in charge of devising a thoroughly styled corporate identity consisting of mascots, team songs, slogans and clothes for each of the teams. It also sold the rights to use J.League designs to several sublicensees and opened boutiques in over a hundred locations to sell J.League merchandise. SCP's intention of displaying cute and cool characters was a deliberate attempt to attract Japan's most important consumer group, young females, who had repeatedly shown their power to move entire leisure markets since the 1980s. The real actors, the players, only entered the stage at the last moment. Six months prior to the kick-off of the J.League (in May 1993), the first J.League (Nabisco) Cup was staged as a trial tournament. The pilot drew high media attention and offered a welcome opportunity to instruct the nation's public on basic football rules and tactics.

A scheme of persistent product placement was devised by the marketing giant Hakuhodo, which readily jumped in when its biggest rival Dentsu declined the risky job of establishing a new sport alongside the popular spectator sports of baseball, sumo and various racing sports. In fact Hakuhodo clearly profited from the experience Dentsu had gained from its 49 per cent partnership in ISL, the sport marketing arm of Adidas. Hakuhodo meticulously copied the basic business principles of 'The Olympic Program' (TOP) – involving income from sponsorship, merchandising and the central negotiation of TV rights sales and the lucrative idea of event packaging – which Dentsu had devised for the International Olympic Committee (IOC).

The J.League has been incorporated as an autonomous, non-profit, organization. Income from broadcasting rights, merchandising and sponsorship is distributed to all members, after funds necessary to cover operational expenses have been deducted. Currently there are 28 full members in the J.League Divisions One (J1) and Two (J2, established in 1999). At the outset, in 1993, the J.League chairman, Kawabuchi Saburō, former manager of Furukawa Electric and a retired 'corporate amateur' of its company team, revealed that the original plan was to begin the J.League with just six teams. In his estimation there were only about 100 players in Japan capable of playing at the professional level at the time. This plan also took into account the allowance of three professionals from abroad for each team (as in Japanese professional baseball). Surprisingly 20 applications were submitted, and after a careful selection process, ten teams were participating in the first stage of the 1993 season. From the beginning, the expansion of J.League was planned to occur gradually over ten years, eventually allowing relegation and promotion between the J.League Division One, a Second Division and the semi-professional/amateur Japan Soccer League (JSL, since 1999 renamed as the Japan Football League, JFL). Teams in the JSL that wished to be considered for J.League status not only had to finish in the top two positions, but also had to pass basic stadium requirements, and other criteria, such as potential level of spectator interest and local community support. During the first five seasons (1993–8), however, lack of competition and the franchise system protected J.League teams from relegation.

Various conditions were imposed on clubs applying to join (see Schütte and Ciarlante, 1998: 221ff). For example, each club had to be a registered corporation specializing in football, a stipulation designed to force the management, as well as players and coaches, to be fully professional. Teams were also requested not to have the names of their owner as the team name. J.League football, unlike corporate football and professional baseball, would not be used simply as an advertising tool. This policy was agreed in the face of strong disapproval from potential sponsors, and the dispute was settled with a compromise allowing the sponsor's name to appear, for a maximum of five years, as part of a club's formal name, on match tickets and club clothing. After a year, however, no company name could be found among the colourful, multilingual team names. The previous amateur side Toyo Industrials turned into professional Sanfrecce Hiroshima, Matsushita Electrics became Gamba Osaka and Mitsubishi Heavy Industries changed into the Urawa Red Diamonds. J.League teams were to have a balanced ownership, representing hometowns (or cities) and regional prefectures as well as sponsors. In addition the J.League was seen as a major tool of urban redevelopment and relocation away from the capital and hence a second condition was the cultivation of a hometown environment. Each club was expected to forge strong links with its local community and teams had to promise to contribute to the promotion of football in their region. In exchange, the regions were expected to support the candidate clubs, most clearly by building the infrastructure and other more direct forms of investment. In the next two subsections we provide contrasting case studies of J.League teams that illustrate these objectives in more detail.

The case of Kashima

Another important condition for J.League membership was the regular use of a 15,000 capacity stadium equipped with floodlights. In order to guarantee full capacity crowds on a regular basis, a hometown population size of less than 100,000 was therefore deemed economically inadequate.

The application of Kashima, a small municipality to the northeast of Tokyo with a population of 45,000, to be listed among the J.League teams was initially considered to have little chance of success. However, while the local football club, owned by Sumitomo Steel, had never played in the highest reaches of the company/amateur league, public support was immense and an alliance of local politicians, business representatives and regional football fans succeeded in convincing the J.League of the sincerity of its application.

With a population of less than 50,000, Kashima did not even hold proper town status in Japan. Like so many other towns and villages in the region, Kashima had suffered from the late effects of failed land use planning. Located 150 kilometres from Tokyo and close to the Pacific Ocean, Kashima had been for most of the twentieth century the centre of a quiet rural district. Until the early 1960s, Kashima was home to a population of just 25,000, who basically lived on income generated from agriculture and the fishing industry. In the surge of economic high growth, the greater Kashima area was chosen as a specially designated industrial zone. First Sumitomo Steel moved in, followed by ten component suppliers and other industries. Up to the mid-1970s, more than 170 new companies settled in the area, a commercial harbour was opened, and numerous apartment buildings for the workers were constructed. The town's infrastructure, social services and leisure programmes could hardly keep pace with the rapid growth of the population that almost doubled within a decade. Under such unpromising conditions of limited quality of living and rising real estate prices, Sumitomo Steel, Asahi Glass and other large enterprises faced difficulties in hiring enough workers even during the heyday of heavy industrial output. These problems intensified in the wake of structural change brought about by the oil crisis: neither company workers nor the young generation intended to settle down permanently in Kashima. Being a hometown to a J.League team thus could be seen as a promising strategy to help counter outward migration and bridge the gap between old residents and incomers.

Without the support of the industrial giant Sumitomo, however, Kashima's application would have been turned down without hesitation. Yet effective lobbying dispelled all initial reluctance within Sumitomo headquarters, whose steel branch concomitantly became the chief promoter of the campaign. Sumitomo managers sought support among local bureaucrats and business leaders, and managed to integrate the surrounding municipalities into the bidding campaign. The J.League's main requirement, a roofed stadium with a capacity of 15,000 spectators, or a seat for every third Kashima resident, was built with generous support by the prefectural government of Ibaraki prefecture that covered no less than 80 per cent of construction costs, estimated at ¥10 billion (Kubotani, 1994: 50). In addition, public money granted by local authorities was used for renovating the traffic infrastructure. A 20-year-old dream was realized when a branch railway line connecting Kashima to the Tokyo-Northeast track of the high-speed Shinkansen train was opened. Additionally public money also financed the refashioning of a freight depot into a commuter station, the construction of parking lots and improvements to sanitary and accommodation facilities (Koiwai 1994: 62ff).

Besides Sumitomo Steel and 40 other companies from the region, five small local authorities became major shareholders of the incorporated Kashima Antlers Football Club. Sumitomo Steel, as holder of the largest share, not only compensated the huge deficits of the Antlers due to the high salaries of foreign star players (such as former world footballer of the year, Zico) but also helped to defray costs coming from the construction of the clubhouse and training grounds. As relying on club sponsors was out of step with the J.League's ideals, the sum of close to ¥2 billion was officially declared as advertising expenses for a small, barely visible, logo on the players' uniforms (Ubukata, 1994: 52ff, 113f).

In terms of results on the playing field, all these investments were justified by the Antlers' success in the J.League. In the first year, they won the first stage of the league but were defeated in the final playoff game by the winner of the second stage and traditional football powerhouse Verdy Kawasaki. The remarkable success sparked interest among local residents, and within a few months the official Antlers fan club increased from just three to more than three thousand members. Since then, the former underdog has been transformed into one of the dominating club sides of the J.League. Winning the championship in 2001 provided the fourth title crown of the Kashima Antlers. The previous season they had even accomplished the treble – winning all three domestic competitions. Only Jubilo Iwata, another powerhouse from East Japan and regular contender for the championship, was able to stop Kashima in 2002. The name of Kashima has become famous throughout Japan, and Kashima town has become a model for regional town planning and development in Japan. Numerous imitators have emerged, attempting to emulate the Kashima story. Whether they can be as successful remains to be seen.

The case of Shimizu

While Kashima town first had to discover its love for football, Shimizu City in Shizuoka prefecture had a long and deeply established football tradition. As early as 1956, the elementary schools of Shimizu had held their first annual football tournament. The football fervour of some school instructors and the pupils gradually spread to higher education and to the schools of the surrounding region. Since then, the entire prefecture has acquired a reputation as 'football country'. Some of the teams that repeatedly succeeded in the annual national schools football championship (originated in 1918) came from this region. No other prefectural football association has more members than Shizuoka's, which registers 13 per cent of all football players, and Shizuoka-born athletes appear in almost all of the J.League teams and the national XI. For example, in 1994, 20 out of 42 national team players and 35 out of 402 professional football players in Japan were originally from Shizuoka (Ōnishi, 1994: 10). Shizuoka's disproportionate representation has begun to dwindle in recent years with the consolidation of the J.League and each club having youth development programmes. Aspiring players, therefore, no longer feel the need to move to the football high schools of Shizuoka.

In 1998, nine of the 22 players in the Japanese squad at the World Cup held in France were from Shimizu (Birchall, 2000: 25), the undisputed centre of the 'football' prefecture of Shizuoka. Of the 240,000 residents of Shimizu, 30,000 are members of the prefectural football association. In comparison with Kashima, all of these circumstances arose out of initiatives and interest of local residents and without the financial support of any large enterprise. Thus Shimizu could be sure that the J.League Planning Committee would consider its membership application sympathetically. Shimizu even served as a role model of a local sports club as it matched perfectly all the expectations outlined in the Ministry of Education's basic plan for the promotion of sport.

In Shimizu, local authorities and the local football association spearheaded the promotion campaign. Hinting at the role of sport in media content of the future, and as a guarantor of high viewing rates in the development of satellite television, the local broadcaster Shizuoka TV, a subsidiary of one of the national commercial broadcasters Fuji TV, became a main sponsor of Shimizu's bid to join the league. While the financial power of the Fuji Keiretsu would have helped to secure a professional team, local sentiment discouraged entering into such a one-sided dependency and the bid went ahead without formal ties to Fuji. For the same reasons, plans to form a partnership with Yamaha's company team (later to become Shimizu's closest rivals, Jubilo Iwata) were cancelled before serious talks had begun. A shareholder company was considered to be the most suitable structure for ownership and control of the club, called Shimizu S-Pulse. When the company that owned S-Pulse went public, Shizuoka TV bought the largest single bundle of shares (18 per cent) and Shimizu City another 2.3 per cent. Local authorities and corporations within the prefecture accounted for 56.1 per cent of shares. The remaining 23.6 per cent were taken up by 2,400 individual investors who bought shares with a minimum value of at least ¥100,000. Demand was so strong that the original goal of raising ¥1 billion was surpassed by ¥600 million (Ubukata, 1994: 83).

In contrast to most other clubs who had to give away tickets in huge numbers to their team sponsors, Shimizu S-Pulse clearly benefited from the long-standing popularity of football in the city. Shimizu matches usually sell out and are played in front of paying customers who reserve tickets months ahead. Even before the first season was completed, the fan club had more than 20,000 members. Shimizu S-Pulse was also first in assuring lucrative contracts with kit (uniform) sponsors. For example, Japan Airlines (JAL) concluded a three-year contract for an annual amount of ¥100 million.

As the unofficial capital of high school football, Shimizu was exceptionally well equipped with football fields and training facilities. The Nihondaira Stadium commissioned by Shimizu City for total construction costs of ¥2.3 billion was opened in 1991, yet at first it could only accommodate 13,000 spectators. In order to meet J.League specifications, the extension of the ground was essential. The ¥300 million required for the rebuilding project could only be obtained because central government deferred the refunding of long-term credit the city had taken out in order to cover the original construction expenses (ibid.: 167). Despite its football fanaticism, Shimizu City with its 20,000 seat-stadium, could not be considered as a suitable venue for the World Cup, since further investment was out of the question.

Local government also paid the bill when Kashima was selected as one of the ten venue cities for the 2002 World Cup. In order to meet FIFA requirements, stadium capacity was expanded from 15,870 to 41,800. Yet, for average league games, even the holder of four title crowns is unlikely to attract more than 17,000 spectators on average at home games because of the size of the host community. At away games, the Antlers are welcome guests because of their ability to attract huge crowds. During the first 13 matches of the second stage of the 2003 championship, Kashima played at home in front of an average of 16,856 fans, yet away games were cheered on by 21,064 Kashima-supporting spectators. Even if the Antlers succeed in attracting 25,000 fans to their new FIFA approved stadium, nearly 16,000 seats will remain vacant.

Success and failure

The J.League's successful kick-off relied on careful market research, clever merchandizing – and borrowed money. The J.League Planning Committee was well aware of the necessity of direct sponsorship in the initial stages. In theory, clubs were required to manage their business affairs independently, and transparency of budgets and discipline in spending were requested from all the clubs. While deficits of up to ¥100 million were to be accepted during the first ten years, in order to compensate for negative balances, sponsorship income from external sources was also required. Hence Urawa Reds and Kashima Antlers, for example, each received an annual subsidy of ¥100 million from Mitsubishi and Sumitomo, respectively. Up to 50 per cent of their club income thus came from the teams' main sponsors who disguised their expenses as promotional expenditure (Katō, 1997: 4ff).

In fact, despite the aspirations of the J.League founders, clubs have remained incapable of becoming self-sustaining business operations. Dependence on sponsorship, which appears in the balance sheets (see Table 8.1) in the disguise of advertisement income, has increased over the years. As can be seen from this table, income from merchandizing flourished only in the first three seasons. The marked decline in spectator turnout put club budgets under additional pressure and eventually forced the Japan Football Association to reduce its 3 per cent cut of gate receipts to 1 per cent in 2001. The declining interest might be due in part to the emergence of new leisure markets, but it has also been due to the rapid expansion of the J.League. The transformation into a body of nearly 30 teams, playing in two divisions and a satellite league (JFL) composed of J.League hopefuls, inevitably has had a downgrading effect on average performance on the pitch. In addition teams originally played each other four times a season. When the total number of games was reduced to playing opponents twice in a season, club revenues from ticket sales decreased, as well as indirect income allocated by the J.League. Broadcasters have also lost interest. Compared to the increase in number of games available, overall revenues of the J.League Eizō, the subsidiary in charge of negotiating broadcasting rights after Sony Creative Products pulled out in 1998, have only changed in 2002 in light of heightened interest in soccer inspired by the 2002 World Cup.

With the formation of two divisions in 1999, the system of distributing J.League income from TV rights and commercial ventures to clubs was revised so that each J2 team received a sum equivalent to half that awarded to J1 clubs, plus payment for broadcasting and product

Table 8.1   J.League club team average income distribution (Yen, million)

1993	1994	1995	1996	1997	1998	1999	2000	2001	2002	2003*

Income from:

(Division 1 only – J.1)

Admission fees

| 840 | 1,481 | 1,530 | 886 | 580 | 533 | 456 | 393 | 595 | 570 | 630 |

Advertisement

| 803 | 997 | 1,128 | 1,394 | 1,486 | 1,301 | 1,251 | 1,332 | 1,347 | 1,255 | 1,286** |

Others

| 523 | 659 | 559 | 526 | 487 | 417 | 401 | 414 | 518 | 564 | 417** |

Allocation funds

| 601 | 679 | 475 | 346 | 275 | 237 | 241 | 230 | 267 | 334 | 286 |

Prize money

| 48 | 24 | 36 | 59 | 48 | 43 | 41 | 33 | 48 | 53 | 25 |

Merchandising

| 251 | 253 | 138 | 88 | 32 | 20 | 13 | 7 | 20 | 27 | 18 |

TV rights

| 54 | 172 | 138 | 87 | 134 | 114 | 137 | 103 | 130 | 131 | 118 |

Start money

| 248 | 229 | 183 | 112 | 70 | 60 | 50 | 88 | 70 | 123 | 124 |

Total

| 2,767 | 3,815 | 3,690 | 3,151 | 2,827 | 2,487 | 2,349 | 2,370 | 2,727 | 2,724 | 2,601** |

Av. attendance

| 17,976 | 19,598 | 16,922 | 13,353 | 10,131 | 11,982 | 11,658 | 11,065 | 16,548 | 16,368 | 17,848* |

Home games

| 18 | 22 | 26 | 15 | 16 | 17 | 15 | 15 | 15 | 14 | 14 |

J.League teams

| 10 | 12 | 14 | 16 | 17 | 18 | 16 | 16 | 16 | 16 | 16 |

Note: *first stage, only; **estimates.

Sources: On income distribution from the J.League, *Newsletters*, 56 (August 1999), 64 (November 2000), 73 (June 2001). All other data are from the J.League Yearbook 2002 (Nihon Puro Sakkā Kyōkai, 2001) or from other information distributed by the J.League via the official website (http://www.j-league.or.jp).

royalties. A team relegated to J2 received the same revenue as J1 teams for the first year they were out of the top division. While the J.League officially states that it 'employed a "scarcity value" for televised games by limiting nationwide broadcasts to one game in each time frame in order to prevent overexposure on TV' (cf. J.League homepage), demand noticeably weakened after the initial *sakkā būmu* (football boom). Nationwide broadcasts failed to draw more than 5 to 7 per cent viewing rates in the second half of the 1990s (Okada, 2000). Therefore, by the end of the 1990s, live football matches were largely shown either on local or on regional TV. Broadcasting fees were fixed by J.League Eizō and, in conformity with the J.League policy to popularize football in hometown regions, were not granted simply to the highest bidder but to the broadcaster with the closest affiliation to the home team.

The policy of controlling all broadcasting rights ensures that no team dominates airtime, and no broadcaster dominates the J.League. Yet whether the procedure of a system where nobody loses benefits all is questionable. Cut off from direct broadcasting revenues, clubs remained highly dependent on direct sponsorship. In most cases success on the field, the number of foreign players a team held and popularity measured in terms of live attendances, correlated. The wage bill became the heaviest burden on club accounts. Kashima Antlers, for example, received $5 million from its main sponsor, Sumitomo Metal, for 'advertising' when it was revealed that they would be in deficit to that amount in the first season. Kashima's expenditure on players and other personnel already amounted to half its total expenses (Oga *et al.*, 1996: 150). According to J.League Club Finances 1998, out of 16 teams in Division 1 (J1) nine recorded a loss and five broke even, only because sponsor companies had made payments equivalent to their club's losses. Money supplied to teams by their parent companies in order to cover debts was hidden in commercial and marketing income that provided almost half of all revenues.

The wages bill fell from ¥1.75 billion per team in 1996 to ¥1.2 billion per team in 1999, but this remained more than twice the amount received from gate receipts. A new system of player contracts was established with a salary cap, introducing a limit of only 25 players per club being allowed contracts worth more than ¥4.8 million a year. This coordinated action was partly to avoid any over-expansion of playing staff. In addition, the number of foreign players was reduced from three per side being on the pitch at any one time to three in total per team squad. Consequently the number of foreign players fell, yet the decline in their salaries did not match that of Japanese players whose wage bill on average was three times smaller. Sponsors such as newspaper giant Yomiuri Shinbun started to withdraw from pumping ¥2 billion a year into advertisements as Verdy Kawasaki failed to rise to expectations about their performance. In 1999, Nihon Terebi took over as the main sponsor of Verdy after it acquired the newspaper publisher's 49 per cent stake and the 2 per cent share held by Yomiuri Land, the operators of the amusement park close to the clubhouse of the team. When Verdy moved to Tokyo, the team roster was consequently reduced from 41 to 25 players. In Hiratsuka (Kanagawa prefecture), the Tokyo-based construction company Fujita shed the 69.88 per cent stake it and affiliated companies hold in the J.League soccer team Bellmare Hiratsuka. Since Bellmare was capitalized at ¥800 million when it was registered with the J.League in 1994, Fujita had spent about ¥500 million a year to cover the club's deficits. The former minority owners, including the hometown government, established a new owner company, Shōnan Bellmare Co. Ltd., consisting of Hiratsuka City and more than 320 local companies.

The restrictions on clubs' expenditure came too late to prevent AS Flugels Yokohama from collapsing in 1998. Similar to Fujita, one of the team's main sponsors, the construction company Satō Kōgyō, suffered severely from the recession. When Satō Kōgyō quit and the remaining sponsor All Nippon Airways (ANA) failed to talk any other company into co-sponsoring, Flugels were forced to merge with the other Yokohama-based club, Marinos. Both companies were reported to have been paying ¥1.5 billion annually to cover Flugels' losses (*Nikkei Weekly*, 1998). The merged club, renamed as Yokohama F. Marinos, was 70 per cent owned by Nissan and 30 per cent owned by ANA.

As a result of the business downturn after the attack on the World Trade Center on 11 September 2001, ANA ceded its share in the team to Nissan. In the short run, to keep the name (and the 'F.') ANA agreed to continue to contribute about ¥200 million annually. The closure of Flugels stimulated strong local feelings, especially after a fairy-tale victory in their last game, the JFA (Emperor's) Cup Final in January 1999. English journalist Jonathan Birchall (2000) paints a sympathetic account of the campaign organized by Flugels supporters against the closure decision. Their commitment sparked the emergence of the 'new Flugels', Yokohama F.C., which was initially financed by International Management Group (IMG), the large international sports marketing agency founded by Mark McCormack, Citibank and the German tool company Bosch, and provided the most interesting development to result from the first closure of a J.League team. After a single season with the JFL in 2000, Yokohama F.C. proceeded to the J2 division where it currently seems to have found a regular home. We now turn from the problems of finance in the J.League to stadium expansion and construction for the World Cup.

World Cup soccer stadiums and the Japanese construction state

The costs of staging the Football World Cup, and the potential gains from doing so, have been rising dramatically. The 1966 competition in England realized £2 million, but USA '94 and France '98 made considerably more both for FIFA and for the host countries. It has been estimated that the organizing committee for France '98 made $65 million (¥7.8 billion: Walker, 2001). Tourism surveys suggested that over 10 million people visited France because of the World Cup, spending in excess of £0.5 billion on hotels, travel and food (Chaudhary, 1999). Before the co-hosting decision, although it was anticipated by the Japanese bidding committee that 2002 would cost more than ever, it was hoped that it would also earn more, thus helping the Japanese economy to recover from the recession that began in the late 1980s. After the co-hosting decision, any realistic hopes of such high returns were dashed. According to an estimate of revenue shortfalls released three months after the decision became public, Japan stood to lose as much as ¥50 billion by co-hosting the World Cup 2002. While FIFA requires a minimum of eight venues, South Korea and Japan each provided ten, with most of them built especially for the World Cup. Total construction cost for the ten new and refurbished Japanese stadiums was approximately $2.881 billion, while Korea spent nearly $1.513 billion (see Table 8.2; Nogawa and Mamiya, 2002).

Each of the 15 host city candidates in Japan had contributed ¥235 million to the World Cup bidding campaign. The planned elimination of five cities intensified inter-city competition and readiness to spend on the campaign. Why cities with a great football tradition, such as Hiroshima or Nagoya, were not selected was never made explicitly clear, though insider accounts hint at a centralized decision-making process. Japan was divided into five regional zones, and each zone would receive a fair allocation of venues. In addition, the existing infrastructure and scheduled sports tournaments of the ensuing decade were taken into account. Hiroshima was thus disqualified for three reasons: first, it already possessed a huge football arena, the 'Big Arch', which had been built for the 1994 Asian Championships; second, the high 'brand recognition' value of the city was not considered to need additional international promotion; third, Ōita, which was in the same 'south-west Japan' zone, received the go-ahead instead, largely because it was governed by a former member of the ministerial bureaucracy who used his personal connections to the central administration in Tokyo very effectively to develop roads, railways and industries in the economically underdeveloped region. Nagoya may have been dropped because it was hometown to Grampus Eight and its main sponsor Toyota, rival to Nissan and main sponsor of the Yokohama F. Marinos. Its citizens are also notorious for running citizens' movements against unwanted large-scale public programmes (including the Summer Olympics in the mid-1980s). In the long run, local authorities in Nagoya or Hiroshima might have been

Table 8.2   The economic burden on Japan's 2002 World Cup venues

Awarding authority of construction project	Construction cost (Yen, million)	Capacity crowd	Population (millions)	Burden per capita	Burden per 4-person household
Sapporo City 'Sapporo Dome Hiroba'	42,200	42,300	1.82	¥23,190	¥92,760
Miyagi Prefecture Miyagi Stadium	27,000	49,133	2.36	¥11,440	¥45,760
Niigata Prefecture 'Big Swan'	31,000	42,300	2.48	¥12,500	¥50,000
Ibaraki Prefecture Kashima Soccer Stadium[1]	23,600[2]	41,800	2.99	¥7,890	¥31,568
Saitama Prefecture Saitama Stadium 2002[1]	35,600	63,700	6.98	¥5,100	¥20,400
Yokohama City International Stadium Yokohama	60,000	72,370	3.35	¥17,910	¥71,640
Shizuoka Prefecture 'Ecopa'	30,000	51,349	3.74	¥8,020	¥32,080
Osaka City Nagai Stadium	40,100[2]	50,000	2.61	¥15,360	¥61,440
Kobe City Kobe Wing Stadium	23,100	42,000	1.51	¥15,300	¥61,200
Oita Prefecture 'Big Eye'	25,100	43,000	1.22	¥20,570	¥82,280

[1] Football-only stadium.
[2] Including renovation costs for World Cup purposes.

Sources: Population size at year end 2001 according to prefectural data; construction costs according to *Nihon Keizai Shinbun*, 8 April 2002.

quite happy with the decision, as the Japan Organizing Committee insisted on the successful candidates providing further new investment and abstaining from recouping income generated by renting the stadiums to FIFA (Nogawa and Mamiya, 2002).

Pumping public money into the construction of huge sport stadiums does not find unanimous consent. Sports venues are often utilized by dominant forces to articulate particular memories and 'a' version of the past rather than the plurality of inconsistent and contested meanings. Yet, since the 1998 Winter Olympics in Nagano, which failed to reproduce the atmosphere of the Tokyo Olympics and the mystical experience of national rebirth, negative sentiments against boosterism abound among many of the inhabitants of the debt-ridden prefectures in Japan.

The unfulfilled promises of reviving the economy and reinstalling trust in the future have contributed to widespread pessimism and a dismissive stance against the construction of mega-sites for a single occasion. However the construction sector is at the heart of Japan's political economy, and growth machine ideologists are central actors in political parties, lobbying groups and non-governmental organizations. One prominent representative is the industrialist and real estate tycoon Tsutsumi Yoshiaki, one of the richest men in Japan and official member of many influential sports committees. Under his presidency, the Japan National Olympic Committee was turned into a professionally run sports agency, and it was probably his presidency of the Japan Ski Association that single-handedly drew the Morioka World Cup (in 1994) and the Nagano Winter Olympics (in 1998) to Japan. While the Nagano Olympics were reported to have generated a surplus income of ¥4.5 billion, the profits largely bypassed national taxpayers (Jennings and Sambrook, 2000).

Nogawa and Mamiya (2002) discussed the impact of the 2002 Football World Cup for those cities that constructed new sport facilities with substantial public investment. Heated debates about urban development took place in many of the World Cup venue cities, and also about the prospects for post-tournament usage, since these cities had spent an excessive amount of public money on their stadiums. In this respect the situation in Japan has begun to reflect developments in North America, Western Europe and Australia. Nogawa and Mamiya also drew a rather negative picture of the current state of public facility management in Japan in their analysis of the economics of the World Cup venues. Mid- or long-term regional government bonds (city and prefecture) had provided 70 per cent of funds for the construction of the World Cup stadiums. For example, the construction cost of the Niigata 'Big Swan' Stadium was $250 million and consisted of 82.5 per cent from the prefecture budget and 17.5 per cent from city sources. The construction cost of the Oita Stadium was approximately $210 million and over half ($125 million) of the total funds was collected from general obligation bonds issued by Oita Prefecture. Nogawa and Mamiya argued that many if not all of the World Cup stadiums would leave a negative heritage of the 2002 World Cup. Both the scheduled repayment of loans and interests and maintenance costs of running the facilities after the circus left town would remain as heavy burdens on local taxpayers. The citizens of Kobe, for example, will only see the last interest payments for the Wing Stadium paid back during the 2030s. Operating the prestigious Sapporo Dome, a multifunctional state-of-the-art leisure complex, costs a minimum of ¥2.6 billion per year, and thanks only to a densely scheduled calendar of events, including large-scale cultural spectacles, commercial exhibitions and the only available calendar of professional football and baseball games in Hokkaidō, northern Japan, were balanced books achieved in 2002. In all other cases, sound management systems have not been established. The newly built National Stadium in Yokohama started to look for a name sponsor immediately after the World Cup: so far (early 2004) in vain. The arena of Nagai has also put its owner city into the red. While both Shimizu S-Pulse and Jubilo Iwata – teams that have a home stadium of their own – promised to patronize the new Ecopa Stadium in Shizuoka as regular customers, the nearest J.League team to Miyagi Stadium, Vegalta Sendai, refused to move to the inconveniently located stadium. According to a forecast by the *Yomiuri Shinbun* (5 May 2003), the 'lack of accountability', that Hirose (2002) attributes to local politicians when it comes to public spending on regional construction projects, was predicted to accumulate to ¥2.5 billion in 2003, only slightly less than the ¥2.8 billion recorded in 2002.

Notwithstanding these widespread concerns, a new variation of the 'bidding war' emerged in 2001. More than 80 localities applied to be nominated as the official training camp for a national team participating in the World Cup. Some of the more eager municipalities were ready to bear a team's whole expense, including accommodation and travel costs, during their stay in Japan. For example, the city of Tottori negotiated with the federation of Ecuador, which requested guarantees amounting to ¥100 million. The Nigerian federation commissioned an agent to bargain with two localities in Yamanashi prefecture. According to sources close to the municipalities, the agent demanded as much as ¥100 million, including accommodation expense and a ¥20 million bonus for himself. Other municipalities already convinced their assemblies to allocate parts of the budget for the purpose of hosting a foreign team. Izumo (Shimane prefecture) was ready to pay ¥60 million in order to host the Irish, Matsumoto (Nagano prefecture) and Kuriyama (Hokkaidō) each invested ¥80 million for the guest athletes and their staff from Paraguay and Mexico (*Asahi Shinbun*, 22 December 2001). Whether the high expectations of paybacks reaching up to ¥800 or 900 million were justified is unclear as the actual impact on the local economy turned out less impressive. The Systems Research and Development Institute of Japan, based in Tokyo's Shinjuku Ward, sent a questionnaire to 43 former host municipalities in France. The survey revealed that, during the last World Cup, hardly any municipality paid money to lure a team. The heated competition among Japanese municipalities raised the price of hosting national teams, and at the same time it documented the undiminished attractiveness of the growth machine that is football.

Despite the almost unanimous conclusion of numerous studies that public investment in sports facilities yields only minimal economic benefits, officials continue to push for new facilities, and public money continues to be spent on them (Crompton, 2001). In many cases these projects are trumpeted as successful not because of any objective assessment about their benefits to local residents, but because of the symbolic power of the edifices themselves (Schimmel, 2001). In considering the situation in Japan, it is also very important to recognize the extent to which construction and civil engineering have long underpinned its political economy. McCormack (1996, 2002) refers to this as Japan's *doken kokku*, or 'construction state'. This can best be understood as an equivalent to the phrase 'military–industrial complex' applied to the USA since the 1950s. It focuses attention on the construction industry and public works as Japan's major industry and the close links between construction, the bureaucracy and government. In 1993, for example, 43 per cent of national investment went into construction and Japan outspent the USA on construction by a ratio of 2.6 : 1 (McCormack, 1996: 33).

Following the administration reforms carried out in 2000, the Ministry of Construction merged with the former Ministry of Transport and other planning agencies to form the National Land and Transport Ministry. It is currently responsible for 80 per cent of tax money available for public works. Japan's public works programme is three times the size of that in Britain, the USA or Germany. It currently employs 7 million people, or 10 per cent of the Japanese workforce, spending ¥40–50 trillion ($350 million) per year. This amounts to 8 per cent of Japanese GDP. The result is that Japan has more dams and roads per unit of land than the continental USA. Half the Japanese coastline and most of its rivers are wrapped in concrete. Some 90 per cent of its total wetlands have been drained and lost, and its biodiversity is threatened. McCormack argues that the centrality of construction and public works in Japan's economy is the product of the operation of an 'Iron Triangle' of construction industry chiefs, senior bureaucrats and politicians. Rather than providing a Keynesian kick-start to a troubled economy, however, many construction projects, including the World Cup

Table 8.3   **The impact of the World Cup on spectator turnout at**
           J.League matches

Name of stadium	Estimated annual income (Yen, million)	Estimated annual balance (Yen, million)	Capacity crowd	Home or would-be home team	Av. home attendance prior to World Cup 2002[2]	Av. home attendance after World Cup 2002[2]
Sapporo Dome 'Hiroba'	2,300	100	42,300	Consadole Sapporo	10,520	23,980
Miyagi Stadium	30	−340	49,133	Vegalta Sendai	22,230	19,390
Ibaraki Prefect'l Kashima Soccer Stadium	270	break even	41,800	Kashima Antlers	25,490	24,610
Niigata Stadium 'Big Swan'	no estimate	no estimate	42,300	Albirex Niigata[1]	18,480	28,890
Saitama Stadium 2002	300	−400	63,700	Urawa Red Diamonds	26,040	28,090
Internat'l Stadium Yokohama	435	−600	72,370	Yokohama F Marinos	33,230	26,560
Shizuoka Stadium 'Ecopa'	no estimate	deficit	51,349	Shimizu S-pulse	14,300	14,920
Nagai Stadium	79	−620	50,000	Cerezo Osaka[1]	4,850	8,780
Kobe Wing Stadium	250	deficit	42,000	Vissel Kobe	13,245	9,270
Oita Stadium 'Big Eye'	50	−250	43,000	Oita Trinita[1]	6,870	14,610

[1] J.League Division 2 (J2) in 2002: 8 home matches before and 10 after the World Cup.
[2] J1 only first stage matches: after 7 matches the leg was stopped (March 2 to April 21) and resumed for the remaining 8 encounters (July 13 to August 17).

Sources: Averages are own calculations; crowd numbers according to official J.League homepage (http://www.j-league.or.jp), financial balance sheet numbers according to Nogawa and Mamiya (2002).

stadiums, may have 'served as steroids, bloating rather than strengthening the economy' (McCormack, 2002: 11–14). See Table 8.3.

Conclusion

The latest Monbukagakushō Basic Plan for the Promotion of Sports published in 2000 reflects a quite familiar approach to sports policy taken by the Japanese government in the midst of the long 'Heisei recession'. Its preamble states in familiar terms that

> the promotion of sport also produces economic spin-off effects in that it helps expand the sports industry and thereby create employment opportunities. Sport thus contributes to the economic development of our country and is apt to make a major contribution to the

maintenance and enhancement of national health both in mind and [in] body. In this sense, it has the potential of saving medical costs. Sport is thus a contributory element to the national economy.

Yet neither in the chapter on the role of the national government nor in the section dealing with local authorities does the Basic Plan indicate the government's intention to invest new money in sport facilities and sport programmes. Instead it suggests that the future lies with private funding initiatives (PFI) – opportunities that have been largely expanded since the passing of the Private Finance Initiative Law in July 1999, allowing new forms of cooperation between public and private enterprises – and the 'creative usage of all spaces deemed to be suitable for sport or recreation activities'.

The Basic Plan puts forward targets for localities and regions to achieve by 2010:

Creating at least one Comprehensive Community Sports Club in each municipality (city, town, village) nationwide;

Creating at least one Sports Center Covering a Wide Area in each prefecture nationwide.

...

In the future, the ultimate goal will be to establish comprehensive community sports clubs in local communities at the level of the junior high school catchment district and to build sports centers covering a wide area in communities at the municipal (cities, towns and villages) level.

The expansion of professional association football in Japan in the 1990s and the co-hosting of the FIFA World Cup Finals in 2002 were expected to deliver many non-sporting benefits. Some J.League clubs may be able to assist in reaching the Basic Plan targets, as they are already developing into multi-sport clubs (see Kinohara, 2002). Particularly in terms of ownership, the joint efforts of local authorities, citizens and companies from the region of the football teams seem to provide a promising new model of sport business which is in marked contrast to traditional Japanese arrangements or modern business models prevalent in the USA or in Europe.

However, there still are a number of grounds for concern about the development of the football infrastructure in Japan. Firstly, the J.League and the World Cup have not been really successful in terms of achieving regional balance. While the number of football pitches and high-quality facilities has increased considerably over the past decade, the overall concerns about unipolarity and hyperconcentration in the Japanese economy have not been mitigated. Despite J.League conditions governing team location, most of the teams that have prospered since 1993 have been located in the large population centres stretching out from Chiba Prefecture in the east to Hiroshima in the west. The most successful clubs – in 2002 as well as in 2003, 14 out of 16 J1 teams – all came from the densely populated Kantō and Kansai area. The former reservations against permitting a Tokyo-based team were overthrown when Tokyo finally opened its own purpose-built football stadium. The stadium in Tobitakyū in western Tokyo was a joint project of Tokyo Metropolitan Government and the private sector. Managed by a private company, its naming rights were sold to a major food production company. The total cost of construction was estimated at 34 billion yen, of which 24 billion yen had to be borrowed (*Asahi Shinbun*, 1 October 1997). Since 2001, two J1 teams (the renamed Tokyo Verdy and F.C. Tokyo, the former corporate athletes of Tokyo Gas) even share the Ajinomoto stadium in the capital.

Secondly, concerns about the usage of the large stadiums built for the World Cup continue to be voiced (Watts, 2001; Hirose, 2002, *Yomiuru Shinbun*, 5.5.2003). Some provide venues for J.League teams, but the capacity will rarely, if ever, be reached for regular league matches. Local residents in many cases will be saddled with large tax burdens to cover annual maintenance costs (as happened in Nagano after the 1998 Winter Olympics were staged there – see Jennings and Sambrook, 2000). Thirdly, the overall concern with the mega-event and professional football threatens to distort the financial basis of community sports. The primary objective of starting a Japanese football lottery (*toto*), which was formally introduced in March 2001 after long disputes about the moral effects of public gambling, was to help local sport organizations and community sport clubs to operate, not for the 2002 World Cup and football stadiums. But the Japanese Organizing Committee (JAWOC) received a massive allocation of the *toto* for its operations in 2002. A number of non-hometown municipalities and sports associations strongly opposed what they considered to be illegitimate allocations of lottery-generated funds, particularly because financial resources for sports promotion and corporate sponsorships have become so limited in the last ten years.

However, as soon as the World Cup closing ceremony was over in June 2002, and shortly before dissolving, JAWOC officials hastily indicated that hosting the finals was very likely to end in an economic 'draw' (*Hōchi Shinbun*, 4 July 2002). When the books were closed, the Japan Football Association (JFA) could even present a surplus of approximately

¥6 billion in its interim report (*Nihon Keizai Shinbun*, 9 September 2002). It was speculated that the actual surplus was even considerably higher, amounting to ¥12 billion (*Sankei Shinbun*, June 2003). JAWOC officials were possibly ashamed to confess that they had unnecessarily squeezed money out of public and private corporations to secure the national project. They were probably also reluctant to back down on the demands of the National Agency for the Advancement of Sports and Health, the government agency in charge of managing the *toto* funds, to pay back certain parts of the grants.

Thus the future of community sports for all and the fate of professional football in Japan are invisibly linked. While community sports continue to struggle with the scarcity of facilities, staff and funds, the political economy of football is arguably suffering from the rapid expansion of the J.League. Within a decade, more than 30 professional teams have been established, dozens of large stadiums erected and hundreds of players, coaches and staff put under contract. As the economic decline forces private corporations to withdraw from sponsoring, public corporations jump in to fill the gap. Yet the companies owning the teams are still in the red, and it is an open question whether the same corporations will ever be able to pay back society by establishing 'such an environment in which anyone could enjoy sports appropriate to their age, physical condition ability and objectives'. So far this long-term goal, as quoted from the J.League's 'The Mission', has hardly been achieved. In the original Japanese, 'The Mission' is rendered as 'The Centennial Plan'. To us, such a long-term vision is more than justified when challenging the 'Iron Triangle' of politics, administration and business that guided Japan through the years of reconstruction and high economic growth. To use another sporting metaphor, this alliance is still playing on centre court, while those in civil society watch from their comfortable seats in the grandstand. Yet, with the Japanese economy in the doldrums, the seats become less and less comfortable, and the number of voices asking for the replacement of players, is increasing. As long as the 'Iron Triangle' continues to steer Japan's economy, however, the J.League will face trouble realizing 'its long term vision of making sport an integral part of the culture and lifestyle of the Japanese people'.

References

Baade, R.A. (1996), 'Professional sports as catalysts for metropolitan economic development', *Journal of Urban Affairs*, **18** (1), 1–17.
Baade, R.A. and R.F. Dye (1990), 'The impact of stadiums and professional sports on metropolitan area development', *Growth and Change*, Spring, 1–14.
Birchall, J. (2000), *Ultra Nippon*, London: Headline Books.

Chapin, T.S. (1996), 'A new era of professional sports in the Northwest: facility location as an economic development strategy in Seattle, Portland, and Vancouver'. Paper presented at the Sport in the City Conference, Memphis, Tennessee, November.

Chaudhary, V. (1999), 'Golden goals', *The Guardian*, 22 October, p.23.

Crompton, J. (2001), 'Public subsidies to professional team sport facilities in the USA', in C. Gratton and I. Henry (eds), *Sport in the city*, London: Routledge, pp.15–34.

Funck, C. (1999), 'When the bubble burst: planning and reality in Japan's resort industry', *Current Issues in Tourism*, 2 (4), 333–53.

Gratton, C. and I. Henry (eds) (2001), *Sport in the city*, London: Routledge.

Harada, Munehiko (2002), *Supōtsu ibento no keizaigaku. Mega ibento to ōmu chiimu ga toshi o kangaeru* [The economics of sport events. Mega events and home teams change the city], Tokyo: Heibonsha (= Heibonsha shinsho), 145.

Hirose, I. (2002), 'Dare ga Wārudokappu no 'higaisha' datta no ka' [Who was the victim of the World Cup?], in Asano Tomoaki and Harada Hiroshi (eds), *Shūshi kessan Wārudokappu. Kaisai shite hajimete wakatte iru kane, seiji, fukumaden*, Tokyo: Takarajima Sha, pp.185–7.

Horne, J. (1996), '*Sakka* in Japan', *Media, Culture and Society*, 18 (4), 527–47.

Horne, J. (1999), 'Soccer in Japan: Is *wa* all you need?', *Culture, Sport, Society*, 2 (3), 212–29.

Horne, J. (2001), 'Professional football in Japan', in J. Hendry and M. Raveri (eds), *Japan at play*, London: Routledge, pp.199–213.

Horne, J. and W. Manzenreiter (eds) (2002), *Japan, Korea and the 2002 World Cup*, London: Routledge.

Horne, J. and W. Manzenreiter (2004), 'Accounting for mega-events: forecast and actual impacts of the 2002 Football World Cup Finals on the host countries Japan and Korea', *International Review for the Sociology of Sport*, 39 (2), 123–37.

Ikeda, M., Y. Yasuo and C. Makoto (2001), *Sport for All in Japan*, Tokyo: Sasakawa Sports Foundation.

Jennings, A. and C. Sambrook (2000), *The great Olympic swindle*, London: Simon & Schuster.

Katō, H. (1997), 'J.Riigu to mesena, firansoropii' [The J.League, sponsorship, philanthropy], *Waseda Daigaku Taiikugaku Kenkyū Kiyō*, 29.

Kinohara, K. (2002), 'Bellmare looking at more than just soccer', *The Japan Times*, 29 January, p.21.

Kishino, Y. and T. Kyūzō (1959), *Nihon kindai gakkō taiikushi* [History of modern school sports in Japan], Tokyo: Tōyōkan.

Koiwai, Z. (1994), 'Sokkā ni yoru machizukuri' [Urban development by football], *Toshi Mondai*, 85 (12), 59–69.

Kubotani, O. (1994), 'Supōtsu shinkō ni yoru kiban seibi. Genjō to kadai' [Maintaining the basis through sports promotion], *Toshi Mondai*, 85 (12), 43–57.

Manzenreiter, W. (2002), 'Japan und der Fußball im Zeitalter der technischen Reproduzierbarkeit: Die J.League zwischen Lokalpolitik und Globalkultur' [Japan and football in the age of technical reproduction: The J.League between local politics and global culture], in Michael Fanizadeh, Gerald Hödl and Wolfram Manzenreiter (eds), *Global Players. Kultur, Ökonomie und Politik des Fußballs*, Frankfurt/Vienna: Brandes and Apsel/Südwind, pp.133–58.

Manzenreiter, W. (2003), 'Wenn der Zirkus die Stadt verlassen hat: Ein Nachspiel zur politischen Ökonomie der Fußball-WM 2002 in Japan' [After the circus left the town. Aftermath of the political economy of the 2002 World Cup in Japan], *Japan Politik und Wirtschaft 2002/03*.

Manzenreiter, W. and J. Horne (eds) (2004), *Football goes east: business, culture and the 'people's game' in China, Japan and Korea*, London: Routledge.

McCormack, G. (1996), *The emptiness of Japanese affluence*, Armonk, NY: M.E.Sharpe.

McCormack, G. (2002), 'Breaking the iron triangle', *New Left Review*, Second Series, **13**, 5–23.

MEXT/Ministry of Education, Culture, Sports, Science and Technology (2000), Supōtsu shinkō kihon keikaku nitsuite [Basic plan for the promotion of sports]. Retreived 18 Feb 2002 from the World Wide Web: http://www.mext.go.jp/b_menu/houdou/12/09/000905.htm

Nagazumi, J. (1999), 'Kōkyō supōtsu shisetsu no manejimento' [Management of public sport facilities], in H. Munehiko (ed.), *Supōtsu sangyōron nyūmon*, Tokyo: Keirin Shoin, pp.157–73.

Nakayama, M. (2000), *Chiiki no supōtsu to seisaku* [Regional sport and policy measures], Okayama: Daigaku Kyōiku Shuppan.

Nogawa, H. and T. Mamiya (2002), 'Building mega-events: critical reflections on the 2002 Infrastructure', in J. Horne and W. Manzenreiter (eds), *Japan, Korea and the 2002 World Cup*, London: Routledge, pp.177–94.

Nunn, S. and M. Rosentraub (1995), *Sports wars: suburbs and center cities in a zero sum game*, Indianapolis: Center for Urban Policy and the Environment, Indiana University.

Oga, J., K. Kazuhiko and S. Masanobu (1996), 'Influence of J-League on local community', in European Association for Sport Management (eds), *Third European Congress on Sport Management Official Proceedings*, Budapest: European Association for Sport Management/Hungarian University of Physical Education, pp.147–54.

Okada, T. (2000), '*J.riigu no mesasu atarashii supōtsu bunka sōzō. Kigyō kara shimin e. Urawa rezzu no rei o chūshin ni*' [The creation of the new sport culture the J-League is aiming for], class paper prepared for the Industrial Management course at the Faculty of Economics, Meiji University.

Ōnishi, T. (1994), 'Supōtsu to chiiki kasseika' [Sports and regional revitalisation], *Toshi Mondai*, **85** (12), 3–14.

Roche, M. (2000), *Mega-events and modernity*, London: Routledge.

Rosentraub, M. (1996), 'Does the emperor have new clothes? A reply to Robert A. Baade', *Journal of Urban Affairs*, **18** (1), 23–31.

Satō, M. (1990), *Rizōto rettō* [Resort archipelago], Tokyo: Iwanami Shoten.

Schimmel, K. (2001), 'Sport matters: urban regime theory and urban regeneration in the late-capitalist era', in C. Gratton and I. Henry (eds), *Sport in the city*, London: Routledge, pp.259–77.

Schütte, H. and D. Ciarlante (1998), *Consumer behaviour in Asia*, New York: New York University Press.

Seki, H. (1997), *Sengo Nihon no supōtsu seisaku. Sono kōzō to tenkai* [Sport policy in post war Japan], Tokyo: Taishūkan Shoten.

SSF (Sasagawa Sport Foundation), S. Zaidan (ed.) (1997), *Supōtsu hakusho. 2001 nen no supōtsu foa ōru ni mukete* [Sports white book. Towards 'Sports for all' in 2001], Tokyo: SSF Sasagawa Supōtsu Zaidan.

Sugimoto, A. (1995), *Supōtsu bunka no henyō. Tayōka to kakuichika no bunka chitsujo* [Changes of sports culture], Kyoto: Sekai Shisōsha.

Tamaki, M. (2001), *Nihonjin to supōtsu*, Tokyo: NHK Shuppan.

Ubukata, Y. (1994), *J.Riigu no keizaigaku* [The economics of the J.League], Tokyo: Asahi Shinbun Sha.

Walker, J. (2001), 'Ex-organizer predicts long-term gain for Japan', *Asahi Shimbun*, 30 November 2001, retrieved 30 November 2001 from the World Wide Web: http://www.asahi.com/english/sports/K2001113000534.html.

Watts, J. (2001), 'The grand folly', *Scotland on Sunday*, 25 November 2001.

9
The 'Green' Games Sydney 2000 Played

Gordon Waitt

Introduction

According to the Olympic Charter, increased understandings of cooperation, solidarity, tolerance and environmental sustainability are all social outcomes of hosting an Olympic Games. This chapter explores one of these claims, environmental sustainability, in the context of Sydney 2000's 'green' games. See Waitt (2003) for a discussion of social affects. The Olympic Charter's apolitical social movement claims are juxtaposed in this chapter by examining the games as urban spectacle. The games become a political mechanism to revitalize deindustrialized localities along the lines of consumption activities, such as those offered by sporting, culture and entertainment activities (Harvey, 1989a). As urban spectacle, the Olympics provide an important instrument by which a city is argued to differentiate itself within an increasingly global world economy, thus securing overseas investments and tourists (Ashworth and Voogd, 1990; Hambleton, 1991; Whitson and Macintosh, 1993; Loftman and Nevin, 1996). Designing, marketing and constructing Olympic venues within a globalized economy is demonstrated to call upon establishing an elite urban development authority informed by entrepreneurial urban planning polices of the New Right (Harvey 1989b). Sydney's 'green' games is thus explored as an example *par excellence* of a hallmark event in the context of economic globalization, deindustrialization, commercialization of sport, the global shift to the service sector and entrepreneurial planning processes. In this context I argue that emphasis is given to image over substance and budgets over social welfare. My evaluation of the 'green' games is firmly situated within both the attributes of the Sydney Olympic site, Homebush, and the site's political economy, explaining conflicting appraisals of the site in terms of different ideologies and power relations between actors (individual or collective). In doing this I help challenge the commonly held view that the relationship between Australian sport and the state is neutral. Sport is portrayed by the state as simply a 'good thing' (Dempster, 1985: 121). In helping to destroy this myth that Australian sport is unspoiled and untainted by any political ideology, I reveal different interpretations of Sydney's 'green' games. Furthermore I question the assumption that the Olympics are an appropriate forum for the modelling of environmental sustainable development (ESD). The Olympic Charter spins a pretence that the Olympics is a social movement, yet, in short, it is a commercial sporting spectacle.

Competing to host an Olympic Games

Economic globalization is argued by some poststructuralist geographers to have generated a situation where the material and symbolic characteristics of place have never been more important (Cox, 1997). Potential investors have access to information about more places than ever before and differentiate between investment locations on the basis of local attributes: the quality of the local environment, telecommunications network, transport infrastructure, regulatory regimes, and lifestyle and attributes of the labour force. Localities therefore attempt to create a combination of investment conditions to attract entrepreneurs, a competitive process that has begged the question of whether localities are participating in a 'race to the bottom' or a 'race to the top' (Porter, 1991; Clarke, 1993; Waitt, 1997). Place marketing and its essentialist language of 'biggest', 'safest', 'cheapest', 'most deregulated', 'most pristine environment' and 'most profitable location' is an integral part of every locality's quest to secure investment. Perceptions of differences between cities are becoming virtually indistinguishable (Holcomb, 1994). Augé (1995) termed this marketing tendency towards the loss of local variety '*non-lieux*' (non-places). Ironically, as global competition brings a new emphasis to the geographical differences between places, the universal language of place marketers replaces distinctive attributes with stereotypes and superficial gloss. I argue that Sydney's bid, as a place-marketing exercise, generated a 'green' symbolic landscape far removed in space and time from the material substance of Homebush.

Olympic city marketers prioritized the imagined 'green' symbolic landscape over the material landscape, I argue, because of the intensified 'place wars' between vying host cities. The stature of hosting an Olympics arguably provides a higher city profile in world markets, enhancing the city's promotional curricula vitae compared to their rivals' (Ward and Gold, 1994). Furthermore, since 1984, the profits generated by marketing broadcasting rights ensured the IOC would never again have to partially fund the Games, as when Los Angeles was the only candidate. Through marketing the Olympic symbol and selling worldwide television rights, the IOC became in reality a multinational corporation, franchising and subcontracting the operation of the games to organizing committees in host cities. For the 2000 Games, Sydney was positioned in contention with Beijing, Berlin, Istanbul, Manchester and Milan. 'Victory' not only attracts the spending of large international audiences, but is also believed to help foster positive images for potential corporate investors (Bonnemaison, 1990). Victors in sport, whether the competitors are nations, cities, teams or individuals, always make claims about their superior performance (Bale and Sang, 1996). Indeed, in 1993, Australian Prime Minister Paul Keating said Sydney's victory would put Australia 'in the swim with the big boys' (*Australian*, 1993).

Placing an Olympics in Sydney: Homebush, deindustrialization and brown sites

Sydney's economic and industrial base was restructured following the economic crisis of the 1970s and 1980s that resulted in the closure or 'downsizing' of manufacturing activities in older industrial regions and cities everywhere. Brown sites marked the location of Sydney's former industrial activity. Taking a lead from the global shift towards the service economy, property developers promoted Sydney's former industrial area as business (Australia Centre, Homebush) or 'high-tech' industrial parks (Redfern Technology Park, Redfern). Simultaneously the New South Wales (NSW) state government refashioned the city to facilitate consumption activities associated with the culture economy, particularly tourism (Craik, 1991). Place marketing reinvented places to attract tourist dollars by offering one or more tourist experiences: shopping, heritage, relaxation, entertainment, fine dining, accommodation (see Hall, 1995, for a list of urban redevelopment projects in Australian cities). In 1985, the first urban redevelopment programme specifically designed to generate a planned tourist landscape occurred in Sydney, with the establishment of the Darling Harbour Authority (Huxley, 1991). In 1990, the 760-hectare Olympic site at Homebush Bay became the focus for a NSW government urban redevelopment programme. The objective was to transform the physical and symbolic attributes of this locality from a domestic dump and abandoned industrial site into an environmental award-winning locality, sustained by emerging culture economies. This new economic base required massive state infrastructure investment in sports stadiums, showgrounds, transport facilities and parklands.

In 1990, the site had already been identified as the only available location in Sydney that could be used for constructing new showgrounds for the Royal Agricultural Show and sporting venues required for an Olympics. This decision was based upon four key factors. First, the land was mostly government-owned. Second, Brown sites were located at Rhodes Peninsula from the abandoned chemical factories of Union Carbide, ICI and Berger Paints. Third, redundant space also appeared from the closure of the remaining noxious industries, deliberately located on what was Sydney's urban periphery in the early twentieth century: the NSW State Abattoir (1907–88) and the NSW State Brickworks (1911–88), which included a quarry for clay and shale. The Royal Navy Armament Depot (RANAD Newington) was also relocated. Finally, the Olympics provided an opportunity to provide a public legacy of remediated land, housing, parkland and Olympic sports facilities in Sydney's socially disadvantaged west. The NSW Property Service Group, the agency then responsible for managing state government lands, adopted a business master plan prepared for the site by design and architect company Keys Young (Young, 1992). The master plan contained two options, an 'Olympic Mode' and a 'No Olympic Mode'. However, before construction could begin on either 'mode', a land remediation strategy had to be decided and implemented. The site (Figure 9.1) has not only an industrial legacy associated with heavy metals, waste oil products, asbestos and dioxins (from the former Union Carbide factory) but also a history of unregulated waste disposal. Since the mid-1960s, fill was a mixed composition of domestic, commercial and industrial waste. At the former ELCOM site contaminants from predominantly power station ash included lead, zinc, copper, cadmium, chromium, polycyclic aromatic hydrocarbons, petroleum hydrocarbons and organochlorine pesticide residues. Newington's East and North Landfills also contained heavy metals, asbestos, ammonia and monocyclic and polycyclic aromatic hydrocarbons. On the south bank of Haslam Creek, fill created an 18 metre-high dump at Kronos Hill, from unregulated disposal. Contaminants at this site were found to include heavy metals, asbestos and dioxins. The highest levels – the dioxin (2378 TCDD), allegedly dumped by Union Carbide – appear at the Gold Driving Range. The total volume of landfill is estimated at approximately 9 million cubic metres, covering about one-third of the Homebush site to a depth between 0.5 and 4 metres. Homebush had to be materially and symbolically reinvented from a brown site of noxious

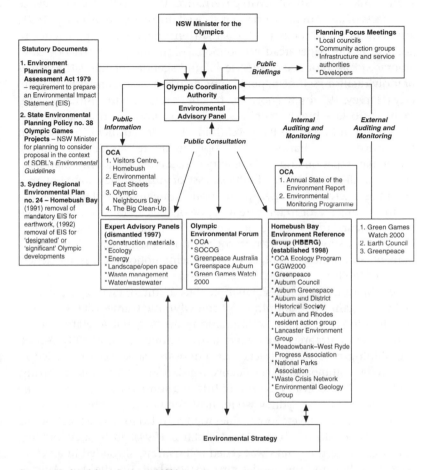

Source: Updated from James (1997b).

Figure 9.1 Siting of the Olympic Games

industries and dump to a new, clean, 'green' economic base sustained by consumptive practices of culture economies, primarily sport.

Acts of governance: transforming a brown toxic site to a 'green' showcase

The reinventing and redevelopment of cities within the broader process of economic globalization has called upon a more entrepreneurial rather than managerial form of urban governance. In Australia, the emergence of aspects of an entrepreneurial state is well documented by Pusey (1991) and Winter and Brooks (1993). Urban entrepreneurial approaches to addressing the widespread economic erosion and fiscal crisis of cities embrace ideas informed by the 'New Right' agenda, including the virtues of individualism, self-help, public–private partnerships and private property (Harvey, 1989b). In short, the task of entrepreneurial urban government is 'to lure highly mobile and flexible production, financial and consumption flows into its space' (ibid.: 11). Government intervention is regarded as a hindrance to redevelopment, as are planning regulations, public participation and social equity considerations. Rather than policies of welfare provision, the 'business' of urban redevelopment programmes increasingly uses promotion strategies and tactics of the profit-making sector to increase its share of the capital investment from entrepreneurs, tourists or local consumers (Roche, 1994). Indeed this is hardly surprising, given direct participation of private capital in redevelopment 'authorities', and objectives embracing notions of 'cost-efficiency' and profitability.

The bidding by Sydney Olympic Bid Limited (SOBL), design by Sydney Organising Committee for the Olympic Games (SOCOG), and coordination by Olympic Co-ordination Authority (OCA) epitomize the non-elected entrepreneurial governance. Public accountability regarding bidding process, contracts and proposals was effectively veiled in secrecy by commercial-in-confidence legislation. As a private company, SOBL was cleared from Freedom of Information requests. Following the announcement that Sydney would host the Olympics, the Freedom of Information Act for New South Wales was amended to ensure that SOCOG documents could not be retrieved (Totaro, 1994). In Sydney, bidding and organizing the games was ceded to business, shrouded in a veil of secrecy, following the model first established by the Los Angeles Olympic Organizing Committee.

SOBL's 'green' bid

The SOBL's 'green' promises were integral to differentiating Sydney's bid from its competitors'. Sydney followed the lead of the Lillihamer 1994 Winter Olympics in Norway. Since 1993 the IOC had declared that bidding cities must assess the environmental impact of proposals (IOC, 1993). The SOBL outlined specific details in the *Environmental Guidelines* (SOCOG, 1995). This publication espoused the concept of ecologically sustainable development, first advocated by the Bruntland Report (1987) and again sanctioned by the Earth Summit (1993). In short, ESD is development that improves the total quality of life both now and in the future in a way that maintains the ecological processes on which life depends.

SOBL's 'green' promise incorporated two main aspects. The first was to remediate the degraded Homebush Bay environment; testimonies to its noxious industrial past combined with decades of landfilling and waste dumping. The second was to construct facilities and conduct the remediation process by incorporating ESD commitments to five areas: (1) energy conservation; (2) water conservation; (3) waste avoidance and minimization; (4) improving air, water and soil quality; and (5) protecting significant natural and cultural environments. Through incorporating ESD principles the bid claimed it made a contribution to international issues of global warming, ozone depletion, biodiversity, pollution and resource depletion. SOBL's objective was to 'make Sydney's Olympic plan a prime example of ecologically sustainable development in the 21st century' (SOBL, 1993a). The Federal Minister for Environment, Sport and Territories, Ross Kelly (1993), confirmed this, suggesting that a vote for Sydney would be a vote for the environment, while the NSW minister responsible for the Olympic bid, Bruce Baird, claimed that Sydney's Olympics would be an environmental showpiece, a model for other cities to follow (SOBL, 1992).

Credibility of these environmental claims was achieved through appealing for endorsement to international environmental authorities and celebrities. Greenpeace Australia's cities and coast campaigner Karla Bell (1993) made a representation to the IOC supporting the environmental merits of the Sydney bid. Film stars Nicole Kidman and Tom Cruise were enlisted to voice their support for the environmental organization ARK's endorsement of the bid. In both these statements no mention was made of the contamination. The unlikely allegiance between Greenpeace, ARK and the SOBC not only gave credibility to the 'green' promise but also helped prevent any public concerns over the potential environmental implications of the proposal, given the site's toxic history. For Greenpeace, the organization could reposition itself as preventing environmental problems rather than generating awareness of their existence. Ironically other local environmental groups (including the Australian Conservation Council, the New South Wales Nature Conservation Council and the Total Environment Centre [TEC]) distanced themselves from the bid's claims (Cook, 1993). The director of the TEC, Jeff Angel (1993a), argued that Sydney's environment had been misrepresented, lamented the potential loss of local ecosystems and claimed that

Sydney had a waste crisis. These groups forced SOBL to retract a statement that expressed their support.

It is not certain how much this component swayed the IOC or the delegates who voted on the venue. In 1999, the exposed corruption of the bidding process through lobbying IOC delegates suggested that the intense competition had also resulted in a series of unofficial 'rules' breeches. Previously Jennings and Simpson (1992) had alleged that 'gifts' of this lobbying process stooped to the lowest ethical base. Apparently the only constraints on lobbyists were their consciences and scruples. Those involved in Sydney's campaign repeatedly claimed a 'clean' bid despite confirmations of paid holidays, jobs and training for IOC members and payments towards the 1993 world youth soccer tournament (Burroughs, 1999). Nevertheless Frank Sator, Sydney's Lord Mayor, did concede when reflecting upon the bidding process that 'we prostituted ourselves to try to get one more vote for Sydney' (Bowers, 1993). However the concept of an environmentally friendly games resonated well with IOC President Juan Antonio Samaranch, who had commented that environmental considerations were a criterion for evaluating candidate cities (North, 1992). In 1993, an IOC report specifically praised Sydney for its emphasis on environmental protection and working with Greenpeace. However, in securing second preferences (transfer votes) in the final ballot, it was the flow of eight of 11 votes from eliminated Manchester to Sydney in the deciding round that secured Sydney's position above Beijing; both Manchester and Sydney had employed the 'Athletes Games' theme.

The Olympic Co-ordination Authority Act: incorporating 'green' promises into legislation

Following the award of Sydney's right to host the 2000 Olympics, the Olympic Co-ordination Authority (OCA) was established on 30 June 1995 to plan and provide Olympic venues and facilities. The OCA had an initial budget of approximately A$2 billion (US$1.4 billion), of which 25 per cent was destined for environmental issues. Comprising four major Divisions, one of which was Environment, Planning and Estate Management, the OCA was obliged to take into account the *Environmental Guidelines* to the fullest extent practicable following the Olympic Co-ordination Authority Act 1995. The environmental legislative responsibilities as they relate to the *Environmental Guidelines* were given effect under New South Wales legislation by their incorporation into the State Environmental Planning Policy (SEPP no. 38). This legislation required

Self-censorship is certainly implied in the remark by *Herald* journalist Mark Coultan: 'Journalists who write stories which might be seen as critical are reminded of their boss's support and told that their stories would be used against Sydney by other cities' (quoted in Bacon, 1993: 4). Content analysis of media reports suggests that, throughout the bidding process, few critical comments were made. In 1992, when the levels of toxic waste at Homebush were measured, reports in the *Sydney Morning Herald* captured only the dismissive comments of Phil Cox, the site design team-leader, who reputedly said 'It's not as though we have Chernobyl on our hands here – they are toxins from household garbage'. Rod McGeogh, chief executive of SOBL, added that 'toxins on Olympic sites are not new. Barcelona, Atlanta, Munich and even Melbourne had to deal with toxins on their sites' (cited in Hawley, 1992). Apparently, given that toxins were not new, they were also not of public concern. Instead Sydney's 'green' environmental credentials were sustained through the media. For example, under the headline 'Sydney's odds on, and Deservedly So', the *Herald* journalist Sam North (1993) confirmed in a special supplement the city's assets and beauty, raising the question that the lack of disadvantages itself might inhibit the bid's success. The same special report described the competing cities as unattractive, suffering from chronic traffic congestion and industrial pollution. Even the British media's critical headline 'Aussies Build Olympic City on Poison Waste Dump' in the *Daily Mirror* (9 July 1993) was rejected and belittled as 'Sydney-bashing' by the British populist press. The integrity of Sydney's bid was emphasized in the Australian media. A win for Sydney was equated with a triumph for the 'true spirit' of the Olympics because of Australia's policies on drug testing, its environmentally progressive planning and its focus on sport and athletes (Fensham, 1994).

At times during the bid when media vigilance became more apparent, the various Sydney Olympic authorities resorted to verbal threats and condemnation of 'unAustralian'. Such threats drew their jurisdiction from the role sport occupies in the mythology of Australian nationalism. Sport, in the absence of a defining national war of independence, can bestow victory in its pseudo-warlike role. Traits apparently demonstrated on sporting fields have been appropriated as desirable, unique Australian characteristics, including persistence, stoicism, determination and resilience (Kell, 2000: 26). Labelling reproaches as 'anti-' or 'unAustralian' the games authorities positioned any criticism as contrary to the legitimate national interest. Compliance of the individual was called for in demonstrating loyalty to the nation. For example, when the *Herald* journalist Alan Kennedy (1992) ran the byline 'We'd win a gold medal for

that, before consent for an Olympic facility was granted, it must have the approval of the Minister for Urban Affairs and Planning, who must consider the consistency of proposed Olympic developments within the *Guidelines*. Given that the environmental requirements were unprecedented in Australia, the Department of Urban Affairs and Planning produced its own document to help developers of Olympic facilities to meet the environmental standards in their applications (*Environmental Planning for ESD: Guidelines for Compliance with the Environmental Guidelines for the Summer Olympic Games*). The legislation required the integration of ESD into all the games business aspects, from purchasing criteria, to merchandizing and sponsorship guidelines.

Internal environmental monitoring and auditing was provided by the OCA preparing an annual State of the Environment Report, and the New South Wales government incorporating a case study in its biennial State of the Environment Report 1997. The process of environmental monitoring, it was argued, was to be further facilitated by annual independent reviews conducted by the Earth Council (a body established after the World Conference of the Environment in 1992) and Green Games Watch 2000 (a body established by the NSW government as the environmental 'watchdog'). The Olympic Co-ordination Authority Act 1995 set the stage for showcasing Sydney's 'green' games utopia.

'Sydney 2000: greenwashing' or a 'green' utopia of the twenty-first century?

In this section I critically examine the SOBL 'green' marketing claims and the outcomes of the SOCOG and the OCA's 'green' planning process. Planning processes, informed by urban entrepreneuralism, have been argued elsewhere to result in a blurring of the distinction between public provision for social goals and private production for economic opportunity and individual profit (Syme *et al.*, 1989; Munro-Clark, 1992; Hall, 1992, 1994; Troy, 1996; Dunn and McGuirk, 1999). In this context, entrepreneurial public–private authorities tend to look upon urban environment as a place of spectacle, where image takes precedence over substance. Discourse analysis of the SOBL's selective promotional textual and visual images appears to confirm such arguments, also suggesting that entrepreneurial planning is informed by decisions that will sell the city as a bourgeois playground (Mommaas and van der Poel, 1989).

To evaluate the outcomes I draw on the reports of the Earth Council, the Green Games Watch 2000 and Greenpeace Australia. These reports highlight that the practices of Homebush's various entrepreneurial authorities tend to suggest that, in an era of intensified global competition, where rival places attempt to surpass each other, a tension develops between the principles of ESD and economic imperatives of time and budgets. I demonstrate how this tension is played out in the entrepreneurial planning process through the subsidizing of private sector interests at the cost of public concerns; the dilution of local planning powers; the limitation of public participation in the development process, and the homogenization of community opinion. I explore how these generate problematic outcomes for any claims of a 'green' games in the context of Homebush's land remediation strategies.

Image versus substance

SOBL's advertising company, Clemenger Sydney, portrayed Sydney's environment as both 'clean' and 'green' by employing signifiers of Australian landscapes as paradise (vibrant colours, sunshine, sunsets, dolphins, beaches and palm trees), wilderness (deserts and mountains without human presence or artifacts) and timeless (outback landscapes, Aboriginal Australians). Clemenger Sydney simply recycled images from an Australian Tourism Commission campaign. SOBL's bid book invited IOC delegates 'to sail to sheltered bays and coves; to run across the warm white sand of coastal beaches and dive into cool, clean waters' (SOBL, 1993b: 59). Sydney, despite being home to four million people, is suggested to have, if not a pristine environment, an extraordinarily unsullied one (Waitt, 1999). Counterarguments abound for such environmental representations. Archaeological evidence suggests that so-called 'wilderness' has been home to Aboriginal Australians for many thousands of years (Head and Fullagar, 1997). Evidence from environmental scientists, activist groups and geographers in regard to air, water and land quality suggests that Sydney exemplifies 'in their most pronounced forms the range of urban environmental problems' (Burnley et al., 1997: 100).

Indeed, at the time of the bid, the last in a series of environmental reports was completed for the NSW Property Service Group that suggested Homebush had extensive environmental contamination problems. The first, in 1991 by Coffey Partners International, was commissioned by the NSW government to conduct extensive sampling in the surface and subsurface soils at Homebush Bay. Results showed that a number of chemical substances, particularly heavy metals (arsenic, chromium, copper, iron, magnesium, zinc) and organic chemicals including dioxins and pesticides, existed in concentrations above 'normal' background levels (Property Services Group, 1992). The contamination was worse at the old brickworks, a site of industrial waste disposal since the early 1970s,

and near Haslam Creek. The contamination in some areas migrated through surface water runoff, groundwater seepage and erosion to adjacent aquatic ecosystems. Fishing is banned in Homebush Bay because of contamination. Conclusions drawn by a second report by the environmental consultants Dames and Moore (1991) suggested that the site's most contaminated parts posed potential health and safety problems to workers and site visitors during redevelopment. Furthermore there could be public health risks to users of these areas arising from possible seepage of contaminants and gases after redevelopment was complete. This conclusion was confirmed by later reports prepared by environmental consultants Inner City Fund Pty Ltd (1993). Such material evidence contradicts SOBL's imagery of Sydney's pristine environment.

Such counterconstructions of Homebush as a toxic landfill, however, within the bidding environment were effectively silenced by SOBL's institutionalized power matrix. Public concern over the level of contamination was stifled because, first, these reports were never published. Sharon Beder, an environmentalist, only secured access to these documents through the Freedom of Information Act. However her attempts to publish these findings in *New Scientist* were also restrained by the Homebush Bay Development Corporation (Beder, 2000). The editors of *New Scientist* decided not to run the article, citing political reasons. They feared that, without articles on the environmental credentials of competing cities, the magazine would be blamed if Sydney lost the bid. The article was published in the *Current Affairs Bulletin* three years later, after Sydney had won the right to host the Olympics.

Second, Beder's (2000) allegations of Australian media self-censorship at bidding time also sustain the argument that opposing portrayals would not be circulated. Certainly Kerry Packer (owner of Consolidated PressHoldings), Ken Cowley (chief executive of Rupert Murdoch's News Ltd) and John Alexander (then editor-in-chief of the *Sydney Morning Herald*) all accepted invitations to sit on the SOBL committee. In addition, a number of radio stations and all three commercial television channels were either direct sponsors of the bid or members of the SOBL (Darcy and Veal, 1994). The critical role Sydney's media played in creating a favourable climate for the bid and kindling euphoria is also acknowledged by bid chief Rod McGeoch (McGeoch, 1994). Indeed it was Australia's media that tagged Sydney 2000 Games unofficially as the 'Green Games' to help differentiate the bid, almost masking the official label of the 'Athletes' Games' and 'Millennium Games'. Therefore Richard Palfreyman's (1997: 98) suggestion that the media were 'extremely enthusiastic about the games' must be placed within the games' broader political economy.

burying heads in the smog', Rod McGeoch, the chief executive of the SOBL, deemed the media unpatriotic. All criticisms were dismissed in a similar fashion. John Valder, corporate chairperson of SOBL, on the ABC Radio programme *AM*, scathingly spoke of the 'double-A BC'. This, he explained was the 'Anti-Australian Broadcasting Corporation', which the ABC had become because of its 'constant negative putting down of this country' (reported in a *Herald* editorial by Hickie, 1993). In the case of the *Four Corners* investigation into the bidding process, to be aired in July 1993, Bruce Baird, then NSW minister for the games, asserted that 'anyone who threatens Sydney's Olympic bid better watch out' (PM Australian Broadcasting Commission Radio 16 July 1993, quoted in Booth and Tatz, 1996: 10). Such threats suggested that anyone who voiced opposition to the games spoke against the national interest.

Even after the bidding process the *Herald* environmental reporter Murray Hogarth (1997a: 101) asserted that, to Sydney's Olympic authorities 'the Games has had the status of a scared cow ... to publish ill of the Olympics was sacrilege, if not outright treason'. Hence, in 1995, when the remediation process had begun, the *Herald* journalist Rollin Schlist (1995) described the containment process as producing 'spectacular landscaping' and the highly contaminated brickpit as a 'spectacular element'. Those reporters who were more critical of the land remediation process allegedly received verbal threats from a former state minister (Hogarth, 1997a). Wendy Bacon (1993: 2), the director of the Australian Centre for Independent Journalism, also concluded that the few journalists who scripted critical articles were 'attacked as unpatriotic, eccentric, inaccurate and negative'. Sydney's 'green' environmental bid credentials exemplify how, through the operation of a matrix of institutions, a priority can be established for place image over substance. Sydney Olympic authorities attempted to silence such concerns by positioning themselves as the legitimate voice concerning the 'green' games, rejecting all criticism as unpatriotic and against the 'public interest'.

The Olympic Co-ordination Authority Act 1995

Successive, detailed qualitative evaluations of the environmental performance relative to the *Guidelines* were compiled by the Earth Council (2000), the Green Games Watch 2000 (2000a) and Greenpeace International (2000). Overall the Earth Council's final evaluation of the OCA's performance was generally positive on each area of ESD. David Chernushenko of the Earth Council evaluated Sydney's 'green' games as a significant accomplishment, providing an environmental legacy and benchmark for future stadiums. He summarized the strengths in five areas: (1) the breadth of issues covered, (2) the environmental tendering process, (3) water conservation, (4) on-site ecology programmes such as the endangered Green and Golden Bell Frog in Homebush Bay's brickpit, and (5) energy efficiency (Chernushenko, 2000).

Such favourable evaluation reiterated earlier claims by University of New South Wales Centre for Olympic Studies academics Richard Cashman and Tony Hughes (1997), who identified the Sydney 'green' games as a mechanism that strengthened the IOC's environmental credentials, amending its charter in 1994 and embracing the environment as the third dimension of Olympism (after sport and culture). In the Australian context, Deo Prasad (1999), the director of the SOLARCH Group at the Faculty of Built Environment at the University of New South Wales, also praised the legislation. He argued that these guidelines not only increased awareness within the community and construction industry of ESD issues, but also provided a new set of regulations requiring energy performance of buildings. The incorporation of a life cycle approach to major building projects, he claimed, would encourage changing industrial practice from, often, an environmentally short-sighted capital costs-driven approach. In short, for Prasad the guidelines demonstrated the first commitment of both government and the industry to move beyond the rhetoric of ESD towards a practical solution. His views must be seen in context, however, as he was a member of the Energy Expert Panel at the OCA and author of a number of guidelines for low-energy building design. Additionally OCA officials interpreted the legislation as a mechanism to secure a position of international competitiveness for Australian business. Grant (1997) and Ottesen (1997) claimed that new environmental expertise and technology would be spawned, having relevance to cities everywhere, particularly in Asia. In the later interpretation of the 'green' games, environmental legislation was entwined within wider New Right policy arguments of international competition, the race-to-the-top, best-practice and profit (AMC, 1992).

The Green Games Watch 2000 and Greenpeace International also agreed that areas of greatest achievement were in the life cycle assessment provision and the substantial environmental legacies of energy conservation, transport, biodiversity and the planning and construction of Olympic facilities. Both commended the Olympic Village in its orientation, 50 per cent reduction in consumption of potable water through application of a dual-pipe water system and use of solar panels, halving the amount of greenhouse gas emissions compared with conventional homes. The Olympic water management system consists of the Water Reclamation and Management Scheme (WRAMS) that the GGW (2000b) described as 'a progressive environmental initiative'. Using filtration technology, village stormwater, sewage and swimming pool backwash are collected and treated on-site within the WRAMS. The Royal Agricultural Showground's environmental features involve the incorporation of passive design concepts to optimize natural ventilation and daylight to save energy, and considerable attention to material selection, examples including the use of plantation and recycled timber and significant reduction of PVC use through polyethylene pipe. Stadium Australia's environmental legacy includes almost 75 per cent construction waste recycling, a commitment to buy 100 per cent green power, and storage and re-use of roofwater to meet pitch watering needs.

Yet both reports were more critical, with GGW 2000 awarding a final score of 5/10 to the 'Green' Games, highlighting earlier concerns of Beder (1996) and Lenskyj (1998). Their final reports raised greatest concern for the failure to address improvements to air, water and soil quality, particularly the use of polyvinyl chlorides (PVCs) and HCFC in refrigerants in venues. The GGW 2000 lamented the lack of educational facilities during the games, and the missed opportunities to combine complete life cycle analysis and eco design with Olympic merchandising and corporate sponsors. Perhaps most significantly, all three organizations expressed concern over the OCA's continued failure to communicate quickly, effectively and transparently with the public. The Earth Council concluded that the delay and selective release of environmental information was secretive and excluded the public from the decision-making process. GGW 2000 noted how the 'commercial-in-confidence' provisions surrounding all Olympic transactions effectively excluded the public from many decisions. The next subsection examines the controversial subject of Homebush's land remediation to illustrate how private sector interest could effectively be prioritized over public concerns through diluting public participation within the planning process.

Diluting public participation in local planning powers

In 1991 and 1992, public participation in the local planning process was diluted through the implementation of successive modifications of the Regional Environmental Plan (REP) (James, 1997a). In 1991, the NSW Department of Planning exempted all earth works from the mandatory requirement to prepare an Environmental Impact Statement (EIS), and, in 1992, all 'designated' or 'significant' Olympic developments. One key objective on an EIS is to alert the decision maker, members of the public and the government to the consequences of a project and to explore alternatives. Effectively, under the new legislation, the state government is accountable only to itself. Without an EIS the NSW Minister for Planning had full authority to give consent for development of Olympic facilities. Justification by the NSW Minister for Planning for such exemption was facilitating the Olympic projects within budgetary, time and performance constraints (North and Cook, 1993). However, without the transparency of an EIS, questions were continuously raised by concerned residents and some environmentalists over the social and environmental 'costs' of such 'fast-tracking' practices (Dunn and McGuirk, 1999). As Jeff Angel (1993b), the director of the Total Environment Centre, noted, the plan enabled the government to be 'a law unto itself'.

In 1992, within this diluted planning environment, workshops involving contractors and the community took place as the NSW Property Service Group prepared its remediation strategy. The group conferred on-site containment rather than treatment of toxins as the most 'suitable' remediation strategy. This planning process, in the absence of an EIS, exemplifies a series of mechanisms employed by the entrepreneurial state that arguably fast-tracked development in private sector interests. The NSW Property Service Group considered various options, including segregating and treating the wastes, sealing up and walling in the wastes in a secure landfill and a containment landfill (capping the toxic materials and collecting the leachates as they percolate into the underlying groundwater). At Homebush the third option was pursued for the majority of the site in view of the expense of the secure landfill trial at the Olympic swimming facility. In greater detail this consisted mainly of capping the old dump site, moving contaminated soils to the worst toxic sites, contouring the capping material and constructing leachate drains to remove the wastewater seeping from the dump sites, which, if toxic, is pumped to the on-site Aqueous Waste Treatment Plant. On-site containment justifications included reducing the risk by preventing human, animal and plant exposure to the toxic contaminants, and removing the contaminated soil off-site simply transferred the environmental problem elsewhere (OCA, n.d.).

These justifications are not a source of critique; rather contestation lies in the decision for on-site *containment* over *treatment*. A containment strategy was implemented despite the Australian and New Zealand Environment and Conservation Council (ANZECC) and the National Health and Medical Research Council (NHMRC) published guidelines for contaminated sites that prefer *treatment* of the soil either on or off-site. According to the ANZECC/NHMRC (1992), the general choice in Australia to remediate contaminated soil has been removal to a secure landfill. Furthermore Greenpeace International has long campaigned against landfills, arguing that 'landfills ... have major environmental impacts' (Greenpeace International, 2001). The precautionary principle, upon which ESD is based, suggests that treatment, not landfill, should be used to dispose of toxic materials. The containment landfill, at least a 20-year old technology, appears a remarkable choice as the most suitable remediation strategy for a site set to stage a 'green' world showcase.

Beder (1996) draws the conclusion that, within a diluted planning process, the most suitable strategy for the Olympic site became defined as quick and low-cost. Evidence for expediency was demonstrated by a NSW Property Services Group officer who is reputed to have said that 'theirs [containment] was a more practical solution that got things done while the United States authorities were still mucking about' (ibid.: 17). Although the containment cost about A$69 million, this is a small budget in comparison to the more secure landfill option, estimated at A$190 million. The precautionary principle of ESD was therefore arguably compromised in the interests of budget and time constraints.

Another principle of ESD was arguably compromised, that of genuine public involvement and consultation on decisions and public access to information. Genuine citizen participation in the decision-making process, according to Arnstein (1969), requires establishing forums that incorporate citizen control, delegated membership or partnership. Community consultation is regarded as a critical component of ESD and remediation of a site. Indeed, the ANZECC/NHMRC (1992) guidelines are quite explicit about the need for community involvement, given the health implications of long-term exposure to dioxins. During this initial land remediation process the OCA claims public hearing occurred through involvement of environmental consultants, the construction industry, environmental organizations (Greenpeace), local environmental groups (Greenspace) and the Trade and Labour Council (OCA, 1997). Yet the remediation work went ahead without any of the options being publicly discussed or an environmental impact statement (EIS) being prepared and publicly displayed because of the amended Regional Environmental Plan. In 1992, when the remediation had already commenced a survey conducted by a local environmental group, Greens in Lowe (1992), reported that, of the 100 local residents surveyed, 71 per cent answered that they had not received enough information about the process. Almost an equal percentage indicated that they had not received enough information to reassure them that the Homebush Bay area would be safe for people to live and work. With access to information denied, public concern mounted in opposition. In 1997, local anxieties intensified following Greenpeace Australia's allegations that they had evidence suggesting that the Olympic site is the 'dioxin capital of the world' (Ruchel, 1997). Greenpeace revealed that, according to their findings, dioxin contamination on the Olympic site itself had levels of toxic rating 1500 times higher than the 'safe' United States standard for residential areas. Public alarm only heightened when Colin Grant, OCA's executive director, was forced to apologize when his statement that the site did not contain any 2,3,7,8,TCDD (a toxic dioxin) was proved false (Hogarth, 1997b).

Early in 1998, the Minister for the Olympics established the Homebush Bay Environment Reference Group (HBERG) after the dioxin controversies. HBERG was to facilitate community consultation on site contamination and the OCA's contaminated land remediation programme. Membership of HBERG comprised a combination of local community interest groups, resident action groups, conservation/environment groups, scientific/academic experts and the OCA. A series of Extraordinary Meetings of HBERG were held with the aim to allow input from the wider community on priority remediation issues. Controversy exists over the effectiveness of the group in facilitating community consultation. On the one hand, the OCA's Ecology Program claims that the 'HERG process was based on a commitment to open, honest discussion' (OCA, 2000). On the other, Beder (2000: 252) describes the forum as 'carefully staged public relations events aimed at creating the appearance of public consultation'. Whatever the positive outcomes of HBERG established through its interactions with the public, the level of local resident involvement was never that required by an EIS.

Conclusion

As an urban redevelopment programme conceived in an era of economic globalization, commercial sport and entrepreneurial planning, the redevelopment of Homebush through hosting a hallmark event cast as a 'green' Olympics provided a set of promises and actions. Different evaluations of these 'green' pledges and deeds reflect a spectrum of different political ideologies and positioning of actors within complex layers of the planning process. At one extreme, the authoritative voices of organizations established by New Right policies, SOBL, SOCOG and the OCA, always positioned the 'green' games unequivocally as an international showpiece of innovative environmental design and technology. The Olympics is seemingly embraced by these public–private partnerships uncritically as a social movement that can successfully address environmental issues. Symbolically these Olympic authorities portrayed their legacy in terms of transforming 'dirty' dumps and derelict industrial landscapes into Sydney's new 'environmentally friendly' heartland. To sustain the argument that the material outcomes were also 'green', the OCA employed a list of environmental awards. For example, in 1999, the OCA won the Department of Land and Water Conservation's River Care 2000 Award for WRAMS; in 2000, the OCA was awarded the Banksia Environmental Foundation Award in recognition of its contribution to environmental protection; and in 2000, Bovis Lend Lease won the Prime Minister's Environmental Award for living cities for the residential development in Newington. Independent evaluations of the Green Games by approved environmental organizations unquestionably added further support to some of the 'green' environmental legacy claims.

At the other extreme are the voices of some environmental activists and local residents who regarded the Olympics as a sporting spectacle and the 'green' games as alibi. These voices were marginalized through the operation of powers given to the entrepreneurial partnerships of the New Right planning policies. Members of Sydney's Olympic authorities clearly used their privileged position in government or business to cast any criticism as unAustralian. Australia's frequently discussed obsession with sport was capitalized upon to ensure censure. Additionally various members of Sydney's Olympic authorities have been purported by Beder (2000) to employ their political status or business connections to prevent critical academic publications or media reporting. 'Commercial-in-confidence' legislation ensures that the actual extent of the way these organizations utilized their empowered positions remains secret for 30 years. Only then will the various confidential workings of Sydney's Olympic authorities be known. Further marginalization of concerned local resident voices also occurred through the dilution of public participation in the local planning process and lack of transparency regarding the level of contamination and selection of the remediation process. These residents and environmentalists developed a counterrepresentation of the consolidated landfill, portraying it, at best, as a managed toxic waste dump. Mark Oakwood, Greenpeace Australia's toxic campaigner, and Geoff Angel, director of TEC, argued that toxic landfills are a temporary solution, given the volume of material leaching out of them (Radio National, Australian Broadcasting Commission, 1999, 2000). According to these environmentalists the next phase is on-site treatment. However the state may regard remediation at the site as completed. The government has not made any commitment to undertake further remediation. Today the OCA no longer exists, having been devolved in July 2001 into the Sydney Olympic Park Authority.

In the post-Olympic context, Homebush's official image remains unquestionably 'green'. In the initial vision statement for commercial, retail and residential development at Sydney Olympic Park, the image makers once again depicted the consolidated landfill of the Millennium Parklands as a 'Green Oasis' (OCA, 2001). The ecology of Millennium Parklands was positioned as 'unique', 'diverse' and 'sensitive' and seemingly relatively untouched by humans. Homebush's planning documents adopted the predictable, ubiquitous language of place marketing. Homebush becomes described as containing the 'largest urban parkland in Australia', which is argued to provide a 'magnificent' setting for commercial and residential development. Continuing commercial development was positioned as essential if the site was not to become a taxpayer's burden, a 'white elephant'. In the Sydney Olympic Park Authority's (2002) master plan, reassurances were once again given that the environment will remain a planning priority of the commercial and residential developments. Previous environmental planning implemented at Homebush was uncritically accepted as 'best practice' (ibid.: 64), a showcase for 'energy and water conservation, waste minimization, pollution avoidance, and the protection for the unique natural environment'.

Unquestionably aspects of 'best practice' do exist on the site and have been recognized by awards and reports of various environmental agencies. Yet it is the very fact that 'greenwashing' has also been embedded through the planning legacy of the site that created concerns amongst ardent critics. The envisaged high-technology centre and entertainment district will attract tens of thousands of extra people to live and work permanently at the site in coming decades. This caused Geoff Angel concern because of potential health risks arising from their continued exposure to toxins over many years (Radio National, Australian Broadcasting Commission, 1999). His concerns were confirmed by Greenpeace. According to Mark Oakwood (Radio National, Australian Broadcasting Commission, 2000) results of chromosomal sampling done by Greenpeace on residents in the area indicated that, 'of 18 individuals tested, 12 came back with at least one chromosome affected, showing they'd been exposed to probably environmental toxins of some form, at this stage undetermined'. Such results will be of little comfort to homebuyers in Newington. Although each purchased their homes with certification that their home was not built on contaminated soil, the remediation strategy of the 'green' games has left a legacy where, in their immediate vicinity, the toxins remain in Homebush Bay's sediments, seep into the groundwater of consolidated landfills and are potentially blown into the air as dust.

References

Angel, J. (1993a), 'Sydney's green Olympic bid: Issues of concern', Total Environment Centre Media Release, 24 June.

Angel, J. (1993b), 'Sydney's Olympic bid fails key environmental test', Total Environment Centre Media Release, 17 June.

Arnstein, J. (1969), 'A ladder of citizen participation', *Journal of the American Institute of Planners*, **35** (4), 216–24.

Ashworth, G.J. and H. Voogd (1990), *Selling the city: marketing approaches in public sector urban planning*, London, Belhaven Press.

Augé, M. (1995), *Non-lieux: introduction à une Anthropologie de la Surmondernité*, Paris: Seuil.

Australian Manufacturing Council (AMC) (1992), *The environmental challenge: best practice environmental management*, Melbourne: AMC.

Australian and New Zealand Environment and Conservation Council and the National Health and Medical Research Council (ANZECC/NHMRC) (1992), *Australian and New Zealand guidelines for the assessment and management of contaminated sites*, Melbourne: ANZECC/NHMRC.

Bacon, W. (1993), 'Watchdog's bark muffled', *Reportage*, September, pp.3–5.

Bale, J. and J. Sang (1996), *Kenyan running: movement, culture, geography and global change*, London: Frank Cass.

Beder, S. (1996), 'Sydney's Green Olympics', *Current Affairs Bulletin*, **70**(6), 12–18.

Beder, S. (2000), *Global spin: the corporate assault on environmentalism*, rev. edn, Melbourne: Scribe Publications.

Bell, K. (1993), 'Australia's environmental record and the Olympic Village, in Sydney Olympic Bid Limited', *Significant Speeches*, 1039–5695.

Bonnemaison, S. (1990), 'City policies and cyclical events', *Design Quarterly*, **147**, 24–32.

Booth, D. and C. Tatz (1996), 'Sydney 2000: the games people play', *Current Affairs Bulletin*, **70** (7), 4–11.

Bowers, P. (1993), 'We're top in "big Australian crawl" at Brothel de Paris', *Melbourne Age*, 24 September, p.2.

Bruntland Report, World Commission on Environment and Development (1987), *Our common future*, London: Oxford University Press.

Burnley, I., P. Murphy and R. Fagan (1997), *Migration and Australian cities*, Sydney: Federation Press.

Burroughs, A. (1999), 'Winning the bid', in R. Cashman and A. Hughes (eds), *Staging the Olympics: the event and its impact*, Sydney: University of New South Wales Press, pp.35–45.

Cashman R. and A. Hughes (1997), 'Introduction', in R. Cashman and A. Hughes (eds), *The green games a golden opportunity*, proceedings of a conference organized by the Centre for Olympic Studies, The University of New South Wales, 12 September, pp.11–13.

Chernushenko, D. (2000), 'The environmental legacy of the Sydney Olympics: how green was your Games?' Environmental Institute of Australia, New South Wales Division, Novotel, Olympic Boulevard, Homebush Bay, November.

Clarke, G. (1993), 'Global competition and the environmental performance of resource firms: is the "race to the bottom" inevitable?', *International Environmental Affairs*, **35**, 147–67.

Cook, D. (1993), 'Green Groups attack Games bid claims', *Sydney Morning Herald*, 29 May, p.7.

Cox, K. (1997), *Space of globalisation: reasserting the power of the local*, New York: UCL Press.

Craik, J. (1991), *Resorting to tourism: cultural policies for tourist development in Australia*, Sydney: Allen & Unwin.

Daily Mirror (1993), 'Aussies build Olympic city on poison waste dump', 9 July, p.1.

Dames and Moore (1991), 'Site remediation works: state sports centre, Homebush Bay development', Report prepared for Property Services Group, NSW.

Darcy, S. and A.J. Veal (1994), 'The Sydney 2000 Olympic Games: the story so far', *Leisure Options: Australian Journal of Leisure and Recreation*, **4** (1), 5–14.

Dempster, G. (1985), 'Challenges in department of sport and recreation and tourism and Australian Sports Commission', *Australian sport: a profile*, Canberra: Australian Government Press Services.

Dunn, K.M. and McGuirk, P.M. (1999), 'Hallmark events', in R. Cashman and A. Hughes (eds), *Staging the Olympics: the event and its impact*, Sydney: University of New South Wales Press, pp.18–34.

Earth Council (2000), 'Sydney 2000 Olympic and Paralympic Games: environmental performance of the Olympic Co-ordination Authority, Review III', prepared by the Earth Council, 18 February 2000, San Jose, Costa Rica.

Fensham, R. (1994), 'Prime time hyperspace: the Olympic city as spectacle', in K. Gibson and S. Watson (eds), *Metropolis now: planning and the urban in contemporary Australia*, Sydney: Pluto Press, pp.171–85.

Grant, C. (1997), 'The infrastructure of the games', in R. Cashman and A. Hughes (eds), *The green games a golden opportunity*, proceedings of a conference organized by the Centre for Olympic Studies, The University of New South Wales, 12 September, pp.41–6.

Greenpeace International (2000), *How green the games? Greenpeace's environmental assessment of the Sydney 2000 Olympics*, Sydney: Greenpeace.

Greenpeace International (2001), 'Greenpeace International', retrieved 22 February 2002 from the World Wide Web: http//www.greanpeace.org/^toxics/html/content/pvchearing/pvchearing.ppt.

Green Games Watch 2000 (2000a), *Environmental performance review report New South Wales Olympic Co-ordination Authority*, Bondi Junction, NSW: Green Games Watch 2000 Inc.

Green Games Watch 2000 (2000b), 'Water conservation – Olympic solutions. Green Games Watch 2000', retrieved 12 December 2000 from the World Wide Web: http://www.grengameswatch.org.

Greens in Lowe (1992), *Survey – Homebush Bay development*, Sydney: Greens in Lowe.

Hall, C.M. (1992), *Hallmark tourist events: impacts, management and planning*, London: Belhaven Press.

Hall, C.M. (1994), *Tourism and politics: policy, power and place*, London: John Wiley and Sons.

Hall, C.M. (1995), *Introduction to tourism in Australia: impacts, planning and development*, South Melbourne: Longman Cheshire.

Hambleton, R. (1991), 'The regeneration of U.S. and British cities', *Local Government Studies*, **17** (5), 63–5.

Harvey, D. (1989a), *The condition of postmodernity: an enquiry into the origins of cultural change*, Oxford: Blackwell.

Harvey, D. (1989b), 'From managerialism to entrepreneurialism: the transformation of urban governance in late capitalism', *Geografiska Annaler*, **71B**, 3–17.

Hawley, J. (1992), 'An Olympian brawl over quay west', *Sydney Morning Herald*, 25 January, p.38.

Head, L. and R. Fullagar (1997), 'Hunter–gatherer archaeology and pastoral contact: perspectives from the NW Territory, Australia', *World Archaeology*, **28** (3), 418–28.

Hickie, J.D. (1993), 'Editorial: Un-Australian Olympic Games', *Sydney Morning Herald*, 13 August, p.12.

Hogarth, M. (1997a), 'The media, the community and the green games publicity', in R. Cashman and A. Hughes (eds), *The green games a golden opportunity*, proceedings of a conference organized by the Centre for Olympic Studies, The University of New South Wales, 12 September, pp.101–2.

Hogarth, M. (1997b), 'Toxic talk poisons Olympic relations', *Sydney Morning Herald*, 19 July, p.16.

Huxley, M. (1991), 'Making cities fun: Darling Harbour and the immobilisation of spectacle', in P. Carroll (ed.), *Tourism in Australia*, Sydney: Harcourt, pp.141–52.

Inner City Fund Pty Ltd. (1993), 'Health and environmental risk assessment for dioxins: Homebush Bay Redevelopment Area', report prepared for Property Services Group of NSW, 5 February.

International Olympic Committee (1993), *Olympic message: environment*, Lausanne: International Olympic Committee.

James, P. (1997a), *Environmental performance review report Olympic Co-ordination Authority: compliance with the environmental guidelines for the summer Olympics*, Sydney: Green Games Watch 2000 Inc.

James, P. (1997b), 'Environmental performance for the Olympics', *Australian Planner*, **34** (2), 650–65.

Jennings A. and V. Simpson (1992), *Lords of the rings: power, money and drugs in the modern Olympics*, London: Simon & Schuster.

Kell, P. (2000), *Good sports: Australian sport and the myth of the fair go*, Sydney: Pluto Press.

Kelly, R. (1993), 'Media Release. World Environment Day and our environmental Olympics', 5 June.

Kennedy, Alan (1992), 'We'd win gold for burying head in the smog', *Sydney Morning Herald*, 5 June, p.15.

Lenskyj, H. (1998), 'Green games or empty promises? Environmental issues and Sydney 2000, Global and Cultural Critique: Problematising the Olympic Games', University of Western Ontario, Centre for Olympic Studies.

Loftman, P. and B. Nevin (1996), 'Going for growth: prestige projects in three British cities', *Urban Studies*, **33** (6), 991–1091.

McGeoch, R. with G. Korporaal (1994), *Bid: how Australia won the 2000 Games*, Melbourne: Heinemann.

Mommas, H. and H. van der Poel (1989), 'Changes in economy, politics and lifestyles: an essay on the restructuring of urban leisure', in P. Bramham, H. Mommas and H. van der Poel (eds), *Leisure and urban processes*, London, Routledge, pp.254–76.

Munro-Clark, M. (1992), *Citizen participation in government*, Sydney: Hale & Iremonger.

North, D. (1992), 'Sydney's green village aims to be envy of Olympic bidders', *Sydney Morning Herald*, 22 December, p.4.

North, S. (1993), 'Sydney's odds on, and deservedly so', *Sydney Morning Herald*, 23 June, p.1.

North, S. and D. Cook (1993), ' "Immediate" benefits if Games come', *Sydney Morning Herald*, 17 June, p.7.

Olympic Coordination Authority (OCA) (n.d.), *Greening up for the games*, Sydney: OCA.

Olympic Coordination Authority (1997), *State of the environment 1996*, Sydney: OCA.

Olympic Coordination Authority (OCA) (2000), 'Ecology Program. Formation of the Homebush Bay Environmental Reference Group. OCA', retrieved 11 February 2002 from the World Wide Web: http//www.oca.nsw.gov.au/ecology.

Olympic Coordination Authority (OCA) (2001), 'Sydney Olympic Park vision for beyond 2000, OCA', retrieved 28 August 2001 from the World Wide Web: http//www.oca.nsw.gov.au/oca/html/about.stm.

Ottesen, P. (1997), 'The Olympic vision', in R. Cashman and A. Hughes (eds), *The green games a golden opportunity*, proceedings of a conference organized by the Centre for Olympic Studies, The University of New South Wales, 12 September, pp.32–9.

Palfreyman, R. (1997), 'The media, the community and the green games publicity', in R. Cashman and A. Hughes (eds), *The green games a golden opportunity*, proceedings of a conference organized by the Centre for Olympic Studies, The University of New South Wales, 12 September, pp.97–100.

Porter, M.E. (1991), 'America's green strategy', *Scientific American*, **264** (4), 96.

Prasad, D. (1999), 'Environment', in R. Cashman and A. Hughes (eds), *Staging the Olympics: the event and its impact*, Sydney: University of New South Wales Press, pp.83–92.

Property Services Group (1992), 'Briefing documents on site remediation and environmental investigations at Homebush Bay', March 1992.

Pusey, M. (1991), *Economic rationalism in Canberra: a nation-building state changes its mind*, Melbourne: Cambridge University Press.

Radio National, Australian Broadcasting Commission (1999), 'Will the green Olympics make the finish line?', Saturday 6 February.

Radio National, Australian Broadcasting Commission (2000), 'Sydney's Green Games!', Saturday 5 August.

Roche, M. (1994), 'Mega-events and urban policy', *Annals of Tourism Research*, **21**, 1–19.

Ruchel, M. (1997), 'Lethal hazardous waste stockpiled next to "green" Olympic site', press release, Greenpeace, Sydney, 3 June.

Schlist, R. (1995), 'An Olympian Challenge', *Sydney Morning Herald*, 1 April, p.12.

Sydney Olympic Bid Limited (SOBL) (1992), 'Committee to ensure Sydney Games are green', news release, 21 December.

Sydney Olympic Bid Limited (SOBL) (1993a), *Sydney 2000 Olympics Bid: bid documents*, Sydney: SOBL.

Sydney Olympic Bid Limited (SOBL) (1993b), *Sydney 2000 environmental guidelines*, Sydney: SOBL.

Sydney Olympic Park Authority (2002), 'Sydney Olympic Park Master Plan SOPA', World Wide Web (http://www.sydneyolympicpark.nsw.gov.au), accessed 27 November 1993.

Sydney Organising Committee for the Olympic Games (SOCOG) (1995), 'A summary of the environmental guidelines for the summer Olympic Games', Sydney: SOCOG.

Syme G.J., B.J. Shaw, D.M. Fenton and W.S. Mueller (1989), *The planning and evaluation of hallmark events*, Aldershot: Avebury.

Totaro, P. (1994), 'Ombudsman attacks new FOI exemption', *Sydney Morning Herald*, 8 August, p.5.

Troy, P. N. (1996), *The perils of urban consolidation: a discussion of Australian housing and urban development policies*, Sydney: Federation Press.

Waitt, G. (1997), 'Environmental standards and industrial restructuring: the case of the Australian paper industry', *Australian Geographical Studies*, 35 (3), 324–41.

Waitt, G. (1999), 'Playing games with Sydney: marketing Sydney for the 2000 Olympics', *Urban Studies*, 36 (7), 1055–77.

Waitt, G (2003), 'Social Impacts of the Sydney Olympics', *Annals of Tourism Research*, 30 (1), 194–215.

Ward, S.V. and R.J. Gold (1994), 'Introduction', in R.J. Gold and V.W. Ward (eds), *Place promotion: the use of publicity and marketing to sell towns and regions*, Chichester: John Wiley and Sons, pp.1–18.

Winter, I. and T. Brooks (1993), 'Urban planning and the entrepreneurial state. the view from Victoria, Australia', *Environment and Planning C*, 11, 263–78.

Whitson, D. and D. Macintosh (1993), 'Becoming a world-class city: hallmark events and sport franchises in the growth strategies of western Canadian cities', *Sociology of Sport Journal*, 10 (3), 221–40.

Young, B. (1992), 'Homebush Bay master plan', *Australian Planner*, 30, 221–6.

10
Conclusion: The Political Economy of Sport in the Twenty-first Century

John Nauright

During the period of producing this volume there have been numerous challenges to existing sport cultures and structures as well as a multitude of sporting 'scandals'. Examples are widespread and include sexual exploitation of women in the recruiting process and murder in American university sport, gambling scandals in international cricket, the use of performance-enhancing substances in American Major League Baseball, widespread bidding scandals in the Olympics and the problems of Athens in its preparations for hosting the 2004 Summer Olympic Games, to name but a few.

Despite an overall climate of growth in the sports industry, some sporting leagues failed during the 1990s and early 2000s. The Canadian Football League (Nauright and White, 1996) and the XFL (Newman *et al.*, 2003) both failed in attempts to establish new gridiron football competitions in the USA, while the Women's Professional Soccer League was unable to capitalize on the enormous popularity of the US Women's National team, with globally recognized stars such as Mia Hamm, and went out of business after only a couple of seasons. While there have been setbacks in some sports, the overall growth machine in sport showed no signs of slowing in the first years of the new millennium. And, while many decry the apparent assault on 'traditions' that corporatized and mediated sport have unleashed, attendances at most major professional sporting events continued to rise in the decade after 1995, and this even as many spectators were priced out of the live attendance market and relegated to spectating via pay television or at sports bars.

There are still plenty of examples of genuine outpourings of local pride and attachments evident in sport when the local team or local boys or girls go on to become international sporting celebrities. At the same time, the trends in elite professional or achievement sports point to increasing centralization of resources, while a rhetoric of purity, fair play and expanding opportunities abounds.

The chapters in this book have all pointed to the dramatically shifting role of sport in society, from diversion to consumption, to spectacle and beyond, where sports events and teams have become vehicles to promote strategies of growth, investment, capital accumulation, global and regional positioning for further capital accumulation, local, regional and national political success and as sites for the solidification and regeneration of national or regional identity. Throughout the world, developed nations utilize sport and major sporting events as ways to jockey for position and visibility, while, in the developing world, countries and cities use sport as a way to elevate their polities onto the developed world stage where they hope to achieve acceptance in the 'world class' stakes and further capital investment.

While there has been a modicum of expansion by major sporting events into the developing world, this process has been slow, uneven and reluctant, a process carefully managed under the guise of stability, security and willingness to conform to the dominant expectations of the industrial and post-industrial core. It is, therefore, not surprising that the neither the Olympic Games nor the World Cup of soccer have been held on the African continent. Furthermore the Olympics have never been staged in South America, and in Asia the Olympics and the World Cup of soccer have only appeared in Japan and South Korea. Even the 'Friendly' Commonwealth Games, while venturing to Kuala Lumpur in 1998, returned to Manchester and Melbourne in 2002 and 2006, both Olympic hopefuls during the 1990s. Adelaide, a city of a million people and capital of the state of South Australia, pulled out of the running for 2006 because many there came to the realization that the potential for limited reward did not justify the cost. FIFA, the governing body of world soccer, has, however, stated that its 2010 World Cup would be held in Africa. At the time of writing, South Africa had just won the right to host the event. Indeed fewer and fewer countries and cities are able to deliver mega-sporting events. During the first half of 2004, for example, reports circulated widely that Athens, Greece would not be able to deliver all the facilities for the 2004 Summer Olympic Games on time and that the ability to supply adequate security for athletes and spectators was of great concern. Even within the European Union, the bastion of twenty-first century regional trading cum political blocs, the ability to deliver a high-quality Olympic Games or soccer World Cup is limited to a handful of nations. Most nations able to host such major events are located in Western Europe or North America and comprise the most developed economies.

As the stakes climb ever higher, the resources required to win the right to host and then to complete successfully the staging of the event create economic demands that cannot be realized in most nations or cities. Michael Hall points out that many in Toronto were not prepared to risk diverting necessary resources into an Olympic Games there for 1996 or 2008, even calling their protest group 'Bread not Circuses', after the famous Roman axiom of providing entertainment for the masses through handing out free food at major spectacles. As Gordon Waitt shows, even in Sydney, Australia, which, according to then International Olympic Committee President Juan Antonio Samaranch, delivered 'the best Olympics ever', the stakes were so high that democratic debate was stifled through a government–media–corporate alliance that successfully labelled dissent as 'un-Australian' at the least and 'treasonous' at worst (see also Lenskyj, 2002). Serious public debate about the toxic nature of the Olympic site, about the behind-the-scenes machinations to win the event, and many other issues was thus averted and the games organizers, sponsors and governments were allowed to frame the games on their own terms with little coherent opposition. Sydney, of course, is not the first or indeed the worst example of attacking democratic rights and dissent for the sake of sport or the Olympics. In both Mexico City and Seoul, student protests met with violent repression from the state to preserve an international public image untarnished by opposing voices.

In the United States, sport has become a huge commercial enterprise with major professional and intercollegiate sports earning multi-million and even billion dollar television contracts. A similar process took shape in Europe during the 1990s and early 2000s as pay television operators entered the marketplace and bought many broadcast rights for leading sports, particularly major soccer competitions such as the English Premier League, the Serie A competition in Italy and the Champion's League in Europe. In Chapter 2, Giulianotti argues that this process is now so far advanced that opposition must be strategic and precisely aimed. Indeed, when the major multi-national media empires are more valuable than most nations' national economies, how can fans of teams like Featherstone Rovers in English rugby league fight back? Even when successful, as the South Sydney club was in Australian rugby league, resistance soon takes on a corporate and market focus guise, as Phillips, Hutchins and Stewart outlined in Chapter 5. As Falcous showed in Chapter 4, however, some clubs and fans excluded from the media–sports complex that controls elite competitions have opted to reform at lower levels and participate with the club at a more grassroots level. In Australia, the Newtown rugby league club did the same thing when they were excluded from the elite competition in the 1980s. While there have been examples such as these, they remain as much exceptions as patterns. Clearer patterns have emerged in the professionalization of sports management and marketing and in the promotion and sales of leading sports brands.

The sport management and marketing industry has taken off internationally and hundreds of academic programmes now exist to train students in these specialisms where they learn about how to sell, sell, sell, about market segmentation, promotions, corporate sponsorship and hospitality. The application of science to sport continues to produce faster, higher, stronger champions with each molecule, muscle fibre and movement analysed, digitized and scrutinized in the search for that extra hundredth of a second or quarter-inch in stride or stroke angle that may make the difference between a first and fourth place finish. Thus, with increasing professionalization, commercialization and multinational media corporate interests in sport, it is clear that the tensions we have highlighted in this volume will continue to be central in the political economy of sport for the twenty-first century.

With the rapid expansion of the Internet and digital television, opportunities for direct broadcasting have led many professional soccer clubs in Europe to explore direct transmission of matches to subscribers. While this opens up possible avenues for some clubs and organizations, the divide between the haves and have-nots in sport may well increase as a result, though the balance may tilt from media conglomerates to clubs. Several English soccer clubs, such as Manchester United, Leeds United and Chelsea, have established services from match broadcasts and highlight packages to financial (including mortgage), travel, insurance and other services whereby fans/supporters can purchase almost every necessity of life from the club and its licensees.

Furthermore political struggles of women for recognition in sport are being subsumed under marketing opportunities. A prime example of this was the hype that surrounded women's world number one golfer Annika Sorenstam's participation in the 2003 men's PGA tour event at Colonial. That Sorenstam received more press for this one event than her 50 LPGA tour wins combined demonstrates that the political economy of sport is indeed highly gendered. We acknowledge that too little attention has been paid to the intersection of political economy and gender in sport, other than to examine ways in which the 'sex sells' approach has been used to expand (male) audiences for women's sporting events and stars. After the 1999 Women's World Cup of Soccer, *New York Times* journalist Richard Lipsyte wrote a column entitled 'Sport and Sex Are Always Together'. In the article he argued that 'sexuality may be so intrinsic to sports that unless the audience is sexually comfortable, the game just won't sell' (quoted in Miller, 2002: 13). He went further and stated, 'I say the more flesh the better'. Toby Miller (2002: 13) echoes this sentiment, arguing that 'Sportsex is everywhere – sold as such'. The Anna Kournikova phenomenon of the late 1990s and early 2000s is a case in point. Kournikova became the best-known tennis player in the world, not because of ability (she never won a singles tournament), but because of good looks that were marketed widely with little regard for on-court records.

Much greater analysis of the gendered nature of the political economy of sport is needed. As Mariah Burton Nelson puts it, 'Sport constitutes the only large cultural institution where men and women are (sometimes) justifiably segregated according to gender. It is one of the few remaining endeavors where male muscle matters' (quoted in Miller, 2002: 109). As a result, Nelson argues, 'The stronger women get, the more men love football' (Nelson, 1994). In the United States much debate emerged in the 1990s and early 2000s about gender equity in sports. With the passage of Title IX in 1972, the US Federal government mandated that no discrimination could be practised in educational institutions that received any source of public funding. While enforcement of Title IX has been sporadic at times, it has served to increase more than tenfold the number of sporting opportunities for women in American universities. At the same time, in order to meet the gender equity requirements of Title IX, many universities have eliminated a few men's non-revenue-generating sports in order to comply (Goddard and Nauright, 2004).

While I have highlighted a number of key themes in the political economy of sport raised by the contributors to this volume and alluded to others, as a group we do not view this volume as being the comprehensive compendium on the political economy of sport, but rather, a volume that brings sport into wider discussions of political economy and society and of the role of political economy in sport.

Final thoughts

As I write I eagerly await my season ticket seating assignments for the University of South Carolina Gamecocks football games for the Fall, and I am watching anxiously each week to see if Aston Villa will qualify for European competition for the next soccer season. At the same time, I have begun reading a book written by the then well-known New England sportswriter Warren Kellogg in 1954, entitled *No Gold Footballs*, in which he critiques 'commercialized sport' that had infiltrated high schools and colleges in the United States by that time. In the book, Kellogg examines one school's model for participation, rejecting the economic model of sport he saw in existence 50 years ago. In my own town, the high school principal faced the wrath of some community members for daring to stand up to the football coach who brought a state championship, runner-up and semi-final finish in the past four seasons. Why? Because the coach believed that football and football players were above and beyond other students. The mentality is little different from that of civic boosters and national governments who suggest that sports team owners, stadium and event contractors and sport events are so important that democratic rights and freedoms are suppressed and public largesse is doled out while education languishes, hospital wards are closed (see Booth and Tatz, 1994, for this argument in the Australian context) and other forms of welfare are attacked. Indeed, while many have argued that the welfare state is in danger of disappearing in advanced capitalist societies of the early twenty-first century, the welfare state for sports team, facility and event owners and operators has continued to expand. While corporate welfare has come under attack in the period since about 1995, the system of public support for largely private sporting events remains intact.

Sport remains a highly contradictory enterprise that, on the one hand, brings people and communities together, albeit for short periods of time, such as in South Africa's 1995 win in the rugby World Cup, Australia's successes at the 2000 Sydney Olympics or Phil Mickelson's dramatic breakthrough win at the Masters golf tournament in 2004. On the other, it divides people through its very nature of having winners and losers. As Giulianotti reminded us in Chapter 2, even wars have been started and murders committed in the aftermath of international soccer matches. The question that we must continually examine is who are the winners and who are the losers when big-time sport comes to or leaves town and whether locally based and focused participatory models of sports and sporting participation are more worthwhile in terms of both public cost and public gain. We hope that, in some measure, our collective efforts in this volume have illuminated key issues in the international political economy of sport that will spark further investigation, policy analysis and debate, and that this book will contribute to an increase in vigorous debate about the roles of politics and economics in sport so that human rights, equity, democracy and dignity are considered alongside growth, profit, sales and skyboxes when sport is discussed in the public domain.

References

Booth, D. and C. Tatz (1994), 'Swimming with the big boys? The politics of Sydney's 2000 Olympic Bid', *Sporting Traditions*, **11** (1), 3–23.

Goddard, H. and J. Nauright (2004), 'Facing the unintended consequences of Title IX: the elimination of men's non-revenue sports to achieve compliance: a case study', seminar paper, Department of Hospitality, Tourism and Family and Consumer Sciences, Georgia Southern University.

Kellogg, W. (1954). *No gold footballs: a study of the physical education program at Phillips Exeter Academy*, New York: Twayne.

Lenskyj, H.J. (2002), *The best Olympics ever? Social impacts of Sydney 2000*, Albany: State University of New York.

Miller, T. (2002), 'SportSex', Philadelphia: Temple University.

Nauright, J. and P. White (1996), Professional sport, nostalgia, community and nation in Canada, *AVANTE*, **2** (4), 24–41.

Nelson, M.B. (1994), *The stronger women get the more men love football*, New York: Harcourt Brace.

Newman, J., D. Grainger and D. Andrews (2003), 'Even better than the real thing? The XFL and football's future imperfect', *Football Studies*, **6** (2), 5–21.

Index